Roy 'the Boy' Brindley was born in 1969 and brought up in Southampton. The first European poker professional to be commercially sponsored, he is enjoying his sixth year endorsing and promoting a bookmaking PLC. Roy writes for several poker publications and commentates regularly on poker tournaments for Sky Sports. He lives in Ireland with his partner Mags and their two young children, Sebastian and Elise.

www.roytheboy.net

LIFE'S A GAMBLE

The High Stakes and Low Life
of a Poker Professional

Roy Brindley

BANTAM PRESS

LONDON • TORONTO • SYDNEY • AUCKLAND • JOHANNESBURG

TRANSWORLD PUBLISHERS
61–63 Uxbridge Road, London W5 5SA
A Random House Group Company
www.rbooks.co.uk

First published in Great Britain
in 2009 by Bantam Press
an imprint of Transworld Publishers

A CIP catalogue record for this book
is available from the British Library.

ISBN 9780593062081

Addresses for Random House Group Ltd companies outside the UK
can be found at: www.randomhouse.co.uk
The Random House Group Ltd Reg. No. 954009

The Random House Group Limited supports The Forest Stewardship
Council (FSC), the leading international forest-certification organization.
All our titles that are printed on Greenpeace-approved FSC-certified
paper carry the FSC logo. Our paper procurement policy can be found at
www.rbooks.co.uk/environment

Typeset in 11.5/16pt Sabon by Falcon Oast Graphic Art Ltd
Printed in the UK by CPI Mackays, Chatham, ME5 8TD

2 4 6 8 10 9 7 5 3 1

Contents

Acknowledgements

First and foremost this book is dedicated to my dearly departed grandmother, Nora. I'm afraid I put her through hell: always in a heap of trouble, always borrowing money desperate to pay off a gambling debt or fund a bet. Between myself and my granddad she cannot have had a very happy life, but sadly, now that I am older, wiser and in a position to rectify things, she is no longer here. That breaks my heart.

My mum has not fared much better down the years. Apologies, and thank you for bringing me into the world, and for dispelling the rumour that I came from the womb clutching a deck of cards too! Dad, thanks for trying your best, especially with my education, which I know was a struggle.

Mags, you have stuck by me during the reliving of the difficult years described in these pages. What can I say, what more can I do? One day our baby son Sebastian and daughter Elise will read this book and I hope their hearts will always be filled with the love that we have for them.

Actor James Woods, in a single conversation which he has

doubtless long since forgotten, gave me so much encouragement to write *Life's a Gamble*. When a Hollywood A-lister tells you to 'do it, write it, and I want to see the finished article' you become inspired.

My friend Jesse May, the 'voice of poker', also gave me plenty of encouragement and single-handedly provided the contacts to get this project both dealt and turned into a winning hand. My sincere thanks go to him.

Obsession and compulsion are the cancer of mental health . . . thankfully I'm all better now.

Foreword by Jesse May

A word. That's all a gambler has. For those who have chosen this way of life, the word of a gambler is all they have. And that is quite simply because to be a gambler means to be sometimes left with nothing else.

What is the most you have ever lost? The question itself is the gulf between those who have seriously gambled and those who never will. The question is simple but the answer is simpler, because it is the same for every gambler of any blood. The answer is: everything.

I first met Roy Brindley when he became Roy the Boy. He was a guy wearing a suit and a Discman when everyone else was unkempt; he understood promotion when everyone else was thick; and he had talent and gamble in scary amounts. Roy shot poker full of life when the rest of us were walking in place. I was on the rail when he nearly won a world championship event, and the poker he can play is glorious indeed. When he's on top of his game, he has the stuff that you dream of. He is a million-dollar Roy the Boy, and he has won sums to prove it.

I also know another Roy Brindley. Dark and sad, broke and scared, reckless and hopeless, drunk and weak. This is the life of Roy the Boy Brindley. This is the life of a gambler.

I was a nineteen-year-old kid just dropped out of college, working days at a desk on Wacker Drive in Chicago. Everything was for gambling. Lunchtime there was the off-track betting on Jackson Street, and on weekends the trip to the racecourse at Arlington. Nights were for studying the form, making charts, and dreaming of the gamble. I had won nine days in a row when I left the office at lunchtime and never returned, hopping the train to the track and every day thereafter.

It was a beautiful Saturday in the middle of summer when I went broke hard. I bet it all on a horse named Carborundum, everything I had except the return train ticket, and that only because I had coolly calculated the money I would save on the return was more than I would make by betting the extra on the horse. It was that sure a thing.

The day came back to me in a flood when I read the story of Roy the Boy. This writing of his took me right back to that sunny afternoon, throwing up in the white-stalled bathroom of the clubhouse box, binoculars still dangling around my neck as I puked. That ride home in a daze on the train. Pacing the streets and digging around the corners of my room to scrounge up change, and then lying on a creaky box spring with a cover pulled up and staring at the wall. It was not the first time I went broke or the last, but it had an intensity that Roy speaks of on every page of his life.

How does Roy know? Roy knows because he's been there,

he's done it, he's making nothing up. Roy knows because he's done or watched through his father Roy and his grandpa Jack all the tricks of a gambler trying to find that extra edge. I did not come from gambling stock. Those who were gamblers in my family were secretive, or they died long before I was born. Roy was full flung from the moment he could walk.

This is a poignant treatise. It's the one I could not put down. This is a blasting, naked account of what it is to be a gambler. Roy reveals what we all try to leave in the box to bring out on dark days and evil nights. This is the secret of our greatest triumphs and also the weapon of our great destruction. This is that thing called gamble.

Here in this book is Roy the Boy Brindley with all his flaws. Perfect? No way. He's not even close. But Roy has been higher than most of us can dream and lower than we can imagine. Your jaw will drop with his staggering wins; your head will shake with his biggest losses. Just take Roy in all his glory, because he's coming at you with nothing left out.

This is not a fiction, nor is it a fantasy. Desperately, we want Roy to win. We want to hear that he has purchased a pension or a bond or an investment that will set him up for life. We want to shake Roy the Boy Brindley and yell, 'Don't! Don't gamble it all away!' But then I think back to the words I have told myself over and over again. This is the life we choose. This is the life we have chosen.

Will Roy win in the end? He's winning right now. The legendary gambler Nick the Greek was known to live by these words. 'The next best thing to gambling and winning,' he said, 'is to gamble and lose. The main thing is to play.' Roy has that special talent to win. It is not luck. You might tell yourself that you'd do it different, but to do it at all you must have what it takes. And as long as you have both talent and gamble, both the top and the bottom are just one step away.

I've known Roy the Boy Brindley since the day he came barrelling into the poker world at a million miles an hour. I've known him long enough to know two things. He's a gambler in the truest and purest sense of the word. And when he's left with nothing but his word, he still has plenty left indeed.

1

Heads-up

As I scoop in the pot once more the audience delivers a rapturous round of applause but, in truth, they don't know if
William, in passing his cards, has made a good play or a bad
one. All they know is I'm stacking up a mountain of chips.

They simply love it. This isn't big money on the line for
opening box number seven, or for answering a trivia question
correctly. This isn't a game show, it's a skill game, where
bravery is the dominating factor and not only can contestants
win big, they can lose big too.

Things have clearly changed a lot since my first televised
poker tournament some five years ago. There too I was in a
tense head-to-head confrontation, but back then the studio had
the atmosphere of a wake.

Poker has been likened to snooker in the eighties: it's big
money, it looks easy, it's constantly on the television and

everyone is trying their hand at the game. Judging by this enthusiastic crowd, not to mention the masses watching the action – with the insight the all-important under-table cameras bring – in their living rooms, who can argue?

William Thorson is my opponent. Nine months ago he collected $900,000 at the World Series of Poker – not for winning but for finishing thirteenth. (As I said, like snooker in its heyday, poker boasts big money.) Just two of us remain at this final table of the Poker Masters of Europe competition being filmed for television in Hammersmith's Riverside Studios, and we both want the title badly. The prize is laid out before us: $190,000 in cash and a glistening trophy. Contenders like Tony G and Ram Vaswani have already been fended off and their presence seems like a distant memory now as our intense head-to-head mind game is played.

Unlike William, a cool-looking spiky-haired dude in his early twenties who has hotfooted it over from his Swedish home, I've not had a major cash win during the past twelve months. A couple of $50,000s here and there, but in my world, this messed-up world of high-stakes poker playing, that kind of money does not last long. It's almost small change. I need this win, I need it badly. I have an ambitious agent to appease, I have an expectant major company sponsoring me, I have critics who I want to silence and, most importantly, a young family to provide for.

All this pressure, yet the last thing on my mind is the money. Some people start thinking about the dough when they're in a spot like this but all they are doing is giving themselves one hell of a stressful headache. They subconsciously begin to play with a lack of conviction, timidly, like a lion who, despite being oh so hungry, is afraid his prey will bite him back. For me it's actually easy as I've never had much need for, or concern about, money. All I've ever wanted or needed is enough for my next bet. So I suppose a lifelong disdain for money has given me an edge in battles like this.

Now, having commentated on stacks of televised poker shows, I am well aware that technicians, cameramen, the director, even the dealers are probably keen to wrap up this piece of television and conclude a hectic week's work. They want it over as soon as possible, they want blood to be spilled, but we are in no hurry. Poker is a thinking man's game and methodical decision making cannot be hurried.

None of them has a clue what's going on inside me. It's turmoil. I'm walking a tightrope in the full knowledge and understanding that one slip and it's all over. There is more emotion in me than in the lot of 'em combined.

Once again the cards are pitched across the table, like the colour of the studio decor a peculiar orange baize with the sponsor's logo across the centre. William and I are sat far apart, almost opposite each other. For some reason, despite youth and the benefit of money behind him, I can sense he is nervous.

During the uneasy thirty seconds between hands while the dealer performs a complex shuffle routine, I fathom the reason. Among all his accomplishments and $1 million in career earnings, he has never won a tournament, never collected a trophy, never been called champion. I'm lucky enough to have a cabinet full of silverware, even if there isn't a six-figure pay-day on my CV. It gives me an insurmountable confidence, an edge; now I know I can exploit his desire not to give up his chips easily. It's a fact: the person who wants it most in poker usually loses out.

Move making is what it's all about in these situations, and I take off in a confrontation holding the worst possible starting hand in Texas Hold'em, 2-7. The first three community cards on the table, the flop, comes Ace-2-4. My adversary and I soon go into a battle of wits.

I have no more than a lowly pair of 2s but I am convinced William does not have an Ace in his hand and his raise of my opening bet is no more than a bluff, ironically in the belief that I too do not hold an Ace.

I pound another bet into the Swede when the next card to fall is a 4. It's a great card for me: even if he does have an Ace I can now represent three-of-a-kind.

But he quickly calls my bet and now I'm left totally confused as to the identity of his hand, knowing just one thing: he has something better than my pair of 2s and I have a lot of my chips involved in a pot which I cannot fairly win. By that I mean win with the best hand. No matter what that last card is, I am forced to make a huge bet in the hope that this bluff will make him pass.

As the cameramen urgently shuffle across the studio floor, their cameras doubtless focusing in tightly on our profiles under instruction from an excitable director wanting to sight a bead of sweat, the last card falls. It's a 5.

The table now shows Ace-2-4-4-5. I have to make it look like I have a 3 in my hand, meaning I have made a straight. With my chips neatly piled and orderly displayed I count out a 60,000 bet – a fair proportion of my remaining chips. I have to keep a posture about myself, not demonstrating the truth. I am slap bang in the middle of a valuable televised tournament which I could be blowing right here and now; I must display a confident grace and air, signifying that I am in total control and deciding on the correct amount to bet in order to be called and therein maximize the profit from my winning hand. In poker terms, the perfectly sized bluff; in layman's terms, total bullshit.

Slowly, I slide my three stacks of chips across the line and announce as confidently as I can the bet size 'sixty thousand'. However, the desired response fails to materialize. I was hoping for an immediate pass. The second preference is a slight delay and then a reluctant, softly spoken 'I pass', but that too is not forthcoming. William simply sits there, looking only at his chips, counting out twelve black ones from his stack. They are the variety that are worth 5,000 apiece.

I sit and stare impassively, despite knowing my tournament could be squandered due to my brutal never-say-die approach. I firmly believe he is timid and desperate not to be knocked out of this game in second position, but as the seconds tick by I wonder if maybe I have read him wrong. Could he have a 3 or a 4?

A minute can seem like an eternity in poker so I don't know just how long it took for him to come to a decision, but at the very moment I believed my adversary was going to announce 'call' he paused, sighed and said, 'OK, you win,' while flashing a 4 from his hand as he threw his cards towards the dealer.

Three-of-a-kind is a mighty powerful hand in Texas Hold'em and just what the reasoning behind his big pass was I'll never know. I do know it inspired me, and moments later, when William announced, 'I am being outplayed here,' I was given a licence to rape and pillage every chip on the table. His comments, his demeanour, his attitude and that huge pass led me to raise every pot, regardless of the cards in my hand; in fact most of the time I wasn't even looking at them. I knew, given his state of mind and my chip lead, he could not fight back until he'd picked up a big hand, and that could be an hour away.

But things have to slow down now that my opponent is on life support, with only a small stack of chips remaining – I've stolen the rest – because his next and only play will be an 'all-in' move.

Sure enough, after a few tamely played hands William makes his first announcement of 'all-in' based purely on the value of his two hole cards. Face down I gently squeeze my cards together and then, taking a peek, slowly apart.

The first is a black Ace. I mentally decide that should the second be a 10 or higher I will make the call. To my total disbelief I see the second is also a black Ace. This is the stuff of dreams, a situation I've dreamt about: all the money in the middle, a title on the line, and I have pocket Aces. I know I am at least an 80 per cent favourite to be holding that trophy aloft within sixty seconds.

William looks on aghast, disbelievingly, as I proudly announce 'call' and turn over my Aces. He has to reveal his hand: it's a woeful Jack-4.

A long delay follows, doubtless due to the director ordering his cameramen into position, preparing graphics for the screen and attempting to build the tension with an over-exaggerated pause allied to some ecstatic commentary.

Finally the flop is allowed to hit the table. It features a 4. I'm still ahead, I'm still a huge favourite to win, but another 4 or a Jack spells disaster. The turn card delivers a meaningless 9. Having studied the figures for years I know I'm now an 89 per cent favourite. Just one more blank card for the entire package: the trophy, the accolade, the satisfaction and the money.

The director's long pause once again drives me insane but, as they say, this kind of suspense is akin to sex: it is best just before the end. However, a climax can sometimes be an anti-climax. Another 4, a miracle 4, appears on the table. My chin sinks to the floor. My heart drowns in disbelief.

William is back in the game, and in the face of such cruel luck I have to avoid that urge to throw caution to the wind, to lose my composure – as they say in poker, 'to tilt'. If I make a frustration-induced mistake now, a poor call, a bad bluff or an oversized bet, I'll be going home dejected, a loser. Seventy grand better off maybe but, as sick as this may sound, that will be of little compensation to me.

A full hour of mini-battles follows, during which I get the better of William. When he becomes short of chips once more he is forced to speculatively put his tournament on the line, this time raising 'all-in' with a King-3.

Once again I take a slow squeeze, and once again the first card is an Ace. The second does not match – pocket Aces are a 220/1 shot after all – but a 10 as a companion is good enough and I make the call. This time I calculate I am almost twice as likely to prevail than the now-drained Swedish player. I am a 65 per cent favourite to be precise. For a second time my heart is beating like a pneumatic jack hammer. The expectant audience are on their feet and the winning line is within sight.

I don't believe in luck, but I believe in fate, and its fickle finger delivered both a King and a 3 to the table. I know the laws of probability are not rules, and this sort of thing confirms they are simply guidelines. What do I have to do to beat this guy? I ask myself.

On we go once more. There will be no early finish for anyone. Despite these two adverse results – 'bad beats' we call them in the trade – I'm determined to fight on for as long as it takes to emerge victorious.

The pattern continues, the boxer versus the pugilist. If my young opponent suddenly turns the screw, raises his game, plays his hands a little less predictably, I'll have to reassess my strategy, but, wrestling back the chip lead for the third time, I see no reason to make any adjustments.

Once again William makes what I consider to be an uncharacteristic play. He looks at his hole cards quickly and immediately announces 'all-in'.

If he's holding a hand of extreme strength, such as Queens, Kings or Aces, surely he would have raised a moderate amount. But I know he has a habit of not raising with the likes of Ace-King and Ace-Queen, playing them slowly and setting a trap. Therefore I have to give serious consideration to the strength of his hand when looking down at my Ace-7.

That wonderful reflex in poker, the gut reaction, is urging me to call immediately as I sense I have the stronger hand. But this is not the stage on which to make a rash decision and, as the chip counts are almost level, without doubt this hand will seal the Masters title.

Just hang on here. I retain a gambler's instinct, and that means were we tossing a coin and my adversary was giving me the smallest edge – odds of 11/10 instead of even-money about a head or tail, say – I believe I am not worth my salt unless I put everything I own in the world on the outcome at the price which is bigger than the probability. Twice before I held the best hand and lost, but superstition and the belief in luck, be it good or bad, have no place at the poker table. With all the factors taken into consideration, I have to make the call.

I announce 'call', and the audience rise to their feet. Dismayed at my response, William sits back while flipping over his King-Jack. I pull myself forward to get an immediate view of the flop while unleashing my Ace-7.

This time those laws of probability are paying attention: although essentially I only need to avoid a King or Jack landing, both an Ace and a 7 appear on the table.

In these spots, as a player, you go through a complete mental breakdown. Your mind does not function correctly. The only way William can now win is with a miraculous 10 and Queen landing in succession. It is as plain as the nose on my face, yet my mind simply cannot compute what is going on. The turn and river cards change nothing but I have to wait for the compère to announce the victory: I'm still looking at William's two cards on the table next to the five community cards and trying to find some way they can make a better hand than my Aces and 7s.

I'm eager to shake my opponent's hand and offer both sincere congratulations and commiserations to him. As he turns to depart the auditorium, head bowed, I move on to salute the appreciative audience. It is one of life's sweetest moments, not least because I am about to be reunited with my six-month-old baby son Sebastian. He holds his arm aloft, clutching the shiny winner's trophy with me, alongside the sponsor's representative, who is also handing over $120,000 in cash.

Had I not come a long way in a few short years? I most definitely had. Less than a decade earlier I was living on the streets with no more than a plastic cup in my hand urging people to part with loose change.

Reflecting on those dark and desperate days often holds me together and I have frequently sent myself back to that period of my life in order to remind myself how lucky I am now and, most importantly, how to perform well at a poker table. It is my fear of defeat.

Although not having to employ such drastic measures on my way to victory here, while shaking every hand thrust in front of me I did pause to consider who, from years gone by, would be watching at home bragging to their wives, husbands or friends 'I went to school with that guy', 'I used to punt in the betting shop with that fella', or even 'I used to share tins of Diamond White on a street corner with him!'

Now, one thing you have to understand: tournament poker is not gambling. Trust me, I know, because I've gambled on anything and everything. Gambling is a festering sickness which I was born with. There's a song whose chorus says 'life's a journey not a destination', and while I cannot claim these punchy lines, I have certainly lived by the motto 'Life's a Gamble Not a Destination'.

Poker has been my redemption. It's been like a dock leaf wrapped around a stinging wound; an improbable cure that has done the job admirably. The game is highly skilful and requires massive amounts of patience, self-discipline, mathematical prowess and bravado. In return it can deliver immense satisfaction and financial reward way beyond six miraculous lucky numbers on the Lotto.

Sadly, I discovered this fairly late in life. For most of it, gambling was there for me, sucking the spirit, not to mention every penny, out of me in a way only friends and family of a heroin addict could understand. Don't get me wrong, I've few regrets. I don't think I've been a bad person down the years, although I've undoubtedly done some monumentally stupid things. I just wish I'd unearthed poker a lot earlier. I envy the scores of young men, like William Thorson, who are set up for life simply by using their brain in a skill game called poker.

Then again, there are those often heard words 'he overcame poverty to succeed', and I actually do think an impoverished background is advantageous in life. I just cannot imagine being born into wealth, which must leave you very little to want or need, and, I imagine, with less ability to appreciate what you have. That's about the only downside to poker, I think: people getting everything all too easily and at a very young age. It's not a problem I've had to deal with!

2

Getting Paid

Declaring that I was born with a festering sickness called gambling may sound a bit dramatic, but certainly the first thing I can clearly recall in life is winning a bet.

It was the hot summer of 1976 when the mighty Manchester United took on my hometown side, lowly Southampton from the Second Division, in the FA Cup Final. The match was huge; occasions like that were huge back then. A year later, for example, the whole country came out for a street party, bought thousands of flags, hats, souvenir cups, plates and coins, and patriotically draped their houses in red, white and blue to celebrate the Queen's Silver Jubilee. Unless you were around then you cannot begin to imagine what it was like.

Anyway, the whole family got together to watch Mick Channon, Bobby Stokes, Peter Osgood and co. take on the mighty Red Devils, and as far as my dad was concerned no such occasion was complete without a bet.

I didn't go much on the game of football – never did, never have – but I do recall a sense of nervousness which both excited and stimulated me knowing that my week's pocket money was riding on the outcome. It was as if my life would be seriously affected if Southampton lost. As it was they won at odds of five or six to one. My life was affected all right: football may have struck me as a boring game, but gambling certainly wasn't!

Good old Dad. He's still around, and he's never changed. The poor guy has spent an entire lifetime chasing a dream, doing what all gamblers do: risking what they cannot afford in the pursuit of something they cannot have. Back then, Saturday was the gambling day of the week, the day racing was on television, and my dad's bet of choice was the 'ITV 7', which required you to select the winners of seven consecutive races. He never once got close. His other great delusion in life was winning the football pools. The miraculous string of score-draw results required to do so also failed to materialize. Even the crème de la crème, one of the biggest rip-offs of all time, 'Spot the Ball', he tried every week.

This gambling stuff, it's in the genes. Guess what, his mother, my gran, who was born in 1909 and is still with us, taught my dad pretty much all he knows! I actually know her as 'Nan Happy', which is a light-hearted joke as she's not always been the cheeriest person in the world! Born in Bristol, during the Second World War she worked as a postman, punctuating her rounds with urgent visits to Southampton's air-raid shelters. Her house was destroyed during an air raid and it was a miracle the family wasn't killed in the process. That night, on hearing the sirens, the family dashed out to their Anderson shelter in the back garden but found it had been flooded out by a spring that had cropped up following heavy rain. They were forced to flee to the communal shelter at the end of the street. On returning to their home, they found that it had been flattened while the shelter had taken a direct hit and was now just a hole in the ground.

The story goes her husband, my granddad, who died in 1951 some eighteen years before I was born, was invited to the opening meeting of the Southampton Dog Track in the mid 1920s by a well-known former county cricketer called Bradbury Pratt who'd opened the track. Apparently Pratt tipped him every winner of the eight races on that opening night and thereafter he was hooked.

I sat down with Nan Happy a few years ago to talk about Mick the Miller, the greatest greyhound ever. He raced in front of crowds of fifty thousand in 1929 and 1930. He was the canine version of Red Rum and Desert Orchid rolled into one. Considering she must be one of the last people who can claim to have seen the great dog in action, I found it intriguing. She also recalled visits to Bournemouth, Park Royal, Slough, Hendon, Clacton and Cardiff Arms Park dog tracks. All distant memories . . . supermarkets or blocks of flats are on top of them now.

Back in those days dog racing was the real deal, the sport of the working classes. Before betting shops, before live sport on television, before television come to that, it was one of the few places you could legally gamble and be entertained. There were up to half a dozen dog tracks in major cities in England, more in London, all packed to the gills. That's how popular it was.

Nan Happy also told me of the time during the late fifties when she and my dad went to Brighton horse races and had the day of all days backing almost every winner for ever-increasing stakes. In the evening they went on to Hove dogs where they backed another seven winners and won a fortune in the process. That night the pair proudly booked themselves into Brighton's Grand Hotel, and once in their room started counting out the cash and placing it in piles all over the bed, dressing table, sideboard and any other free space they could find. Things were about to go somewhat awry, though, as a waitress delivering room service entered the bedroom and caught a glimpse of the money. She'd only just heard of a local bank robbery on the radio, and within fifteen minutes the police arrived on the back of her tip-off. Dad and Gran spent the night at the police station rebuffing accusations that they were armed robbers!

Nan Happy was and is primarily a dog person, a love passed down to my father, and one that was eventually to take hold of me. I was just three days old when Dad first took me to the dogs (that's what they tell me anyway). But I inherited my thoroughbred gambler genes from both sides of my family. My granddad Jack, my mum's dad, also had a major say on the course my life would take, and his passion in life was horse-racing. Not the love of the breed, not the spectacle of the sport, but the gambling opportunities it gave him.

That United–Southampton FA Cup Final may have been one of the first recollections of my childhood, but the indelible memory of that mid-seventies period is the day Granddad Jack sat me on his knee and told me about the time he won enough money to buy a row of houses. I'm guessing I was about seven. We were in the front room of the terraced house my gran and granddad lived in on the Flower Gardens estate in Swaything, a district of Southampton. It was a working-class estate, vast and sprawling, built in the 1930s. Milkmen's floats struggled up the long, wide, hilly roads in the mornings, and in the afternoons the clip-clop of horses' hooves echoed around as the coal needed to heat the homes was delivered by cart.

The front room of 141 Carnation Road was a sacred place on a Saturday afternoon, its heavy green curtains drawn tightly to prevent even the slightest ray of sunshine making the new-fangled colour television, the size of a bank vault, anything other than perfectly clear. Thick cigarette smoke swirled and danced around the room making patterns and appearing to chase and lick at you if you walked through it quickly. Granddad was a heavy smoker. Two of his fingers were coloured yellow from the nicotine and he drew heavily on cigarettes when he had a bet running, while the hand not grasping the ciggie kind of shook, clutching for things such as his lighter or a pen. He never even knew he was doing it.

On this day I knew his final selection, probably his last hope for the week, had got beat as the television was turned off the moment the horses crossed the line. He stubbed out the smouldering butt, pulled the curtains apart and prepared to go to bed for his afternoon snooze – another Saturday afternoon ritual which he did after losing his money. It was like his way of dealing with his loss.

'Granddad,' I asked, 'if you lose your money on the horses every weekend, why do you continue to bet on them?'

He paused, smiling at me in an affectionate way as if the question amused him but it was one he wanted to answer.

'I haven't always lost,' he said. 'Once I won it all. Come and sit on my knee and I'll tell you all about it.'

Granddad Jack was good at telling stories. I loved to hear them, especially at night, but something about his demeanour led me to believe that what was about to come was a true tale, not a glamorized yarn.

'Before you were born and when your mummy was a very young girl your gran and I went to the races at Sandown. We never had much money but it was a day out for us. I thought a horse in the opening race was sure to win and I put pretty much all my money on it – ten bob [50p].'

I listened intently while picturing the scene: a Ford Popular or Austin 8 taking them there, my gran dressed up, a flowery scarf covering her hair, lipstick applied liberally, Granddad clutching his cardboard betting ticket while pacing up and down and drawing on his cigarette nervously as the horses circled the parade ring.

'What happened, Granddad?' I wanted to know. 'Did it win?'

'It did win, and at odds of twelve to one,' he replied.

'Wow, what a good day out you must have had after that.'

'Things did not stop there,' he said. 'I put most of my winnings on the next race, and that horse won too.'

I was excited for him and spellbound by his story. It was as if all these losing Saturdays I had been accustomed to sharing with him were worthwhile.

'How much did you win?' I asked. 'Did you need a wheelbarrow to put all the cash in?'

'No, I didn't, as I didn't stop there. I thought the next race had a certainty in it and I was prepared to put most of my winnings on him. Guess what. That one won as well, and we had netted a fortune. In fact, it was so much some of the bookies couldn't pay me out. They told me to come back after the last race when they could get some more money.

'Now, knowing we had so much money to collect I continued to bet with the money I had left in my pocket. On a roll, I took the plunge and backed a thirty-three-to-one shot each-way. Coming into the final furlong I couldn't see my horse, but suddenly his jockey's red cap became visible in the middle of a tightly bunched pack towards the front. The commentator started calling his name and it looked like he was going to finish in the first three, meaning we would win. However, a whole host of horses crossed the line together in a bunch finish and from where we were stood I had no idea if he had made the frame or not. It was a photo-finish.

'I asked anyone and everyone who had won and if my horse had finished in the frame but no one seemed to have any idea. Even the judge must have been struggling to tell from the photo as it took him ages to announce who had won and who had come second and third.

'Finally the announcement came through. "Here is the result of the fourth race: first, number seven . . ." Number seven! That was my horse! Your gran and I could not believe it. A thirty-three-to-one winner! We had won another fortune.'

This was not fiction. Granddad, excited by reciting his unforgettable day at Sandown, had a huge smile on his face. He was reliving every bet placed and sharing with me the thrill of watching his horses cross the line, and hearing the judge's verdict on that photo-finish. Indeed, Gran came through from the kitchen with one of her homemade currant buns on a plate and a cup of tea and said to me, 'It's true, and I told him, I told him to get his winnings immediately.'

With that statement from Gran I now guessed this story had a bitter twist.

'Did you lose back all of your money, Granddad?' I asked.

'No, that was impossible. All told we had won enough to buy a castle, a fleet of Rolls-Royces and chauffeurs to go with them. In fact, when I went to these bookmakers to collect they too said they had to get more money to pay me out and also instructed me to come back after the last race. At the end of the meeting I had two pocketfuls of betting tickets from maybe thirty bookmakers. I didn't know which ones owed me from the early races or from the thirty-three-to-one shot; some owed me from both. It was incredible. None were very happy though and when they asked me how much winnings I was due and I couldn't exactly tell them, they all told me to come back in fifteen minutes when they would have finished paying other customers, would have worked out my winning total and, if need be, sent off for more cash.'

Gran took up the story as Granddad was becoming choked.

'Jack took us to the bar, where he bought everyone a drink. Dozens of people, people he had never met before.' This was really odd as Granddad never drank. 'He wanted to toast his life-changing win and share his good fortune with everyone. I kept telling him it was time to get his winnings but people kept asking him what he had backed and how much he had won. They all wanted to talk about it. Eventually he stepped outside to see the bookmakers again.'

Downbeat, Granddad picked up his story again. 'I was not expecting what I saw,' he sighed regretfully. 'Each and every bookmaker had slammed their satchels shut, grabbed their stands and run off. All that was left was the wooden boxes on which they stood and piles of torn-up tickets all over the floor. I saw a few of them urgently throwing their equipment into the boots of their cars but they were in the distant car parks, off and gone, never to be seen again. Not one paid me out.'

Now I loved my granddad; to me he was the most special person in the world. Not only did he not drink, I never once heard him swear. I cannot forget the look on his face and the tear in his eye when he told me that story. Make no mistake, from that moment onwards I detested bookmakers, and I was to spend the best part of my life trying to get revenge.

3

Full House

Granddad Jack worked for shipbuilders Vosper Thorneycroft as an electrician, although I'm far from certain how much work he ever got done. I mean, he would go off to work with a flask and a blanket; I suspect he spent much of his time sleeping in a cabin or, when he had money, in the betting shop. He was a likeable character though who would do anyone a favour if he could. There were always people knocking at the front door asking him to fix a car, a bike or a lawnmower.

He loved a small-time scam – you know, the type of bloke who would drive a diesel van because he knew a farmer who could sell the fuel to him for a fraction of the price at the pumps. I can clearly remember a thick cable he installed stretching from one side of his house's electricity meter to the mains, bypassing the coin box in between. It meant the cash box only ever had about £6 in 10p pieces when the electric company sent someone to empty it.

But his good and endearing qualities were somewhat overshadowed by his gambling. He just couldn't stop, no matter how much it affected the people around him, and he really did torture himself with guilt related to it.

Just like the electricity coin boxes, everything was done in cash in those days, and that meant Granddad was paid his wages in cash, every Friday afternoon. He would normally arrive home with half of it gone, forced to claim that he had lent it to a guy at work who needed money for his rent or some other dire emergency. The truth was he had lost it in the betting shop, and he did the other half of it on the Saturday afternoon races. As a result my poor gran had a hard time of things, never knowing what, if anything, she would have to run the household for the week.

Like I said, once that last horse got beat on a Saturday he went straight to bed and often spent the rest of the weekend there, fighting a type of depression. As I was to discover when times were hard for me, when you're asleep you forget all your troubles. The problem is, you then don't want to get up. It's a vicious circle.

He did get up, for work on a Monday, but would spend any free time immersed in Raceform Update form books trying to identify winners for the coming weekend. By the time Friday afternoon arrived the cycle would start again. Despite a life-time of trying he never repeated that magical day at Sandown Park.

Here's an example of how badly gambling got hold of him. One Christmas Santa, who in this era delivered only one or two presents, brought my mother, a mere child at the time, a beautiful wooden doll's house. She played with it from first thing in the morning to last thing at night and could not wait to get up on Boxing Day morning to play with it some more.

But by the morning it had disappeared: my granddad had sold it in order to raise the stakes for a bet on an absolute certainty that he had uncovered. Not for the first time it was a certainty that got beat.

Despite all these dreadful happenings – and he knew what he was putting his family through – Granddad Jack simply could not help himself. And I maintain he was a good person. If that certainty had won, he would not only have got the doll's house back, he would have treated the whole family to wonderful gifts.

It was a close-knit family. My granddad served on the *Queen Mary* alongside his brothers, Boff, Rex and Michael. They too liked a bet. Michael went on to own a string of betting shops. The only problem was, he couldn't stay on the right side of the rails – there's no buzz involved in the safe option of just taking bets – and ended up losing the lot through gambling. Michael married Grace, who was one of my gran's sisters, so the large families were close and interwoven.

My mum had two older half-brothers, Trevor and Roy, from my gran's first marriage, but she arrived relatively late, in 1952, and just seventeen years later she was giving birth to me – rather early in life! Dad, who I have briefly introduced you to, was considerably older than my teenaged mum – like, twenty-five years older. He had already been married and had a family of six, but he fell for my mum after meeting her dad (Granddad Jack) . . . in the betting shop. Where else?

The story goes like this. They were both losing heavily and started to chat. My dad explained that he dabbled in anything from second-hand furniture to scrap metal, buying and selling in newspapers, auction sales, and even jumble sales (car boot sales had not been invented yet). Granddad was delighted to hear this and, hoping he could gather together a bit more cash for another bet, declared that he had some scrap copper and brass he wanted to sell at his house. Now copper and brass may be right up there with mercury, silver and gold-dust to a scrap-metal dealer, but when Granddad Jack took my dad to his garage, opened a work cabinet drawer and began removing individual screws, nuts and washers, my dad immediately knew he was not about to strike it rich! Anyway, that's the day he met my mum, who was still at school at the time.

You know, when I think of it, an auction sale is just like one big game of poker, but one that can be corrupt. You have the vendor who wants to get as much for his goods as possible and the purchaser who wants to pay as little as possible. In between those two people you have a stack of duckers and divers all trying to make themselves a few quid. I spent a lot of time at auction sales as a child, every Wednesday at a place called Ringwood in the New Forest, buying furniture with my dad and granddad.

Granddad could have set himself up for life once at an auction sale but didn't. Back in those days, the seventies, there were auction sales organized by the government called 'government surplus sales' where they would sell obsolete goods from the army, navy, air force and police, even hospitals and schools. At one of these sales Granddad looked at the catalogue and saw there were batches of 5,000 (empty) ammunition boxes consigned by the army. There were actually forty such lots dittoed down the sales catalogue, so whoever bought the first batch had the option to buy the remaining thirty-nine lots – that's 200,000 boxes in total – at the same price.

These things were usually just a wooden box with a lid and a rope handle across the top. They were of very little use to anyone for anything, apart from firewood. However, Granddad had discovered that on this occasion these boxes were not wooden, they were aluminium, and were worth an absolute fortune as scrap. He knew this because he'd gone to the Aldershot depot to look at all the lots on offer, and that depot was miles away from the Southampton hotel where the auction, sprinkled with buyers representing Arabian and African governments, was taking place.

The auctioneer was expecting each batch to make about £25, but when the bidding went up to £250 everyone knew something was up. Suddenly, mid-way through this bidding war, a burly and threatening fellow came running across to my granddad. He pulled him aside and menacingly whispered in his ear, suggesting that he stop bidding immediately. On top of the intimidation he promised to give him a pay-off for doing so.

Poor Granddad, he was muscled into taking a £1,000 backhander to stop bidding. If he had gone ahead and bought all those boxes and sold them on for scrap he would have been set up for life.

If you can't tell yet, I spent a lot of my childhood at my gran and granddad's. The main reason for that was the brain haemorrhage my mum was struck down with a year or so after I was born. Only major surgery saved her life, but even that came at a cost: Mum was hospitalized and left blind for a year by her illness. As a further consequence, she was unable to have any more children, and I could sense she was desperate to do so even when I was a little boy. So I was an only child. I did have half-siblings from Dad's first marriage but I knew little of them. They were much older than me, grown up, married and starting families of their own by the time I was reaching double digits.

Granddad's form-book studying and Saturday afternoons apart, those days and evenings in the mid to late 1970s evoke just one memory for me: family gatherings, almost every night of the week, invariably in my grandparents' front room, where cards would be played from early evening until the small hours. At least five times a week my folks would make the short drive from our home to get a seat in the card school. Gran, Granddad, Uncle Trevor, Mum, Dad, Aunty Pat and Uncle Alan were stalwarts, and the action was deadly serious too. (Pat and Alan weren't really my aunty and uncle, just distant relations, but it's what I called them.)

Ninety-nine per cent of the time they played a game called Nomination, a form of rummy. The players would have to 'nominate' how many tricks they would make. Rummy is a simple game, but Nomination isn't because, between you, you cannot nominate the exact number of tricks possible in every hand. Each round there could be up to four winners, but there had to be a loser. Twenty rounds made up a game.

When a hand, or round, was in progress it was deadly silent. They were all deep in concentration (they needed to be). But while the cards were being taken back in and the next hand was being shuffled and dealt there was always a frenetic autopsy. 'I had to play my Queen like that because the clubs had been round four times and it still wasn't the master', or 'If you had led out with your diamonds I could not have trumped your King the second time round'. That kind of talk was commonplace before silence fell once again as the next hand started.

Such was their seriousness I couldn't have the telly on because that would upset their concentration. I'd therefore end up, even as a small child, sitting there watching them play cards for hours and hours on end.

You'd imagine they were playing for fortunes, but the stakes were always 'two bob' (ten pence), no more no less. It was the satisfaction of winning that did it for them, my granddad in particular. He simply loved his cards, but he could go 'on tilt' at any moment, especially when a game was clearly lost from a long way out. My mum was a good player, but Aunty Pat was clearly the most successful. To quote another modern-day poker term, she was a solid grinder: she gave nothing away and she was never reckless.

How did I know so much about their abilities? It came on the back of hours and hours of watching each of them play. I would beg them to let me play, but this was serious stuff and no young child, cherished grandson or not, was going to get into their card school and make a mockery of it. Instead I was offered the rare privilege of watching Granddad play his cards, which he would hold high enough to allow me to see how and what he was playing. I did this for a full six months before concluding that I knew his each and every move inside out.

I had the game cracked, so once again I asked if I could play with them. It was still a resounding no, but in came another offer: 'You can sit behind me and watch me play, how's that?' Fantastic, six months sat behind my mum watching all her plays and moves.

This continued for no fewer than three years, by which time I had sat behind and watched the plays and moves of everyone who had ever played in the game. I had got to the stage where I could interpret pretty much what any player held without looking at anything other than the cards they were discarding, allied to their body language.

Finally, one day, it happened. Alan was on nights, Dad was working, Uncle Trevor was not well, so I was left with the dream: an empty seat in the game and nobody apart from me available to fill it. I think it was Aunty Pat who said, 'If you think you know how to play this game you can play, but you better not mess us around by doing silly stuff or make any mistakes with the rules.'

The cards were dealt, and at long last I picked up my own hand of thirteen cards. Was I nervous? Did I play slowly, methodically, concerned about what a mistake would mean? Not for one minute. Despite having waited years for this moment I played fast and loose, bursting with confidence. In the first game I delivered an almost perfect winning score. It was deemed a fluke, but success in the second and third games, well, it just mystified them. It was no surprise to me. Mentally I'd won hundreds of games in the past.

In addition to knowing my opponents I was good at the game because numbers were involved. Your brain has to keep a running tally of the number of trumps left in players' hands, then the number of cards ahead of your big cards which can beat them; that goes for the three remaining suits too, so there were four running numbers washing around your head at all times. Added to that you have to take notice of what other players are discarding and figure out why, taking into consideration the number of tricks they are trying to make.

I firmly believe that at a young age your brain is like a sponge. You cannot teach an old dog new tricks, we all know that, but the bottom line is . . . you can teach a young dog almost anything, given the right incentives.

These days, with the exception of my mum and dad, everyone who played in that card game is dead. My Uncle Alan was the last to go, in 2007. His wife, Pat, died in 1996, Gran the following year, while Granddad had gone on ahead in 1989. There's no longer a card game down here, but all I can hope, for their sakes, is that there is a great one going on up there somewhere or other, and that one day I can join in again.

4

Flush

Playing Nomination was an art form, like learning the piano or taking dancing lessons is for others, and I strove to get better and better. I never considered it to be much fun, it had to be taken seriously. Card playing of any kind, done well, is a discipline not a leisure activity. The satisfaction comes after the event, not during it.

For me, fun was just around the corner, and it wasn't football or pop music, the things most other kids of my age were getting excited about, it was dog racing.

Since 1977 we had always gone to the Greyhound Derby final at White City. It was a family outing – Mum, Dad and me. We would go to London early in the day, walk around Shepherd's Bush market buying fruit, drinks and everything necessary for an upmarket picnic, then go to the track and queue to be among the first in so we could claim our favourite seats one row below the royal box and spend both the afternoon and evening there. The place was jammed, so you couldn't move even if you wanted to.

But then Dad bought a greyhound, the first he had owned since the early fifties. Getting him was a trade-off with my mum who wanted a pet German Shepherd. It was a big step as Mum had made him stop gambling when they got together, but down the years she slowly relented. The greyhound my dad bought was called Ballyard Stag, and he was a canine win machine. We were going dog racing three nights a week at Portsmouth and I simply loved it.

I'm quite certain these were the happiest times of my dad's life: a fast greyhound, a fast car (he bought a Jensen Interceptor with some of his winning bets on the dog) and some ready cash in his pocket was all he ever wanted. He had worked hard enough for it though.

By all reports, it's fair to say that during his first marriage he too was a compulsive gambler, often leaving his wife and six children with no food on the table, unable to collect a wage packet without taking it to a betting shop. But he had curbed and controlled his habit after meeting my mum and, following jobs in the Standard Telephone Cables factory and at Southampton's Eastleigh Airport, where he loaded suitcases on to Channel Island-bound aircraft, he became a classic ducker and diver who loved the feel of cash in the palm of his hand and wasn't afraid to work for it. He'd stroll around housing estates with a bucket, ladder and sponge offering to wash windows for £2 a pop, and he once had a great business walking door-to-door across Southampton flogging and fitting peep-holes, those things hotel room doors have which you peer through to check that it's room service that has just arrived not an armed robber. The device cost him a couple of quid and the installation required only a drill. He'd have the job done in half an hour and he'd charge a tenner. Not a bad mark-up back in the early 1970s.

Quick cash was what Dad liked best, so it was a natural progression that saw him open a second-hand shop. Second-hand shop . . . evokes thoughts of crooks and conmen, right? Not on your nelly. The old man was so straight he was the only one ever taken for a ride. Even as a kid it would break my heart the stunts people pulled on him.

For example, one day a man walked into his shop saying his mother had died and he needed the entire contents of her house clearing. 'Absolutely everything must go,' the man stated as Dad walked around the house later that day. 'Everything' meant the curtains and carpets right through to the washing machine and freezer, not to mention a vast array of antique furniture and china. It was a valuable job which Dad had to make a seriously high bid on. His offer was accepted almost immediately, catching my father somewhat off guard as he didn't actually have the cash to make the purchase and needed to see his bank manager for an overdraft. In fact, such was the vendor's eagerness to do the deal and have the house cleared, Dad became suspicious and asked for proof that the goods were his to sell.

By the following afternoon, with more money than he could really afford to invest, Dad arrived back at the house with hard cash in his pocket and two hired hands. Sure enough the vendor produced his poor old mum's death certificate, which was correctly dated; there was even a condolence cutting from a newspaper, plus his airline tickets back to Spain where he lived, which was the reason he was in such a hurry to get the house cleared. The hand-shake was made and the contents of this sadly departed lady's home were loaded up on to Dad's clapped-out Transit Luton van.

That night it was dogs as normal, but on returning home at midnight he discovered his van had been stolen. The police, on receipt of his call, quickly soothed his anxiety by stating that they had his van and had impounded it. They asked him to come to the station the following day.

On arrival there he got some bad news. The goods he had bought had not belonged to the son of the deceased old lady. In fact the departed woman was very much alive and kicking. It was her boyfriend who had decided it was a good idea to sell all her possessions and do a moonlight flit to Spain while she was attending her own sister's funeral. The net result was, my dad had both purchased and received stolen property.

Thankfully the police were very understanding and simply ordered him to return all the property to the pensioner. For good measure the lady concerned decided that her partner hadn't really meant to perform such a dirty trick, selling her worldly goods with the use of her sister's death certificate. She chose not to press criminal charges and took him back.

All's well that ends well, right? Not exactly. Dad lost every penny of the money he had borrowed to buy the goods – the conman with no charges pressed against him kept that – which set him back about six months' profits. It gets better . . . a week later he received a solicitor's letter from the woman demanding compensation for a scratch to a dining room table leg, a packet of burgers from her freezer that had defrosted, and the cleaning costs of her curtains which now had dirty fingermarks on them!

As much as Dad was a grafter and often swindled, he was

also very unlucky. Through the shop he once sold for a pound a monstrosity of an ornament which, in fairness, could only have been described as a weird black paperweight. Six months later a picture of it appeared in the local newspaper, the *Southern Evening Echo*. It had just been resold at Sotheby's in London for £250,000.

Dad once viewed the contents of another lady's house. She didn't really want to sell any of her belongings; she had simply called him in to get a valuation for her period furniture and antiques. He was not surprised when he was sent away being told that she would think about his offer and be in touch.

Forty-eight hours later his photo-fit appeared on the local television news programme saying police wanted to 'question this man in relation to an antiques robbery'! Thankfully he got himself straight to the police station before he was recognized and reported by a member of the public and it was soon accepted that his visit and the theft the following day were purely coincidental.

Dad still talks about those times today, particularly his dog, Staggy. 'I had a thousand on him when he won once and five hundred quid quite a few times,' he told me just recently. 'That was a lot of money back then, son.' As for myself, each meeting I was given £2 to gamble with, which represented twenty pence per race and enough for a bottle of Coke and a bag of salt 'n' shake crisps. Back then the old ladies working at the tote windows were happy to take my bets despite my tender age. They saw no harm in it.

I hadn't forgotten my silent vow to seek vengeance for the harm done to my granddad by those Sandown Park book-makers. In no time I figured win bets were no good. Even if I found a 10/1 winner I'd only get £2 back and I wasn't going to change the world with that. Forecast and jackpot bets with greater reward would be my speciality.

As for reading the form, there was virtually nothing I could be told about any of the dogs at the track. I'm serious. Of the 180 dogs that raced there regularly I could tell you what grade of races they ran in, who trained them, what colour they were, what their racing weight was, and explain their style of running, be it finishing fast on the inside, or starting fast and running out of puff down the outside. Once again I maintain that the fertile mind of a child can outstrip an adult's brain in such areas.

At one meeting, during 1980 when Staggy was at the height of his powers, winning almost every week in top grade, with just a single 20p ticket I landed the Ace Pot. That was a string of four straight winners which netted me a whopping £52 – probably the best part of a man's working wage at that time. A week later I celebrated my eleventh birthday and found myself armed with a further £30 in cash from friends and family, who'd popped fivers and tenners into birthday cards. I now 'held' (that's a gambling term; they never leave you) £82, which I then asked my understanding dad to put on his dog the next time he ran. It was outrageous, I know, but Staggy was virtually guaranteed to lead in the race in question. You could make a case for some of his rivals being in with a chance on their fastest times, but only one had ever won from an unpromising position, from way behind.

Before the bet was placed some kind of committee meeting between my mum and dad took place. She plainly wasn't happy about her son turning into a carbon copy of his gambling-addicted father and grandfather. But, much to my surprise, it was quickly confirmed that Dad would indeed place the bet with the on-course bookmakers (while the tote windows would take bets from me, the unscrupulous book-makers with leather satchels perched on wooden orange boxes wouldn't). However, unbeknown to me, my mum was praying that the dog would lose and then my gambling would be nipped in the bud. What better way to turn somebody off betting? A bit like giving someone a stomach pump after drink-ing too many pints of beer for the first time. That's how she looked at it.

I can recall the race as if it were yesterday. It was a summer's evening, the sun was shining, the track, which had grass straights, looked like a bowling green. Perfect conditions for a dog who had stamina limitations and would struggle to last home on a wet muddy track.

The traps opened, and thankfully he avoided a bump. He did so because he was the first to step out of them and that allowed him to display his deadly early speed which carried him into a decisive lead. Rounding the first bend he was a few lengths clear. The chasing pack reached it together and collided.

The coming together increased his lead, but when trap four appeared from the mêlée in second and took up pursuit my heart sank. This was the only rival that had a chance of finish-ing fast and collaring Staggy in the dash to the line. I screamed and screamed at the top of my voice, cheering and urging his stamina to last out, as if to warn him he had a contender behind him and he had to maintain the gallop.

He passed us about fifty yards short of the winning line still in the lead. I was confident he had done enough and he could not be closed down, but that extra second or two it took for him to stride past the winning post delivered an adrenalin rush which I had not experienced before. I don't know how to explain it, like poison and an antidote injected straight into your heart simultaneously. The phrases 'heart-in-mouth' and 'agony and ecstasy' kind of fit the bill; distilled excitement maybe. I don't know if I can describe it. Try putting a month's wages on a dog or horse yourself and watch it go up the home straight neck-and-neck towards the winning line. Such was the power of this fix, had Staggy been nailed on the winning line this buzz, this drug-like hit, was worth losing £82 for.

The track's announcer was soon on the tannoy system: 'Here is the result of the eighth race: first, trap five, BALLYARD STAG!'

The buzz ended, it was a surreal feeling. At odds of 7/4, I had £225.50 to collect, yet I felt calm and composed. I wanted it to be a photo-finish, I wanted this buzz to last longer, I wanted to be on a razor's edge, caught between winning and losing the lot. As it was, I now had more cash in my pocket than most working-class men at the end of a month.

Driving home that night, sat in the back of the car and pretending to be asleep, there was an autopsy. 'What are we going to do now?' my mum said to my dad. She had taken a gamble and lost. The consensus seemed to be to put the money away, invest it for me for the future.

But what use was £225 to me in the bank? I was eleven years old. I was now up and running in every sense of the phrase and ready to pile the lot on my next 'certainty'. If I could spin 20p into £225, what could I turn £225 into? A lot more than the 6 per cent annual interest the banks were going to give me.

I was not going to stop, I was upping my stakes. What was the point in backing small? If I lost £5 or won £5 it was not going to alter the fact that I was a rich little boy and I wanted to get a whole lot richer. The more you put on the more you win, right? OK, if you lose you lose big too, but the prospect of losing never bothered me. After all, the money was never mine in the first place. That mindset has remained with me for decades. It's the same for the majority of gamblers. When they win there is this feeling the money is not theirs and a strange sensation of guilt washes over them. Mix in gambling circles and you will constantly hear people say 'I was gambling with their money' – that saying justifies losses.

Underneath it all, sick gamblers – and there are probably hundreds of thousands of them – have to gamble big, otherwise what's the point? What's the point of a fun bet? 'Big' is as big as your finances will allow and not a penny less; in fact, usually a little more. Victory, a win, has to be ecstasy; a loss, utter devastation.

So there I was, a kid in a sweetshop. I didn't know if my next bet – all £225 if I had my way – would win or lose, and I'll never know whether I would have been instantly cured of my addiction by a big loss because my mum decided in her wisdom not to let me find out. That money was indeed banked at her insistence, and eventually the majority of it was exchanged for a BMX bike, a CB radio (all the rage at the time), a guitar and a record player.

In no time, CB lingo – 'one nine for a copy, any breakers and takers' – was boring me and I broke the strings on the guitar, which were never replaced.

5

The Deal

As I'm sure you can tell by now, I was somewhat different from other kids of my age. Not just because my only pastime was gambling, there were a number of factors, such as being an only child. That really does set you apart.

It's just the way the cards fell. I cannot blame my parents (although I've often unjustly done so), because they always tried their best, especially when it came to education. Stretching way beyond their means, they gave me an expensive private schooling which, looking back on it, was ludicrous considering their often limited resources. Neither had been properly educated and both struggle with writing and arithmetic to this day. They wanted me to have what they missed out on, the best start in life.

You could question, was it all a waste of money considering what I was to become? Undoubtedly the education did not work out according to plan. I never became an academic genius. I fitted in at school like one of those square pegs trying to squeeze into a round hole. No surprise really. I wasn't well spoken, I came from a working-class family and I lived in a house in Binstead Close, Bassett Green, that was built in the early 1970s as part of an estate that featured endless rows of affordable terraced housing. They would call them starter homes these days. For years, buying a house didn't appeal to Dad. Many times he described property ownership as nonsense – 'spending a lifetime trying to pay for something which is no use to you when you are dead' was how he put it. It wasn't until Maggie Thatcher allowed council tenants to buy their homes for a fraction of their real value that he took the plunge, and that was only down to my mum nagging the life out of him.

Snubbed at school for being the son of a junk shop owner, I was then treated like a leper back on my estate for being the kid from the posh school who wore a uniform. Neighbouring kids perceived me as a snob who believed I thought I was too superior to go to school with them, so why should I be good enough to play with them? At home or at school, either way, I couldn't win.

Over a period of time I got used to it, but one incident, on the street in front of our house, stayed with me for years, and had an effect on the course of my life.

It happened when one of my father's sons moved into our street. I was fascinated by this. I'd had no interaction with any of my dad's first family whatsoever – understandable, as they were all considerably older than me. To underline that fact, this half-brother of mine had two children who were just a few years younger than me. Technically I was their uncle. Excited by this, I couldn't wait to meet them at the playground and introduce myself. I'm sure the conversation, when it happened, started something like this: 'Did you know, your daddy is my dad's son? That means he is like my brother, and I'm your uncle!'

The following day, like a bat out of hell, my half-brother's car roared around the corner and headed straight for me. Sat on a go-cart, I froze, transfixed by the chrome grill bearing down on me. At the last conceivable moment – at least that is how it seemed to me – it swerved away, and the car shrieked as it came to a halt, leaving a burning rubber smell in the air. I looked up to see my half-brother urgently unwinding his window, crimson-coloured with rage and anger.

'Now, you listen to me, you illegitimate bastard,' he roared.

I looked up at him not knowing what was going to come next.

'Don't you ever tell my kids you're related to them. Don't you ever come near them. You're not a Brindley, you're nothing but shit. You weren't wanted and you're not wanted. Don't you ever forget it!'

In all honesty, I didn't understand much of what he was saying. I'd never heard the word 'illegitimate', I didn't know the true meaning of 'bastard' – it's true my parents were not married until I was eight years old – and I certainly did not know what I had done wrong. I never told my parents. I bore the burden of his barrage.

Just a few years after the incident, when passing through puberty, I made sense of it all. His grievance I could understand, but to behave like that and to terrify a little boy like that, I had to believe there was something seriously wrong with him. I vowed that one day I would have my revenge for his unforgivable actions towards me, and for years I planned on retribution. As it was, our next meeting was over twenty years away, and, as you may know, things can fester over such a period.

The infant school I'd been to was Woodhill, in Chandlers Ford near Southampton. Mrs Callaghan was my teacher, that much I remember. I also recall a little girl called Deborah Dalton, who was my first crush. Even at such a young age, having a crush hurt, especially when Deborah and her parents moved to Bahrain. I promised myself I'd find her and marry her one day. I was never to see her again.

My secondary school, which I attended from the age of twelve, was St Mary's in Bitterne, Southampton, a Catholic school run by brothers. I found things particularly tough there. For the first term Dad dropped me off and collected me in his old clapped-out Transit van, but I soon told my parents I was old enough to catch two public buses to and from school each day. Anything was better than facing the humiliation of the other kids ridiculing my dad and me by calling us 'Steptoe and son' and 'Brindley the gyppo'. That hurt like hell.

Yes, Dad was delivering second-hand wardrobes and beds to squalid bedsits, or clearing out closed-down factories. No, he wasn't dropping me off at school in a Mercedes or Ferrari on his way to his privately owned solicitor's firm or dental practice.

It was hardly surprising that I became introverted. I had no interest in being educated, friends at school were almost non-existent, my ears stuck out and I struggled with the ribbing I got about them, I was short and dumpy, I didn't like sports much as I was no good at them, and I had no brothers or sisters so I had no one to talk to at home or at school. In fact, I had no interest in anything much so I just sat there day in, day out, simply daydreaming about gambling, oblivious to the teacher and blackboard before me.

The folks did not know; they thought I was getting a fine education. Let me explain. Neither ever asked to see my homework, which I never did anyway, and neither enquired as to what I had done that day at school. It took a few years, but eventually I realized it was the fear that I'd reply about something they didn't understand, or show them something to read which they couldn't.

At school there was only one subject in which I really excelled, maths. I had a natural talent for numbers, and despite O levels normally being sat on leaving school at sixteen, I took and passed the maths exam aged thirteen. I did absolutely no revision either. I didn't need to. Dog tracks, gambling and playing in all those card games had been the best form of revision I could ever hope for. A total of £1,187.50 being paid to a winning punter for a £500 bet must mean his selection won at odds of 11/8; stated as a betting percentage, that price rates the selection's chances of winning at a little over 42 per cent. Similarly, with five hearts left in a sixteen-card deck the probability of the next card to come out of the pack being a heart is 31.25 per cent, or odds of 11/5. How many thirteen-year-olds would know that, or could make those calculations in seconds? At Portsmouth dogs I often stood behind the bookmakers near to those wonderful but sadly missed people, the tic-tac men – that is an art form I fear has been lost for ever – listening to the bets being placed and taking in the calculations between the stake, the price and the payout. Division, multiplication and fractions were my ABCs.

As my final year at school beckoned, the recurring question

of what I wanted to do when I left needed to be answered soon. There was only one legitimate career path that I was interested in and that was the Stock Exchange. I'd be good at that shit. Figures and quick decision making, always looking for an edge, manipulating (betting/trading) markets – it was my thing. Admittedly I just saw it as gambling at the highest echelon, and the more I thought about it and the more I dreamt about it the more I saw it as my path in life. Don't forget, the Big Bang, the day in October 1986 when the stock market finally went computerized, was still on the horizon. For now, traders continued to run around frantically on a trading floor screaming dealings between themselves while urgently signalling their pit bosses with hand signals, working under the motto *dictum meum pactum*, or 'my word is my bond'.

I was already perfectly qualified in this field, because no matter how you look at it, the scenario is no different from the betting market at a racetrack, and there was little about that anyone could tell me. Just like the dog track, which gave me my real schooling, the City of London was one of the places where a working-class boy with minimal education but a quick mind could make something of himself.

So when the big day finally came, the day I was to meet the one person who could steer me in the right direction, a careers officer, I wasted no time in telling him what I wanted to do. 'No, no, you can't do that,' he bit back, 'it's way too difficult to get in there, almost impossible. Barclays Bank is a good place to get a solid career in finance, why don't you apply there?' He'd thrust some leaflets towards me before I'd even told him why it would suit me. A fat lot of good he turned out to be. I have to say, for a full ten years I was bitter towards him, as my life could have turned out so differently given some suitable help, guidance or encouragement from him.

Then again, come the mid nineties I watched the television aghast as the story of the Barings Bank collapse broke. Nick Leeson was the culprit, a young man not much older than me who had become hooked on gambling for big money. He hid his losses, chased his losses and ultimately lost everything. He was the world's biggest gambler, finishing up $800 million down. I sympathized with the guy while the rest of the world, especially those who had lost money with Barings, condemned him. If things had worked out differently, had that careers officer given me all the help in the world, the odds are I'd have done a Nick Leeson, so I look on it as a good thing sometimes. How fitting that Nick, like myself now living in laid-back Ireland, and I are good friends these days.

With the stock market a non-starter, all I craved was a life as a professional gambler. I was aching for the day when I could walk into the Mecca of all Meccas, a betting shop.

I'd first felt compelled to go into a betting shop when my granddad used to leave me sat outside one in his Ford Anglia back in the mid seventies. I'd be clutching a packet of crisps and a bottle of Coke (designed to gag me) while he was stuck inside unable to leave until he'd successfully chased his losses, or indeed lost the lot, despite my tooting his horn endlessly in frustration.

In betting shops back in those days it was commentary only, no pictures. You'd only see horseracing on ITV on Saturdays. Channel 4, which arrived with extensive horseracing coverage from the outset, didn't yet exist. Most of the betting shops didn't give you a carbon-copy slip of your bet either; you would get a small cardboard ticket similar to that given on public buses. Granddad used to walk out with a pocket full of them, all worthless.

A few years had passed since my 20p Ace Pot win was parlayed into £225 and I'd had another taste of a big-time gambling win, on my fourteenth birthday, when my dad asked what I'd like to do as a treat. I wanted to go to Fontwell Races so, equipped with my birthday money once more, off we went. The opening race was a poor 'selling plate', a race restricted to horses of moderate ability where the winner would be offered for sale by auction after the race. I quickly calculated with a form book that a horse by the name of Bell Hop was likely to win. Yet, to my amazement, he was a 16/1 shot.

This is where most punters go wrong. If they fancy a horse which is an even-money shot they will not hesitate in placing a big bet on it. However, if their strong fancy is 16/1 they'll cut their bet dramatically, even back it each-way. They just presume an even-money favourite is that price because his chances of winning are as good as a coin flip, and a 16/1 shot is pretty much a no-hoper. But the horse doesn't know what price it is, and gambling is all about the relationship between probability and the odds offer. In my mind, Bell Hop was a 2/1 shot and I needed to put every penny on him at the much bigger price. Makes sense, don't it?

Bell Hop, at 16/1, won that opening race after I'd invested my lot (£30) on the nose in person (and illegally) with a book-maker for the very first time. I won £480. Now I wanted to get on a Granddad Jack-style roll and fearlessly I waded into three of the next four winners. Just before the last race I turned to my father and asked, 'Dad, if you were winning and you really fancied one in the last race, how much would you have on it?'

Always a fountain of wisdom on these kind of matters, he coolly replied, 'Well, you want to go home winning, so I'd put half my winnings on him. You know, if you are winning twenty have a tenner on.'

I'd already won nearly £900 and that final horse I fancied was on offer at odds of 7/4. Naturally, I ignored Dad, put three-quarters of my winnings on, and ended up with another £1,000 in the pot after a bloodless victory. Sadly I got popped – the notes bulged out of my pockets so much they were spotted – and once more all bar a small amount of my loot was withheld by the parents, put in a bank and ultimately used in part when I was seventeen to tax and insure my first car.

At the age of fifteen I made the big step: I entered a betting office, in Portswood, Southampton, for the very first time. It was where my first bus journey home from school ended and the second one started; the shop was just a few yards from the 13a bus stop. I stashed my tie and blazer into my bag, put a thick jumper over my shirt and ruffled my hair, desperately trying to look three years older than I actually was.

Who was the first person I bumped into? Nan Happy! She used to walk across to the bus stop and take two buses to get to the betting shop, where she would spend the afternoon with her friends placing Round-Robin and Yankee bets, especially on anything her hero Mrs Jenny Pitman trained. Her idea of an afternoon out was not to go ballroom dancing or to the bingo. Those afternoons in the betting shop were her idea of entertainment right up until she lost her sight about ten years ago.

Nan Happy has never drunk or smoked. Gambling is her

only vice. She remains unashamed of that even to this day. I find it amusing that my eighty-year-old father still rings her every Saturday and reads through the list of runners and riders so she can make her selections for the day and he can place her bets. It's not just the horses either. Dad would often take her to the casino, where she would sit next to the roulette wheel listening intently as the croupier announced the winning numbers. She would then ask the dealer to place her chips on numbers for the following spin.

I digress. The most important thing on this day was that she never questioned my being in the betting shop. The subject matter, as I seem to recall, was more 'what do you fancy?' rather than 'do your mum and dad know you're in here?'

It was a fateful day as the staff took my bets without hesitation and over the weeks and months I grew in confidence, strolling into numerous betting offices with poise and professionalism – the professionalism of a mug punter.

6

Big Pot

School was coming to an end, and although I clearly knew what I wanted to do, I had no idea of how to get there or how to achieve it. For certain the commodity in the gambling business was, is and will always be cash. I rarely had any, apart from those winnings in the bank which I could not touch.

To appease my parents, who had invested so heavily in my education, I decided to go to college. The trouble was, I'd passed only three O levels – if I'd applied myself I believe it could have been several more – so I was forced to take a very ordinary BTEC General Diploma in Business Studies at Eastleigh's Technical College. It would equip me with all I needed to become an office clerk, although such a path in life was never really an option.

I was very wary about college. It scared me. An all-boys school featuring little or no interaction with girls for the past five years had left me terrified of them. I can clearly recall sitting between two similarly aged girls on my induction day too frightened to as much as look in their direction. One attempted to talk to me; I replied with no more than a shake of the head.

My introverted, some would argue bizarre, nature apart, I had little interest in college. I would turn up in the morning but during the lunch break I'd find myself in a Jack Grant (the local chain) betting shop, which I would not leave until the last race had finished, therein missing the afternoon lectures. I managed to maintain this betting lifestyle by helping out Dad with his evening deliveries and attending the odd auction sale, buying stock for his shop. But business was not going well for him, and the shop, Goods & Chattles on Lodge Road near the city centre, was also subject to a compulsory purchase order, meaning it would soon be forced to close.

Truth be known, I was just ambling on aimlessly. College was not for me, although I felt obliged to be seen to be making the effort, considering what had been spent on school fees. I could take a job but, as snobbish as it may sound, I felt way too good to spend my life as a factory worker or clerical assistant. What I needed was a big win, and it was just around the corner. Well, it was at the bottom of Gran's street, in Mintrums Betting Office in Swaythling.

Mintrums was a smoky gambling den I'd been going into for the past year or so. It featured none of the assumed trappings of betting shops these days: fruit machines were not allowed in betting offices, neither were drinks machines; display monitors had not yet been devised, and televisions were illegal. In fact, it may have been the case that carpeting was also illegal. Just as well really, as the lino floor was permanently littered with discarded betting tickets, cigarette butts and broken pencils.

The decor was simple, two grumpy-looking characters sat safely behind a caged-off counter taking bets, ragged pages from the *Sporting Life* displaying the form decorated the walls, and a 'board man' equipped with multi-coloured marker pens and a white formica board wrote down the latest betting and results as the information came through an old brown speaker box which lived in the corner of the shop. The punters, most of whom were gambling with the remnants of their giro cheques, perched themselves on tall stools around the sides of the shop. They stared at the speaker when a race was in progress as if they could somehow alter the words that were coming out of it telepathically, or encourage the progress of their selection.

Leaving my BMX bike outside Mintrums on this particular morning – a Saturday morning – I entered equipped with my *Sporting Life* and something like a fiver in cash. As was usual for that time of day Hackney greyhounds were on so I placed a few mandatory bets on the dogs. Thankfully that was a profitable exercise which allowed me to up the stakes on my selections on the horses that afternoon. All of those horses were mixed in doubles, trebles and an accumulator.

I had figured out long before that small win bets were never going to net me a meaningful sum, so it had to be done this way. To this day I struggle with the expression 'fun bet', or the act of betting small once a year on the Grand National or Derby. For a start I can see no point if a loss or win changes absolutely nothing in terms of your state of affairs, even quality of life.

Anyway, on this day I returned home to watch the first of my selections win on television, as did the second, Von Trappe, and the third, Ihaventalight. I was already sitting pretty with a decent return guaranteed, but the final selection, to complete the accumulator, would land me a massive lump of dough: my choice, Bluff Cove trained by Reg Hollinshead, was 14/1 for a marathon hurdle race.

A three-mile hurdle takes a lot longer to run than a 440-metre dog race, so the buzz of having thousands of pounds on the line while watching such a contest also lasts a lot longer, especially when your horse is galloping strongly throughout. That feeling, that adrenalin hit which if it could be sold by a back-street pusher would make him an overnight millionaire, was stronger than ever, and when Bluff Cove took up the lead at the bottom of Cheltenham's gruelling uphill finishing straight I lost total control of my senses. I shook from head to toe, paced up and down, grabbed at objects for no particular reason, just like my grandfather; and when Bluff Cove crossed the winning line in splendid isolation I broke down in tears.

I'd done it, I'd won a fortune. In the mid eighties £3,700 was more than enough to buy a very decent new car, or as a down payment on a house. Such things never crossed my mind at any stage, especially immediately after the race when I called my granddad in a frenzied teary state telling him to 'get round to my house now'; I was too excited to say any more. He arrived within minutes, diving out of his car and pacing down the pathway, expecting to see anything other than me clutching a betting slip shouting, 'I've done it, I've done it!'

Having shown me all his formulas and systems for selecting winners, no one was happier about my win than Granddad. Well, they wouldn't be, as I'd told no one else out of fear my winnings would be confiscated once more.

When it came to collecting those winnings, remembering how those unscrupulous bookmakers had run off and left my granddad clutching unpaid winning tickets, we decided to send someone else in with the winning docket, someone big, burly and imposing – a family friend, a former boxer, whose dad used to go to the dogs with my dad in the sixties. After landing such a big win the last thing I wanted was for Mintrums to say 'we're not paying you out because you're too young to bet and the bet is void as it was placed illegally'.

We got paid and I now had what I wanted, a huge bankroll to send me on my way as a professional gambler. There was no stopping me. In fact, within days I was living the life, taking trips to Plumpton races, Wembley dogs and the like. The only material goods I bought were a jumper and a pair of trousers. They were needed to get me into the posh part of the racetracks, the members' enclosures.

Having thousands of pounds stashed around your bedroom – behind picture frames, among the pages of books, rolled up within socks, even hidden in the battery compartments of games consoles and radios – makes you feel secure when you are a gambler, especially a teenaged one. But as it turned out the money lasted just a few weeks. That's right, I plundered the lot betting on anything and everything for ever-increasing stakes, thinking it was as simple as chasing my losses and eventually I'd find a winner. Easy come, easy go? Not really. Placing the last of my money on a horse in a betting shop knowing I did not fancy it to win but working on the theory that his price was right in order to get back all my losses was the moment I should have known I had become a sick, addicted gambler.

Thinking back, even as a young child the signs were there. I once had a system to beat the fruit machine that resided in the café at Pompey dogs. If I told you I could not lose you will know my scheme wasn't exactly legal, fair or honest. Call it what you want, but then again neither is a bookie who throws his satchel and stand into the back of a car and makes off without paying a once-in-a-lifetime winning punter his money.

The key ingredients were the penny coins taken out of circulation for decimalization in 1971. There were loads of them in my dad's junk shop. Holding the new 50p pieces alongside one, with the help of a hammer and a bit of filing I could batter those old copper coins into the shape of the new 50p, which I then slotted into the fruit machine to give me ten valuable spins. I knocked out two dozen of those fake 50ps every week and they were worth a grand total of £12. The machine would spit out on average £8 in 'winnings' for my fake money. It was a tidy sum for a kid of my age.

So what did I do with my 'real money' winnings? Why, I pumped the money straight back into the very same machine, chasing the £3 jackpot and getting a buzz from watching the reels spin.

It's all a sickness. Having gambled on anything and everything over the years and mixed with the people who swim in that same sea, I've made a lot of observations. I can tell you that people who become addicted gamblers invariably become addicted to games of chance, not skill. I could not begin to estimate how many people, in secret, have a problem with bingo, for example. Similarly, people know that fruit machines cannot be beaten, they know they will lose in the long run, but they cannot help themselves. I'd say they are the worst gambling mediums of all. Nudges, super nudges, super holds, cash ladders and a host of other features make people think they are in control, that there is skill involved, so the money just keeps going in the slot. At the other end of the scale, the stock market. How many people do you think have to go to Gamblers Anonymous (GA) meetings because they have a problem 'gambling' on it? Make no mistake, people win and lose on that beast too, but it's regarded as a legitimate game of skill.

Anyway, I'd gone from nothing to a relative fortune and back down to the basement. Soon after burning my way through the £3,700, while sweeping the floor of my dad's junk shop for £2 an hour I mentally sobered up and considered exploring a different path in life.

First, I wrote a letter to Terry Ramsden quite simply asking the man for a job. Terry Ramsden was my hero, a guy who had come to my attention thanks to the string of racehorses he owned. His blue and white silks were everywhere at the time and soon people were talking about him as he was often backing his horses to win six-figure sums.

A documentary-style piece broadcast on the BBC in the spring of 1986 during the build-up to the Grand National – Ramsden owned that year's favourite, Mr Snugfit, and had backed him to win a £1 million bet – revealed that his millions had come from dealing on the Far Eastern stock markets and he had progressed from an Enfield comprehensive school, to an office clerk – 'licking stamps and filing paperwork' – to a multi-millionaire businessman in a few short years. In addition to his string of racehorses he owned stud farms, houses all around the world, Walsall Football Club, twenty-seven cars, a

Gulfstream jet, two helicopters and a 30 per cent shareholding in Chelsea Football Club. He always had a burly minder walking behind him and a woman on his arm. How could you not envy and admire this guy? And, as the saying goes, if you can't beat 'em, join 'em.

Second, I was now in receipt of my provisional driving licence, and I used it to join Southampton's Tiberius Casino. Obviously I was underage, but in those days your driving licence did not clearly display your date of birth; instead it was jumbled up in coded fashion, meaning I could and did claim that my date of birth was 9/10/1966 not the correct 10/6/1969. If the casino had been caught allowing a child on to their premises, unintentionally or otherwise, they would have been closed down overnight and for ever.

The casino interest came from my Uncle Trevor, my mum's elder brother, who worked in my dad's shop dealing with customers on a day-to-day basis. Unlike my granddad he never encouraged or even talked to me about gambling. He never backed horses, but he had started going to the casino a few years earlier and was clearly doing all right for himself. None of us ever knew exactly what he was winning, we only knew he was playing blackjack and he must have had some run because he was forever buying gifts, costly gifts way beyond his wage, for all those near and dear to him.

This was attractive to me. Influenced by what appeared to be easy money I taught myself all I could about blackjack and devised my own strategy. It took months and I played out thousands of hands before I realized the fundamental rule in the game: big cards are good news for the players and when you are expecting a run of them you have to up your stakes.

Next I worked on a staking strategy. How much did I want to win, and how much was I prepared to lose in pursuit of it? Eventually I believed I had the winning formula. In fact, I had played repeated theoretical scenarios employing my tactics and staking system using a mythical bankroll of £200 against a mythical house. In the process I had beaten the mythical casino for thousands.

By the time I had all the blackjack angles covered, a reply from Terry Ramsden arrived. His letter thanked me for my enquiry and regrettably informed me he had no vacancies. It was nicely written and seemed sincere. I still have the letter. Within two weeks there was a front-page story in the *Sporting Life* explaining that he and his company Glen International had gone bust owing millions! Knowing all that was coming down on him, I appreciated all the more the time he took to reply to my letter. His misfortune gave me added reason to make blackjack my focus.

Now, I knew dog tracks inside out. I could not recall a time in my life before tote windows and bookmakers. I knew pretty much what to expect in a betting office long before I went in one to place a bet – remember, Granddad Jack's brother, Michael, owned several and I'd been allowed in as a tot. But casinos, that was virgin territory.

The Tiberius was situated within an Edwardian terraced building between Portswood and the city centre. It was a stone's throw from Derby Road, which was the red-light district. In fact sometimes the working women would stand on the street corner directly opposite the casino entrance.

I made that first visit, to sign up, one afternoon. The place opened at two p.m. and I thought, considering my shy nature and aversion to people, it would be the best time to attempt to join. It was remarkably easy: a few forms, a flash of that provisional licence, a picture taken with a Polaroid instant camera, and my membership was approved. Precisely twenty-four hours later – a 'cooling-off period', and a legal requirement – I was allowed to enter the gaming area for the first time.

Now came the hard bit: to play at the tables without making a rookie mistake, without looking out of place, and with the confidence of someone who was a seasoned casino visitor. In truth I was crapping it. I was the only person in the casino, apart from the three croupiers who stood motionless at two roulette wheels and a blackjack table. There was also a waitress who was quick to ask me if I wanted a drink of any kind. Essentially I was an alien, the only person out of place in this gathering, a punter not an employee, and I felt more uncomfortable than ever as they all looked at me wondering which table I was going to head for.

The blackjack table was, of course, my target, but I knew nothing about the system: how to buy chips, when it was permissible to place my bets and remove them. Thankfully, that blackjack table was being dealt by a man, unlike the two roulette wheels, which had attractive, scantily dressed women stood attentively at them. They would have intimidated me all the more.

My £10 was taken from my pocket and I held it in my hand as I asked the dealer where I could exchange it for chips. 'You have to give it to me,' he replied. I began to hand it over but he shied away from the note as if it were disease-ridden. 'No, not to me personally, I can't take it. You have to place it on the table.' He pointed at the baize before him. I placed the note on the table.

'How would you like that?' he enquired.

'As chips,' I simply replied.

'Yes, I know that, but fifty-pence, one-pound or five-pound chips?'

I'd been in the building just a minute and already I was failing in the etiquette stakes.

'Um, we'd best make it fifty-pence chips,' I answered.

As my note was being forced down a small slit in the table into a cash box below and twenty 50p chips were being counted out, I took my first glance around the room. It was just like the movies: long red curtains, an imposing crystal chandelier, cherubs in the ceiling corners, gilding along the borders, quality decorative carpets. This was no betting shop.

'There you go, sir, twenty pieces at fifty pence each,' the dealer announced. 'Good luck,' he added as I sat myself on a stool at the table and pulled my stack of chips towards me.

Off I went, winning my first ever hand of blackjack with 50p invested. Actually, unbeknown to me, and despite all my homework, if you are sat at a blackjack table on your own in a British casino you have to play two boxes (hands) at once. But that wasn't a bad thing and had little effect on my strategy. Within half an hour I was sat in front of £40 worth of chips, but as they were small round discs they did not seem the same as hard cash. Far from it. Just like those Nomination card games I played as a ten-year-old, I remained disciplined and not terribly excited about my winnings.

In fact, even on this very first session, I found winning money at blackjack tedious. There was no buzz, no excitement, just a playbook which I stuck to religiously, meaning that inside my head a number of figures were constantly totalling up and, in response to my calculations, I'd place either small or large bets.

There was no euphoria, no adrenalin shot, when I won a hand, as I played hundreds of them, winning as many as I lost. Obviously the secret was to have larger bets on the winning hands, therein making a profit. But it was analytical stuff, robotic, nothing like the rush I got from backing a horse to win hundreds and watching it go neck-and-neck to the line. At one stage on that first visit to the Tiberius I deemed the probability of a plethora of picture cards and Aces being dealt out as huge and I placed my £30 winnings in a single box and just 50p in the second box/hand. I didn't flinch a muscle as I was dealt a King followed by another King, giving me 20, which was way too good for the dealer's Jack followed by a 6 followed by another picture card, meaning he bust. Even this big bet did not send me into a frenzy. I simply asked for the procedure to cash-in and left with my target £60 in winnings – mission accomplished.

The next afternoon, at two p.m. again, and after spending the morning at college, I returned to the Tiberius and completed the feat once more. In fact, I never missed an afternoon there for a fortnight, winning on all but one occasion.

You could say I'd cracked it, I'd found the formula for being a winning gambler. It should have been Shangri-La, everything I had always wanted. But I was not enjoying it anything like I was enjoying the challenge of finding a winner on the horses. In fact, my now considerable casino winnings were going directly into a betting shop where I was chasing another big win instead of doing the obvious: winning it slowly but surely at a blackjack table.

I don't know, it just didn't do it for me. I couldn't even mess with my opponent's head like I could in a traditional card game. I mean, the croupiers simply dealt the cards out according to the rules; it was not a tactical battle. Each visit, analytically, mirthlessly, I collected money, but it felt like a job. I'd seen James Bond in a dozen casinos and when he played it seemed glamorous; for me it was monotonous. If I liked it for anything, it was because it funded my visits to the betting shops. By my third week of playing blackjack I was winning almost £1,000. However, apart from my £50 stake money, my bankroll, at no point did I ever have more than £200 in cash. It was a case of 'win it at the casino, take it to the betting office', day in, day out.

Midway through that third week, there was a bombshell. I happily arrived at the Tiberius at two p.m., walked up the three short but lavish steps to the front door, went through it and on to the reception desk. As I flashed my card to the receptionist I was informed that my membership had been revoked, I was not allowed to enter.

I asked to see the manager – it would have been stupid not to: it would have looked so obvious if I'd simply turned and walked out. The manager soon arrived. I was just about to protest that I was over eighteen and there must be a misunderstanding somewhere, when he said, 'There is nothing I can do for you, Mr Brindley. We run a business and some customers are valued and some are not. Unfortunately, being a successful card counter comes at a price!' That was all he had to say on the matter. I'd been barred, not for being sixteen years old but for beating the system, for walking into their shop every day and taking money straight out of the till. Casinos are commercial businesses and no business tolerates a customer who does anything other than make them money.

Barred for winning in a casino, no interest in college, no money, no income. What the hell was I going to do now?

7

Dogged

My first year at college was drawing to a close. Naturally I had failed miserably with my coursework; after all, I was rarely there. I still felt I had to justify my parents' investment in private schooling and, quite frankly, college was like a front for my gambling exploits, in the kind of way a small business can disguise illegal drug trafficking. I mean, if everything on the surface appears to be hunky-dory . . .

The next course was a BTEC National Diploma, again in Business Studies, and to get on it I had to attain another O-level-type qualification in double quick time. A lack of determination has never been my downfall and I found a crash course which would put me through the exam in English within weeks.

The qualification in question was part written exam and part oral presentation. Here I had a complete result as my presentation to the panel was all about the Australian horseracing legend Phar Lap. I had a brilliant film based on the life in the 1920s and 1930s of this wonder horse which I'd watched so often I'd inadvertently memorized it word-for-word. That went down a storm, and a week later, when the written exam paper instructed me to write about a great sporting event, I had the deal sealed. The history of the Melbourne Cup, a race which Phar Lap won, was the only thing to write about. This was my fourth attempt at the qualification. Thankfully it was successful.

Things were changing. I had turned seventeen, I had passed my driving test and, with the help of my Nanny Nora (my mum's mum) and my mother, not to mention the savings that had been put away for me from my Fontwell win several years earlier, I purchased my first car, an Alfa Romeo Alfasud 1.5 Super. Dad's shop had now been closed, and my parents, along with my grandparents, were planning on selling their houses and buying one big house with adjoining garages and barns somewhere further north where Dad could care for his three retired greyhounds, Granddad could do his woodwork, which had become a hobby, and Mum could care for both my gran and granddad as they approached later life. Pretty soon I would have to fend for myself.

I was still searching for my next big win, but that wasn't going to come in a casino playing blackjack as every casino for miles around had barred me. The Tiberius obviously shared information with other establishments and I was blacklisted far and wide for being a card counter. I needed to feed my betting-shop addiction, so I had to find ways of earning money while also attending college regularly for fear of being thrown out.

I started going to jumble sales, car boot sales, charity auctions and the like, searching for antiques and collectables which I could sell at a profit to the traders I'd got to know through my father. It was profitable all right, but it took up every spare minute, and no sooner had I bought and sold something I squandered the proceeds. Furthermore, for years my father had instilled into me: 'I'm not sending you to an expensive school in order for you to be a junk dealer like your dad. I want something better for you!'

Next, real work, via a job agency that sent me out anywhere and everywhere during college holidays and at nights. I mean, I worked all over the place, from building sites to glue factories, warehouses to removals firms. Gradually this took over my life and I was going to college just a few hours a week.

This taste of real work was a new experience for me. It gave me cash in my pocket, which went to a betting shop, meaning I needed more money, which required more work. Soon there was no free time for college and I was asked to leave on the back of my poor attendance record.

So that was the end of college. It was time for me to get a full-time job.

Through the agency I took up permanent nights in a factory called Square Grip in Eastleigh, a company that would cut and shape concrete reinforcing bars. It was dangerous work – the cutting machines were capable of taking your fingers, even your hand, clean off – but great money. At breaktime the skeleton night staff would play five-card brag and I rarely failed to clean the lads out.

From there I went on to Mother's Pride Bakery for permanent night work once more. This time I was working six p.m. to six a.m. six nights a week (seventy-two hours in total) for a massive take-home wage packet of £180. You see, I needed that kind of income to fuel my gambling habit as I was far more likely to win big with big bets than small ones.

One week I can recall collecting my wages from the bank and putting the entire lot on a horse called Forest Flower, a filly of Ian Balding's. She ran a stinker and I was forced to borrow petrol money for the rest of the week.

I just could not nail a big one. It went on for weeks and weeks. Loser followed loser. I was like a zombie working so hard, yet, as I pissed the lot away, I'd have been better off signing on the dole.

Soon both my parents and grandparents were making their move north and I could either go with them or . . . well, what option did I have? I did have an option, actually, and it came in the autumn of 1987 within an advert in the *Sporting Life*: 'Kennel-hand required for Surrey greyhound kennels with live-in accommodation'. I'd been around greyhounds aplenty, and although I'd never had a job looking after them I simply loved the idea of being a greyhound trainer and enjoying the thrill of training a winner. That buzz would satisfy me, and the live-in accommodation was vital to my existence at this point.

Off I went to a place called Ranmore, a lovely but isolated spot on top of a hill close to Dorking in Surrey. The whole place had been inaccessible for a few days because the great hurricane had gone through a few weeks earlier. The live-in accommodation was actually a Victorian bathroom equipped with a cast-iron free-standing bath, a toilet cistern with a square iron tank overhead and a matching sink. There were mod-cons, such as an old-fashioned Baby Belling cooker, a kettle, a damp carpet and a single bed. The wallpaper was coming away from the walls. The kennels, built into the cellar, were located underneath this room within a mansion that was, according to legend, built in the mid 1800s for an admiral who could see the Channel from his observation post at the top. The entire place was dilapidated, including the kennels.

I got the job, but lasted only for three months or so. It was nothing to do with the £50-a-week pay or the accommodation – in years to come I was to live in a lot worse – it was just a case of the trainer I worked for seeming to me to know very little about the dogs – the simple things like feeding, watering and letting them out into a paddock for exercise apart. All the same, leaving that job was difficult. I'd developed a taste for greyhound training, and I'd become so attached to the dogs, among them Padja, Missy, Sailor and Cindy. Race nights at the tracks were a lot of fun, I loved the breed and their docile nature, and this was the 1980s, a time when money seemed like no object to owners and racegoers. Greyhound training had a lot going for it. It was so exciting, a thirty-second rush every fifteen minutes on race nights after a week of preparation. I decided this was my vocation in life.

Next I moved on to Langley, close to Slough but out in the countryside somewhat. From there you could get a great view of the planes taking off and landing at nearby Heathrow. This was another live-in job with a greyhound trainer, who this time raced his dogs at Walthamstow. It was where all the money was, the Royal Ascot of dog racing. Here I lived in a caravan which I shared with another lad, and this time I soon realized my new boss knew his stuff. He had, after all, just trained the Derby winner, Signal Spark, and was about to land the St Leger with Exile Energy too.

All in all, this was a big step forward for me. Not financially, as my wages had only increased to £70 a week, but career-wise I was to learn about the greyhound, an athlete that can run at forty miles an hour and be prone to every injury its human counterpart can incur.

As for the gambling, well, I was now ideally placed with three nights' 'live racing' at Walthamstow, a Mecca for greyhound fans, plus another night each week at Oxford or Wembley, possibly Catford or Wimbledon. And as I said, at this time money in London was abundant.

Another kennel-hand, a fella called Billy, taught me the ropes in terms of making an extra few quid courtesy of tipping dogs to the general public. He had the game sussed. At Walthamstow, for example, he had half-a-dozen punters all around the track prepared to give him a backhander for a successful tip. He would spin them lines about the times the dogs had done in their trials back at the kennels, or explain how certain dogs had been running with low blood counts but in the past week their latest readings had come back spot-on. He'd also say a dog had finished its last two races with cramp but it had been fed on a special feed for the last ten days ensuring it would not happen again, and it was expected to improve out of recognition on this particular night.

Most of it was pie in the sky; he was simply tipping dogs he fancied. But people love to think they have some inside information, an edge, and quite simply cannot resist a tip on a good thing.

When one of his tips won he would disappear for a few races while he did the rounds, finding all the people he had given his selection to and pretty much holding his hand out.

This was like wheeling-dealing all over again, and I loved

that cash-in-the-pocket lifestyle. There really was some money about back then too. Just one look at Walthamstow's car park – it looked like an exclusive German sports car forecourt – proved that.

In time, Billy and I between us perfected our technique. If one of us went on a bad run we would drop our punter, or he would drop us, but immediately afterwards Billy or I would go in, befriend the racegoer and start up a fresh tipping service. We got greedy too. Well, if you are going to start work at 7.30 a.m. and finish at one a.m. when returning from a race meeting six days a week for £70, I think you are entitled to.

For example, if someone tipped me £50 for a winner after the race I'd look all dismayed and disappointed and come up with a sharp question like 'What price was he? Four to one? So you only put on a tenner for me? Well, thanks, thanks for the tenner, I'll back the next one myself next time and I'll be putting on more than a tenner! I tell you what, keep the £50 and put it on my next tip for me – that's how confident I am about putting you into winner after winner after winner.' A week later I'd give them the biggest certainty on the card; no matter how short their price, it just had to be a winner. It didn't matter who trained it as I could always come out with some shit like 'I've been talking to John Coleman's head lad and he told me . . .' Now, when that won, say at even-money, I'd go and find my punter to collect my winnings, which should have been £100. Invariably they handed me £100 and said something smart like 'When do you think you'll have another [tip] for us?'

'Two consecutive winners, my friend. You have basically given me a tenner and you want more info like this? I've got plenty more where these have come from but from now on I want you to place £50 on each for me, otherwise it's no use to me.'

Sure enough, come next meeting they're eagerly looking for me, seeking secret info and prepared to pay for it, inspired by their own greed . . . and mine.

I remained at this job for a year or so, learning all I could about the handling and training of racing greyhounds, plus the treatment of injuries and a whole lot more. Once again I had my favourites, the dogs I will never forget, such as Hymenstown Trip (pet name Neddy), Gay Starlight, Windsor Lemon and Mr Hills.

Tragically, during my time there Granddad Jack passed away. He was the dearest man to me, everything in my world for so many years. Yet I never once went to see him in his new home in Lincolnshire and I was so upset to be told that every Sunday for months he looked out down the road and said, 'Young Roy will be coming today, you wait and see. He'll be here to visit us.'

Around this time, as we approached the 1990s, what I could best describe as a 'nomadic lifestyle' started. I moved on to another live-in kennel-hand job, this time in Essex. The area was a market gardener's paradise. Greenhouses littered either side of the country lanes we walked the dogs down every day. Here my net income was £60 a week, and I was living in a shed with a corrugated asbestos roof, a single-bar heater and damp walls. Kennel-hands in racing kennels do not have unions like those within the horseracing fraternity, ensuring fair pay and conditions.

The wages didn't matter though; neither did the seven-day-a-week work regime. This job, with a trainer who had the finest dogs in the country under his care – Waltham Abbey, Sail On Valerie, Lissadel Tiger, Mals Boy and Farncome Black – would allow me to receive a professional trainer's licence. I'd be fully qualified, experienced enough to go it alone.

Naturally, to set up my own kennels I needed money, a lot more than £60 a week could give me, so I continued to gamble every day of my life with every penny I could get my hands on. That £3,700 win was already four years behind me but I was convinced a bigger coup was just around the corner.

With the finest dogs in training, everyone wanted to know the kennel's news, starting with which dogs we thought would win. Again I picked up another £100 or so every week with my tipping to punters at tracks all around London: Catford, Romford, Wimbledon, Walthamstow, Wembley, and as far afield as Oxford and Peterborough. But the biggest and best tipper of all was Charlie, or Jock (as he liked to be called), Scott. Amazingly, this guy lived just a few hundred yards away, in a house opposite the kennels. He already had his own tipster called 'One Arm Lou', a form student who always had a stop-watch round his neck and a notepad in his pocket (and he really did have one arm, and one eye, following an attempt to save a schoolgirl who had fallen overboard a pleasure boat on the Thames about thirty years earlier). But, positioned within the kennels, I had a fresh 'insider's angle' and I bene-fited from Jock's generosity whenever I put him on to a winner.

Jock was cooler than a bottle of Moët on ice. My absolute hero, the epitome of the man I wanted to be. He drove a Jaguar XJS, lived in a smart place with its own swimming pool, had a lovely wife with beautiful kids. But at the same time he was also quite a man about town, distinguished, always well dressed, with a moustache that was trimmed immaculately. What's more, he gambled, and gambled big. He always had a big wedge of money on him and spent Saturday afternoons in the betting shop, where he would have his own seat reserved by the management, who would keep cups of coffee on tap for him. He'd punt every race with big chunks of money. People would go into the shop simply to watch him in action.

Truth be known, Jock was like all the rest of us, but I was too blind to see it at the time. I had him perched on a pedestal. Jock's money came from his business but I didn't want to believe it, especially on the nights he took me out gambling for high stakes at Wembley or Catford dogs.

On one occasion after racing Jock took me to the first card club I'd ever seen. It was somewhere on London's North Circular Road, in a commercial shop that doubled as a café during the day. It was a desperate place, completely illegal, like something out of the movies, with hungry-looking characters called Fat Tony and Stef the Greek who munched on thick cigars and who licked their lips like cold-blooded wolves when Jock walked in. Poker is a thinking man's game, a patient thinking man's game, but Jock craved quick action. He lost quick and he lost big with bluffs even I could see were futile.

So keen was I to enjoy this kind of playboy lifestyle for myself, for the first time I got into hock to fund my gambling, desperate to win a chunk of money. It was so easy when I was a schoolboy but I'd not won anything close to a four-figure sum in years now. These days I was in a job that started at eight a.m. and was all done and dusted by 1.30. In the evenings I'd often go racing, but I needed to be at the kennels at five p.m. every day to let the dogs out into the paddocks, so what was I going to do with my afternoons? Sit in my shed and watch *Blue Peter* and *Home and Away* in front of the one-bar electric fire? There was only one place to go: the betting office in the nearby town, Broxbourne.

A few doors down from the betting shop, which was part of a publicly owned chain, was a Barclays Bank in which I opened an account, my first bank account, and to my utter surprise, and without applying for it, they sent me a chequebook and cheque-guarantee card with my welcoming pack. I was earning £60 a week and they sent me thirty cheques potentially worth £50 apiece (the maximum value the guarantee card would allow).

Now, I didn't start off intentionally, but I was soon writing out cheque after cheque made out to that bookmaker's, one a day every day – the most they would take. Before long I was up to my eyeballs with a stonking £1,200 debt – five months' wages. I simply could not win, and every day I was getting deeper and deeper in. Occasionally I'd collect a lump from my greyhound-tipping exploits and would pay off some of this unauthorized debt. That would appease the bank and the nasty letters would stop arriving for a while. They would even send out a fresh chequebook. But the overall trend was downward, and when I was in to the tune of £3,500 or so, more than I earned in a year, a letter arrived saying 'no more chequebooks'.

A desperate last throw of the dice was called for. I walked into my local branch stating that I had left my chequebook at my parents' house and needed a temporary/emergency one to see me through. It was an audacious bluff and I was depending on word of my account's closure not having been passed on from head office to the branch yet. It hadn't been, and I was presented with ten fresh cheques.

I found a horse I fancied and travelled to ten individual betting shops during the course of the afternoon, placing £50 on it in each. It gave me the old-fashioned buzz, the one I was addicted to. Everything was on the line, money that was not really mine, huge amounts. A win would get me out of the mire; a loss ... well, that didn't bear thinking about. As it happened, my selection was beaten by some considerable way. I never even got an adrenalin fix out of it because it was never in with a fighting chance at any stage.

There is a thin line between being a gambler and being a crook, because we are both looking for some kind of edge in life. I've been told about so many gambling scams it's unreal. From the outrageous to the outright criminal.

I know one guy – I know him extremely well – who used to go into a random betting shop and ask the manager if he was allowed to place a bet using a cheque. The reply was always the same: 'Yes, of course you can, but your cheque must be accompanied by a guarantee card.' He'd then rush to the counter as the dogs were going to the traps, waving his chequebook and guarantee card and saying, 'This is the race I want to bet on! Look, put this slip through the till and if it loses I'll finish writing out the cheque after the race.' Now, should his selection win he would stand there bold as brass waiting to be paid out; if it lost he would be out the door, down the road and gone without leaving as much as a cigarette end.

I once saw a fella punting race after race on the dogs for thousands. He was working to a staking system and increased his bets until he found a winner. He went on a great run and won more and more. Eventually his bankroll was so big he could afford to have thirteen losers before he needed to find a winner. With about £25,000 in cash in a bag, a fortune at the time (1992), the betting shop manager agreed it would be easier for him to keep the punter's money behind the counter and they would settle up at the end of the day. Otherwise he would have to count out piles of notes every race, every seven or eight minutes.

Now, just as I've seen thirty-two consecutive red numbers on a roulette wheel, I witnessed this guy back thirteen consecutive losers. He walked to the counter, was kind of commiserated by the manager, who said something like 'Sorry, pal, but your losses come to £24,950' as he handed the punter the large cash-filled carrier bag in order for him to count it out and pay up. The punter started to count it out but then paused, looked up at the sky and said, 'Do you know what, a gambling debt is not reclaimable in a court of law and I've just decided I'm not going to pay you.' He then turned and coolly walked out of the door with his bag in his hand. Fact was, he was right. Until recently there was nothing bookmakers could do about punters running out the door or simply refusing to pay.

My time in Nazeing came to a close. I'd worked in greyhound kennels for over two years and, now aged twenty-one and equipped with references, I could apply for a professional trainer's licence from the National Greyhound Racing Club. Firstly, however, I'd need kennels. Secondly, I'd need some dogs to train. And finally, somehow I had to pay off the bank.

8

Nutted

For the first time in years I returned to live with my parents, although it wasn't home as I knew it. They now lived in Lincolnshire, about ten miles from Boston, a godforsaken place.

Granddad Jack had died, but my gran was there, as was an old distant aunt called Aunty May. She was approaching a hundred and would sit in a chair watching snooker from noon until night (the BBC wallpapered their airtime with it back in those days). Steve Davis was her absolute hero. She was a good old stick and loved me dearly as I had visited her and pushed her around the shops in a wheelchair when she was in an old folks' home a few years earlier.

But my dad had changed. I don't know if it was the despair of his business being closed down on him, the move to isolated Lincolnshire – which is flatter than a pancake; when there is a breeze in the rest of the country it's a full-blown hurricane there – or the invasion of his house and home by elderly family members. I suspect it was all three, the latter having most to do with it. He always wanted all of Mum's attention; even as a child I often felt in the way. From the age of fourteen I spent more of my life living with my grandparents than my parents. He couldn't help it. He was so insecure, paranoid, about the age gap between him and my mum, and this was compounded by the memory of her nearly dying with a brain haemorrhage.

Things did not go smoothly from the outset. There was a lot of friction between us. Still, with financial help from old Aunty May, and a library book about building and brickwork, I managed to construct kennels for seventeen dogs within the barns that were part of the property's outbuildings.

I was right on course. Becoming a greyhound trainer in my own right was what I had worked towards for the last few years, and within three months of my arrival my kennels were finished and my licence application approved. But there was a problem: I did not have a single greyhound in my care, which meant I did not have a single kennel fee coming in. What's more, the bank had tracked me down, they wanted their money, and they had sent a representative to knock on my door and ask for it.

Gradually I took in what could best be described as cast-offs, a rag-tag collection of greyhounds with attitude problems – like they had their own ideas about chasing a mechanical hare and didn't want to cross the winning line with their nose in front – or injuries that impaired their ability to race regularly, such as muscle tears and sprained wrists. Worse than that, none were being paid for. My ex-governor sent me four such dogs, of which only one ever won a race. But that fella was special. We had a bond, and when I left the Nazeing kennels Friendly (race name Kishikirk Taurus) refused to 'eat, shit or do anything other than sit in his kennel and cry his eyes out for you', according to my old boss. Friendly was with me for many years as my pet long after he retired from racing. We were inseparable for a long time.

Neal Foulds, who was the number two ranked snooker player in the world at the time, gave me two dogs which came with a health warning. One of those, a real character called Bertie Small, went on to win a few open races for me – they're the top races – which wasn't bad for a gift dog with more injury problems than Barry Sheene. Neal was a good guy. I met him when he was an owner at the Langley kennels, and he gave me some sound advice from his own experiences such as 'Do not believe in all the promises people make to you. When you are young people build your hopes up and then always seem to let you down. You will have a lot of those knocks in the training game.' How right he turned out to be.

There was another fella who was similarly helpful, a former football player turned greyhound trainer called Barry Silkman. I know absolutely nothing about football, never have, but I know that these days Bazza is a highly successful football agent with half of Chelsea on his books. Back then he was as skint as I was.

One paying owner did eventually come my way, again a guy I had met during my time in Berkshire. He gave me a six-year-old – normally well past pensionable age in greyhound racing – bitch called Rosewood Joy. Rosie had been graded off at Walthamstow, meaning she had not won a bottom grade A8 race for over six months. But somehow I turned her right round and won four open races with her, which, say it myself, was an incredible feat. However, the trade paper, the *Sporting*

Life, was not overly interested and wouldn't give me even an inch of column space. Rosie's amazing transformation should have got me noticed but it was to no avail, and within no time I realized I was in a dead end.

The problem wasn't my ability to train and care for my dogs, it was Boston. It's like the armpit of the human body. You have to travel a long way to find anything of any use and people don't like visiting. I was not in love with the place either. Our property was ten miles from the nearest town and we were surrounded by nothing other than fields of potatoes and cabbages.

Barclays Bank were getting paid £8 a week, just to cover the interest, while I continued to spend all my spare time in an independent betting shop somehow betting on credit. That came to a head one cold, wet and windy night when two heavies came knocking on my door, equipped with shotguns, looking for money. That's some shock to the system I can tell you; it frightened the bejaysus out of me. They got paid courtesy of a bank loan from the TSB, supposedly for my greyhound-training business. It was OK, though, as a big win was surely just around the corner, and that would pay off both the banks, which had let me get in so ridiculously deep.

With a kennel full of dogs that needed feeding and only one or two with owners paying kennel fees, added to the fact that my relationship with my dad was falling to pieces – I believe he thought that once I had left the nest I should not return; all my mum's attentions should now be directed at him – my career as a greyhound trainer was crumbling. I had to move nearer to London, where all the action was, where the wealthy owners were and where I could get dogs to train with much-needed paying owners.

A year had passed, and I had plenty of winners with the few dogs I had, but I was as broke as ever, in a lot of debt to both banks and family members. Then word reached me that there was a range of greyhound kennels for rent near Brentwood, in Essex. I paid the place a visit and they were immaculate so I agreed to take them and moved my dogs in immediately. This was ideal for me. The place was just a few miles away from the likes of Crayford, Romford and Walthamstow, with Ramsgate and Rye House in easy reach.

The money for my deposit and rent in advance came from an American owner I knew from the Nazeing days who sent me five young puppies to train and race. He was a sound guy and very wealthy, an investment banker. The dog of his I'd looked after for him eighteen or so months earlier, Tain Solas, had cost £17,000 – some money in those days!

There were two problems, though. First, I had nowhere to live. I was reduced to living in one of the kennels simply because I couldn't afford to rent anywhere nearby. The kennel in question was about the size of a big double bed with a wooden raised section, a dog bed, which I curled up on to sleep. I didn't really care that much because the most important thing was that I was now near London. I didn't feel at all miserable, it was all a means to an end. My kennels were hygienic, scrubbed with disinfectant every morning, they had a fresh layer of sawdust spread on the floor and I had a quilt around me.

The bigger problem was my landlord, who was dodgy. I'd guess he was a former gangster who hadn't quite retired yet, or couldn't. About a week after I arrived he took me for a walk around his massive forested estate, clutching a shotgun to clear any wildfowl – something I was not keen on. As we talked about dogs he turned and asked, 'Do you like my little estate, then?' I nodded, and said, 'Why, it's lovely.' He chuckled and replied, 'And to think they say crime doesn't pay!' After a pause for me to take on board what he had just said, he then added, 'But I'm not being funny or anything, if anyone tries to screw around with me they'll get some of this, know what I mean?' He looked at me and tapped his shotgun, which was broken at the barrels with the copper ends of the two cartridges inserted into the barrels showing.

One day, about a month later, with things starting to go well – new owners had now joined me and some winners were coming my way at Rye House – I was in my kennel happily grooming my dogs when news of a ram-raid robbery came on the radio. I thought little of it until, when I was walking a few dogs around the woods, two big black BMWs came roaring through the estate's entrance and my landlord came out from his house to talk to the guys in the motors. I looked on, unbeknown to them, from my vantage point behind the trees. The guys got out of the car, walked around to their respective boots and opened them up to show my landlord their contents – a treasure trove of jewellery, most attached to display trays, which had doubtless come from the robbery performed the night before.

Who needs to stay around for that shit? I could have been kneecapped for what I'd witnessed, if they thought I was snooping on them. I was soon on my way back to Boston, as broke as ever, with all the debts closing in on me.

During this short spell in Essex dear old Aunty May, who had financed my kennels and been so good to me, passed away. It was one less debt, but I have never felt good about borrowing money from this very old lady and never paying her back. God bless her.

My sickness was stronger than ever. I was deluded. I still believed I could win a fortune and that would enable me to buy my own house and kennels. The time in Brentwood proved one thing, though: I could attract owners in the south of England. Returning there was still my goal. Meanwhile, as we moved into 1992, gradually all the new owners and dogs I had drawn in near to London left my care. I did, however, have a huge roll of the dice running for me at the Cheltenham Festival that spring.

You see, each and every day I went into a betting shop I would place a small ante-post wager on two horses in a double. It could be anything between 50p and £25, and I'd been doing it for weeks and months. One was a horse called Royal Gait, my fancy for the Champion Hurdle at 20/1, the other The Fellow, at 33/1 for the Gold Cup. It was, of course, Cheltenham racecourse that had delivered me my £3,700 payout.

When Royal Gait landed the first of those races I stood to win over £60,000 if The Fellow, who was now a 7/2 shot, could land the Gold Cup three days later. You don't need to guess that this was the biggest buzz of my life.

In what was one of the most memorable races in the history of the Cheltenham Festival, the French jockey aboard my horse, according to pundit John McCririck, 'gave the outside of the track to no one', meaning the horse ran about a furlong further than any other horse in the race. He looked like a sack of spuds in the saddle, and while trying to give the horse all of his assistance he was as effective as an anchor in a rocky seabed. Conversely, young jockey Adrian Maguire on the 25/1 no-hoper Cool Ground gave his horse a really tough ride, whipping and pushing him for what seemed to me like an eternity and forcing him over the line in the tightest photo-finish imaginable. A full and tense five minutes later the body blow of an announcement that The Fellow had got beat, nutted on the line, came through. I was finished, a once-in-a-lifetime chance of a life-changing result gone. It was agony and ecstasy at their extremes.

Just as I was contemplating a life spent picking cauliflowers out of the nearby fields I got word of yet more kennels available for rent, this time near Andover in Hampshire, something of a 'new town' that was infinitely more preferable than Boston and only forty-five miles or so from Portsmouth, the track where I spent so much of my childhood and where I could race my dogs.

I crammed the seven dogs I had left in Lincolnshire into the back of a tiny fuelled-up Renault 5, which had set me back the princely sum of £80 at auction. (I'd gone through half a dozen clapped-out old motors since the classy Alfa Romeo I had as a teenager – Mark III and IV Cortinas mainly, plus an estate Passat and an Astra, which were better for moving the dogs around – so this Renault was the latest in a long line.) I had a dozen tins of Chappie on the car floor to feed my dogs – totally inappropriate for racing greyhounds – and just £12 in cash in my pocket. I was starting from scratch all over again, and on my arrival, without enough food to feed my dogs the following day, I resorted to knocking on the door of the local Social Security offices to see someone about an emergency loan.

9

Home Straight

Initially I was given temporary accommodation by the social services, but the place in question was no more than a doss-house where I shared the kitchen and bathroom with three other lads who were all off their heads on heroin. It turned out they had been placed there after being released from jail.

I stayed just three nights, feeling desperately unsafe, before finding myself accommodation in a really nice shared house with three women who were business professionals. I lived there for around three months before moving into a mobile home on the farm where the kennels were. I was just yards away from my dogs so it was ideal. Social Security gave me a helping hand for the first few months – I was, after all, essentially unemployed. It's safe to say I look back on those days and fail to see many comparisons with the international poker circuit.

This time there were no issues with my landlord, a farmer called Roy Hares. You could describe him as a miserable, moaning old bastard, but beneath that front he was kind of all right. He'd bet every day of his life too, at 10.30 each morning driving his car to the betting shop, where he would meet up with his circle of friends, chat and place his wagers. It was always the same type of bet and always for the same stakes, meaning that over a period of time he could never come out in front.

Of course I'd turn up at 1.30 after my dogs had had their main feed and were sleeping. I'd certainly not bet the same amounts and same bets every day. I was smart. I knew it was impossible to beat the system that way. But I also knew you could not win betting on every race, yet I did so. The 1.30 p.m. feed time was a window in my kennel routine I had deliberately created. The dogs didn't need to go back out into the exercise pens until 5.30, and that meant I could take in all the afternoon's racing. My dogs didn't go out again after that until ten p.m., so during the summer months I could also get back down the betting shop for evening racing, which I watched while munching through takeaway fish and chips or a Chinese, depending on how my funds were at the time.

Roy the farmer would also punt on my dogs, and when he had a good win he'd bring up a tray of broken eggs from his farm shop as a tip for me. Can you imagine, he once won £1,500 on one of my runners, one I'd prepared and tipped to him, and he gave me a tray of forty-eight broken eggs in return! Well, they are full of protein, and they went down well with the dogs in their cornflake, milk and vitamin-packed breakfasts.

He had a son called Ian, a nice enough fella who was kind enough to show me around locally and introduce me to a few of his mates, which was nice, as when you're nomadic friends are thin on the ground. Together we would drink in the local pub in the small nearby village, Amport, and play the odd game of brag in my caravan. Poker was still no more than a game I was familiar with.

This was a lovely part of the world, idyllic. The villages of Monxton, where my kennels were, and Amport had thatched cottages, a stream rolling through them, greens and a cricket ground. It was like something out of *Midsomer Murders*, simply beautiful. Things went well for me there from the outset. I was immediately happy.

But to achieve my training goals, to land the big races, I needed winners which would encourage new owners who could wave their chequebooks around in order to buy the fastest dogs. Those owners would also pay bills, and that money would pay my rent and keep me afloat. I hatched a plan.

On taking over the new kennels I had inherited two dogs that were drawing pension but were still, to my mind, capable of winning poor-grade races. One was a six-year-old called Turnpike Lass, who had whelped a litter of pups; a bitch like that winning races is as unlikely as Zola Budd making a comeback. The other, Strachen Style, had a very poor win ratio. I had brought down with me another fella, called River Ridge, who had been retired after spending his career with a Walthamstow trainer and was only with me while awaiting a new home and sofa to live on. However, I managed to talk the owners into letting me give him just one more go on the track.

All three of these unlikely candidates had the potential to improve, I thought, and after they'd completed their qualifying trials and once they'd had a race or two I went to work on them. Handfuls of protein-rich raw meat went into their main feed, copious amounts of vitamins B, C and E into their breakfast. I walked them different routes twice a day, with three long gallops during the week; I even gave them a Jacuzzi, which is as beneficial to dogs as it is to humans, relaxing, therapeutic and performance-enhancing.

They were set to race on the same night at the start of the month. The plan was to put on some of my training fees, which would have come through from my limited number of owners by then, and win a decent sum for myself. Naturally, in the never-ending search for owners I wasn't shy about tipping these dogs to anyone, and that included two jockeys I'd met in a nearby pub. There were several racehorse trainers and stables in the area, including Toby Balding, on whose gallops, which prepared the likes of 1969 Grand National winner Highland Wedding and two Champion Hurdle winners, I used to run my greyhounds, and Richard Hannon. Both were at the top of their profession at the time.

When the day arrived I had £200 set aside to back my dogs in the betting shop. However, I got suckered in like every punter in every betting shop across the country does. An announcement came over the tannoy: 'There has been more money for this favourite at Warwick, he is now 6/4 from an opening show of 5/2 as they are loading the stalls.' That in itself was too much for me to resist, even though I should have known better. A £50 bet on this horse would give me another £75 to place on my dogs, and they were sure to win.

The horse lost.

Losing £50 hurt all right, but then I staked another £50 on a 6/4 favourite in the belief that I'd win back my money plus another £25, enabling me to put £225 on my dogs. That same old familiar thought pattern, always spiralling downwards.

I lost.

With £100 left I thought to myself, I've backed two losing favourites, I cannot possibly back three in a row. It was not until all the money was gone and I was walking out of the door that what I had just done hit me like a hammer from hell.

I turned up at Portsmouth track that night before racing to weigh-in my dogs and put them into their pre-race kennels, which is part of the rules and general routine at dog tracks. Without a penny placed on my dogs, the general manager approached me and opened a conversation with: 'I understand your dogs are expected to win tonight!' Not sure how to react, and baffled as to how he knew of their well-being, I simply replied, 'I hope so.' The manager responded, 'Just as well, as someone has tried to place fortunes on them in London today and I'll be watching them carefully.'

I hadn't told anyone in London about my dogs' well-being, so I was completely gobsmacked. I knew that statement was not good news and, everything considered, I cringed as River Ridge – who was to become one of my all-time favourites – pulverized his opponents. One down, two to go. Next up was Turnpike Lass, who majestically turned back the years and overcame some bumping to win as well.

This left just Strachen Style, who was a bit of a thinker and would not perform unless there was nothing between himself and the hare, but if he did take an early lead it would all be over. He did just that, bounding up the home straight a staggering thirteen lengths clear of his rivals – half the track in dog-racing terms.

Standing alongside the running fence, watching him cross the line, I was left scratching my head, ruing my inability to walk into a betting shop without doing some mug punting, calculating what I would have won had I not lost my £200 stake on those horses. As they were big prices, it ran into thousands.

I walked back into the paddock to greet my winner, wash off his paws and give him a well-earned drink. I'd forgotten all about the general manager – until he stormed into the paddock, spluttering out words to the effect that I would never set foot on his effing track again. He was convinced I was 'turning this track into a circus', when I knew nothing about the money that had been put on my dogs, and having had nothing on them either.

Driving home that night I felt strangely muted. I was broke, I had been for years, and even when training my own winners I still managed to fuck up by losing my stake beforehand. Now I was also barred from the track.

I went back to my caravan and took stock of everything. I'd broken no rules. The performance of my dogs was not questioned by the racing stewards, though they did order dope tests, which naturally showed up no irregularities. With no actual inquiry called by those stewards I felt I'd been banned for no good reason. It wasn't just.

I decided to fight my corner, and a phone call to the ever-helpful Jonathan Kay, a journalist at the *Racing Post* whom I'd become friendly with during my time at Walthamstow, did the trick. I protested that my wins had come about simply due to a good training performance, and they ran a series of articles, the first titled 'Portsmouth sack Brindley after he lands hat-trick'. It was actually great publicity as my dogs' owners wrote letters to the paper saying it was disgusting and outlining what a talented handler I was. Eventually I was reinstated, and new owners came on board, inspired by the prospect of having their dogs in a true gambling kennel.

Much later I discovered that the track's tip-off came from a bookmaker who had refused to take bets on my dogs from a character called Brian Wright, who'd been tipped my three-some through his horseracing contacts in the area. Wright, nicknamed the Milkman, was sentenced to thirty years in jail in April 2007 following a conviction for drugs smuggling after an eleven-year worldwide investigation into his activities. He claimed his multi-million-pound fortune came from gambling on horseracing. He was indeed renowned for courting all the top trainers and jockeys, lavishing money, expensive suits, cars, women and a whole lot more on them, but this was his first venture into greyhound racing.

It's a funny thing, but once I started training dogs I never backed dogs trained by anyone else again. What was the point? If I didn't know the form of my own dogs, if I wasn't able to know when they were going to run a stormer, what chance would I have lumping into someone else's? Horses, that was different – I just loved the buzz.

About a year on, River Ridge, or Buster as I called him, had become a virtual win machine, and another inmate, a black dog called Meat Mac, who looked more like a Labrador than a greyhound, also seemed to win to order. Over a period of time I placed nineteen bets on that pair alone and they won fifteen times and finished second on another three occasions. I dared not calculate my winnings on the pair because, as usual, they were going straight down to the betting shop.

I suppose everyone changes down the years, but people who gamble only deviate. Gary Wiltshire also started adult life working in kennels; he is now one of the biggest bookmakers in the business. Ross Jackson, who was a young bookmaker at Portsmouth around these times, moved out to Vegas in the mid nineties to eke out a living punting on American sports. (He married a beauty who ultimately left him to marry country singer Kenny Rogers, but I hope he did all right out of the divorce settlement.)

But you know, as much as I could never stop gambling, and as much as I was unsuccessful overall, I was not a complete mug. I'd bet on two flies walking up a wall, but only if I thought I had a mathematical edge. I still love the challenge of trying to find an edge. For example, I remember backing the Conservative Party and John Major to win the 1992 general election at odds of 6/1 a week before the election. I didn't think they would win, but the true probability was more like 3/1. I don't know how much I won but I can guarantee that whatever I staked was as much as I could afford to lose and not a penny less.

It's all relative, of course. Twenty quid may not sound much, but when you have left yourself just enough for two portions of sausage and chips for the next two days until you get more money together you are at the height of gambling sickness. When someone at a poker table boasts these days they placed a massive bet on something – say, £500 – I don't shudder, I question the ratio of what that sum represents to what they have. They always have plenty more in the bank and can afford to feed themselves for the rest of the week. Technically my £20 bet was bigger.

Other such value bets included a tip-off that Boy George had apparently recorded a brilliant song for Christmas (this was back in 1993 or 1994). As word had reached me in July I'd managed to place enough small bets on it becoming number one over the festive period to ensure a massive pay-off. Sadly, his track was dire and it never made the top thirty. Far more recently I figured out that telephone votes from Indian strongholds like Birmingham and Bradford would make Shilpa Shetty very hard to beat in *Celebrity Big Brother* and a genuinely big touch was landed when the 16/1 long-shot came good.

Back in the early nineties, though, it was always a case of win on the dogs and do the proceeds on the horses, because I loved mug gambling. The trouble I was facing now was actually getting my dog bets on, so here's the sort of thing I got up to.

Once, Meat Mac was running and was, according to my judgement, an absolute certainty. It was that raw meat and vitamin time of the month, plus he had a plot draw – in trap five with the dog in trap four sure to move inwards from the starting boxes, meaning he would get a clear path – and he was back in form following some pretty average performances, which led to him being down in grade on this occasion. However, the most that could be won from the betting ring (the on-course bookmakers) at Portsmouth was likely to be £1,200. Therefore I came up with a cunning plan.

On a Saturday afternoon I collected a childhood friend of mine, Phil Rowles, who didn't know the first thing about gambling, and drove him to every betting shop within miles of Southampton, to Winchester, Salisbury and beyond. He was sent into each clutching a betting slip which I had already written out staking £25 to win on Meat Mac in the 9.23 p.m. at Portsmouth (bets of £30 or more on that meeting had to be phoned through to head office and verified). I sent Phil in to place the wagers as my face would be familiar to the few betting shop managers I knew went to the track. Similarly, we chose a Saturday as it was a particularly hectic day. If shops did start to phone through to head office reporting a string of bets at Portsmouth on this particular dog, they were likely to be too busy to do anything about it. By five p.m., after placing dozens of bets, everything was in place.

Later that evening, as the dogs went out on parade for the 9.23 race, I was ready to implement the second phase of 'Operation Meat Mac'. You see, I had two runners in the race and I knew my second string had absolutely no chance, she was simply outclassed. The bookmakers and general public didn't, though, and they watched a fantastic performance by me, waltzing into the betting ring and openly placing bets on her for everyone to see. Both the bookies and the punters took this as a sign that I fancied her and gave Meat Mac no chance. As a result his price drifted out and out and out. After all, if the trainer fancied his other runner what chance did Meat Mac have?

Betting markets are just the same as a fruit and veg market. You are there to sell your stock, and if grapes are £3 a kilo at nine a.m., by closing time if none of them have been sold and you are faced with the prospect of dumping them into the bin, you will lower your price, knocking them out at £1 a kilo.

Should the pitch next door follow suit, you will then drop the price to 80p, trying to attract the grape buyers to you and clear your stock. When a dog drifts out in price because no bets have been taken on him, the same knock-on effect comes into play, and the price goes out and out. In an ideal world bookmakers want to lay every runner in a race.

In what was one of the most memorable moments of my training career I leant over the rails on that cold, crisp night, plumes of exhaled vapour bursting forth as I cheered Meat Mac home. He usually came from behind in his races and finished strongly, but it was all over after a few yards as he took an early lead.

The net result was a host of small bets landed at the outrageous odds of 7/1 when he had just four opponents to overcome (races at Portsmouth back then were five-runner affairs). Had I tried to get the bets placed at the track, the return on my money would have been minuscule in contrast because the weight of money would have driven his price downwards and he probably would have started as an odds-on favourite.

It was all fun stuff, and I was happy for a while. I was still scratching around most of the time, but at least I had a caravan to live in and a kennel full of dogs that I loved. I didn't need anything other than a daily bet and food and provisions for my dogs. In fact, my demands were ludicrously simple. I was living a kind of crofter's lifestyle on my farm, just ticking over with little thought about the future. I suppose few people have such thoughts in their early twenties. I still firmly believed another string of big-priced winners was going to alter my life one day.

For me, the biggest incentive of all remained the prospect of unearthing a champion, and my young American yuppie owner Sky Lucas was the man to provide one.

When I moved back to Boston he removed the four dogs he had from my care and placed them with another trainer, but with little success. Now that I was situated down south he decided to return Nunny, Bunny, Rosie and Clown to my care. My kennel was small and intimate with just a dozen dogs in my care. Every one had a pet name, every one was given a biscuit at night. The larger kennels could have over a hundred dogs so they missed out on the loving touch. I knew exactly how to handle Sky's dogs.

And they needed some TLC. When I got them back I took them straight to the local veterinary surgeon, seeking answers for their poor form. They underwent a kind of Crypton Tune for canines, and within weeks I had them transformed. Clown progressed from winning an A8 (a bottom-grade race) to contesting open races and had six wins on the bounce. Her sister, Nunny, almost matched her for results.

My success with them led Sky to send me his latest puppy, a youngster called Jacksonflybynite. I have to concede she was one of the ugliest specimens I'd ever seen, with a long, undershot jaw and a curved back, but she went from a raw puppy winning her debut A7 race into an open-race winner in just four outings. It was nothing short of a miracle.

I was on my way up the ladder in greyhound racing, and my reward for these results? A phone call from Sky, telling me that he had decided to send Jacksonflybynite to another trainer. Jacksonflybynite, the potential champion I craved, left me. She was never to win another open race.

I thought he must have got the message when he rang one

day to say, 'Roy, I have four pups that were bred in America and have been brought here. Tain Solas is their daddy and I'd like you to train them for me.' The new recruits bolstered my paying numbers and this time they were not only very good greyhounds, they were exceptional. I mean, you can tell the first time you put them on a track. Fast dogs have a great conformation – everything is in fine proportions – and they usually have a calm, laid-back attitude. It's like they know they are good.

One, American Hot, was a massive brindled bitch who had the word champion written all over her. I brought her on slowly, winning in the bottom grades and then upping her in racing distance, to six bends. She won an open race at Portsmouth and two at Henlow in her seven-race career for me, which featured five wins. There was also Soo Nippy, not quite as talented but still a top-grade winner over the six-bend distance. And then the dream of all dreams, a dog with Derby class speed and potential called Jespair Joey.

I'd worked with some great greyhounds in the Essex kennels, including Derby favourites and Greyhound of the Year winners, and this fella had the same kind of class stamped all over him. Winning an A7 on his debut and an open race in his third public outing was mighty impressive, and I believed he really was the dog I'd been dreaming about. I begged Sky not to take this talented dog away from me but, sure enough, Joey and his siblings were to be shipped to the other trainer. In desperation I called the man concerned, whom I'd never met or spoken to before, and I got straight to the point. 'Mate, I've worked in kennels all of my adult life, I've only got moderate dogs and I've dreamt of having a dog of this class and calibre.

Take the others but, please, leave Jespair Joey with me.' My plea was to no avail. He bluntly replied, 'Son, life's tough, and if you get things too easily you won't appreciate them. I'll send a van to collect the dogs in the morning.'

Disillusionment immediately set in. I had done the same thing for five years now. Not one single day had I failed to walk into a kennel at eight a.m. in order to exercise my dogs. But I was getting nowhere. I'd not trained a big competition winner, not even come close, and the way it was going I couldn't see it happening any time soon. All the top trainers had owners queuing up to buy expensive dogs that had a fair chance of becoming a champion. I had one owner who was insulting my, and his own, intelligence. I was twenty-five. Phil, my childhood friend, my best friend as an early teenager, who I met at Southampton's BMX track, was already a parent and owned his own house.

Around this time he got married and asked me to be his witness. Naturally I was happy to accept, but when the big day came round I had to feed and exercise my dogs before getting scrubbed for the ceremony. Once that was out of the way and the requisite pictures had been taken I had to dash back to the kennels for the main feed of the day. I made it back for the reception but I couldn't drink as I needed to take the thirty-mile journey back home once more for the dogs' evening turn-out.

I thought I had settled in the Andover area, but it was time to move on again – overseas this time as I couldn't bear the thought of watching American Hot and Jespair Joey winning big races for another trainer. America was the place, the land of hope and dreams. Just look at Sky Lucas. He may have been a bad judge of character, but I could not dispute he was living the life: jetting around with a woman on his arm, loads of ready cash, punting away at the finest dog and horse tracks in the country.

I learned there were no fewer than seventeen greyhound tracks in the so-called Sunshine State of Florida. I had absolutely no contacts or any idea where to start looking for a job out there, but I was convinced it was an achievable dream. It was something bigger and better but still with greyhounds, somewhere I might settle down and finally have that elusive big win.

At the time my worldly possessions and assets amounted to a clapped-out van which I rather grandly described to friends and family as a greyhound transporter. I had to leave the mobile home on the farm to cover my outstanding rent while I set up a kennel girl in the greyhound business by helping build kennels in her parents' back yard so I knew my dogs would receive the best treatment. Friendly, my retired pet, one of the very few greyhounds I successfully taught to sit, give me his pay, fetch a ball and play dead, who had become a resident in my caravan and accompanied me to the betting shop and pub and just about everywhere else, needed to be left somewhere very special. Thankfully, my mum and dad agreed to look after him while I was away. If they hadn't, I wouldn't have gone.

So, after five years of knowing and doing nothing other than training dogs, I finally took a day off. That day soon became a week and then a fortnight as I got ready for my American adventure.

I stayed with my nan Nora for about a month as I prepared for my big exit. She had moved back to Southampton, unable to live in Boston with my dad, and had been in a warden-controlled flat there for some time. I loved having her there as I could pop in and see her on Sunday afternoons and in the evenings when I returned from Portsmouth dogs (I drove almost directly past her front door).

Of everything I was going to leave behind, saying goodbye to Nan Nora was the hardest. I took these weeks with her to tell her how much I loved her, and I apologized for making her life so miserable so often down the years. On countless occasions I had shamelessly borrowed the last tenner she had in the world. She knew full well I'd had little chance in life; she knew my bad ways were all gambling-related and that it had been bred into me. Ultimately I almost asked her for per-mission to go to America, explaining that I loved her so dearly that the prospect of her being taken poorly when I was over-seas worried me terribly.

10

Horrible Beat

It's funny how television influences your mind. I can clearly recall my flight to North America on my big adventure, sat on a 747 flying over Greenland and Canada. I looked down aghast at nothing other than barren white ice for hours and hours on end, not quite believing the vastness of this wasteland. To me, the ice cap was about the size of Epping Forest or Salisbury Plain. I mean, that's the impression I got from my TV.

That wasn't the half of it. When I disembarked after a ten-hour flight I realized for the first time that I had flown first-class all the way. That's right, I had been given a free upgrade but had no idea until I walked back down the plane looking at the 'sardine class' seats in the rows towards the back of the aircraft. Such was my ignorance of the world and its workings. I mean, all I really knew was greyhounds and betting shops. I just presumed the quality of service and seat comfort had improved drastically since the last time I'd flown on a summer holiday to Spain with my family, twelve years earlier.

The seats on the jumbo were soft and leather, I had my own TV, and people kept offering me champagne, even before we took off. Naturally I didn't take any because after the sale of my van and purchase of my air ticket I only had £270 left for the trip. I didn't want to be drinking it away.

Despite targeting Florida as the most likely place to find work in the States, I'd actually flown into Vancouver, Canada. I had family there: Aunty Pat's sister Olga, along with her son Rob and wife Debby. Vancouver, and the surrounding area of Chilliwack and Sardis, was a beautiful place, so different from any countryside I had seen before. The breathtaking Rocky Mountains with snow on their peaks simply blew me away. As did the clean air and novel things that were done in this society, bizarre things such as refuse recycling. Rob took me to the local beauty spots, such as Harrison Hot Springs, and also, on my request, horseracing at Hastings Park and Cloverdale, the two racetracks in Vancouver city. There were no bookies on the course, just a window where you put on the bets which went into the tote. It seemed very relaxed compared with the hustle and bustle of betting rings and bookmakers which I was used to back home – less exciting actually.

A month passed while I simply chilled, came to terms with my new-found freedom, and enjoyed the beautiful countryside and my eccentric but oh-so-lovable aunt's weekly routine, which revolved around dancing almost every night of the week at ex-pat clubs where the average age was seventy. But I could not stay with them indefinitely. I needed to get working. I only had two months left before having to take my return flight back to England.

It was a local veterinary surgeon who gave me the contact

details of a lady who lived nearby and kept greyhounds. I made a cold call, explaining that I was a journalist from England who wanted to do a story on greyhound racing around the world. My story was actually true as before my departure I had contacted Jonathan Kay at the *Racing Post* who put me in touch with the paper's editor, Jim Cremin. He issued me with a letter confirming I could supply stories to the paper under the guise of 'US greyhound correspondent'. Of course, the problem was I could not write a sentence which wasn't riddled with both spelling and punctuation errors, and I'd never heard of a fax machine, which I was supposed to use to send back my stories.

The lady concerned was very welcoming, and when I visited she explained, while proudly showing me her cherished pets, that greyhound racing was only done on a fun basis in Canada. She was kind enough to give me a collection of American greyhound magazines though, and armed with them I called pretty much every phone number I could find in their pages.

Eventually I found a greyhound-breeding farm called Greymeadow Kennels, in Abilene, Kansas, that needed some help. I had no idea where Kansas was and had never heard of Abilene, but when a local travel agent quoted $4,500 for a flight there I took the cheaper (and more appropriate) option of a Greyhound bus at $170.

The journey to Abilene took a total of fifty-six non-stop hours, through Washington State, Oregon, Idaho, Utah, Colorado and into Kansas. You could write a book about that journey on its own. It's the best way to see the place and meet typical Americans, the weirdos and the freaks, in places where few tourists ever go. There were some obvious highlights, like seeing the mountain which millions watch obliviously at the start of a Paramount film – yes, it really exists. Other memorable moments include going up the Rockies and admiring beautiful Colorado, and driving over the canyon which Evel Knievel unsuccessfully attempted to cross in a rocket back in the seventies.

Once again my naivety of the world and the power of television led me to believe I'd see little other than yellow taxis and skyscrapers everywhere. There were no yellow cabs where I went but there were seriously straight and long roads punctuated by towns which all seemed identical, and boasting huge signs that protruded out. Those signs were identical too, neon-lit and promoting Super 8 and Best Western Motels, Ford and Chevrolet truck dealerships, McDonald's, Burger King, Wendy's and Taco Bell food joints. It was a culture shock, and I found myself urgently seeking something that would remind me of home, even if that were just a stone building, a church spire maybe, which was a hundred years or so old.

It was late at night when the bus finally pulled into Abilene. It looked just like any other town I'd been through since leaving Denver hundreds of miles back. The bus dropped me off outside a gas station, where I anxiously looked up and down the road for my new friends Jack and Mary Butler. I use the term 'friends' because I was not technically working for them – I never had a work permit. If they didn't turn up I was stranded a good thousand miles from civilization as I knew it, and more than that from the sea, another thought that worried me like some kind of phobia. What's more, I was in dire need of a shave and a shower and I had a grand total of $55 on me. Considering the banks I owed and never paid, I'd never been granted a life-saver such as a credit card.

Eventually they showed up, and the next morning I could see the scale of their property. It was like Southfork Ranch from *Dallas*. Within the sprawling complex were buildings which housed five hundred greyhounds. Yes, five hundred. It was a huge operation, from birth through to the dogs being retired from the track and being transported hundreds of miles away and placed in home adoption programmes. Essentially the place was a breeding farm. Pups ran up and down all day long in ever increasingly sized runs. At twelve months they started their schooling at a training track where they learned to run around bends and out of starting boxes. By the age of fifteen to seventeen months they were ready to be sent off to the tracks to race. The American Way was a conveyor belt system, and a very successful one.

It was so different from what I was used to. Here, the staff dutifully clocked in and clocked out; they were paid by the hour and they worked just forty-five hours a week. It sounded like a doddle compared with working in large kennels back home. My new job was to help cure dogs returning from the tracks of ailments. You have to find their injuries – a trapped nerve, a torn muscle, heat, swelling or inflammation on a joint – through patience and understanding.

In many ways the area was similar to Boston, Lincolnshire, with cornfields all round, and we were positioned slap bang in the middle of nowhere. I lived in a spotless trailer home with all the mod cons which looked out on to an empty expanse of land for miles. The town itself, about twelve miles away, was like something out of *The Dukes of Hazzard* (another eighties television series). Red-neck territory is the term, where dungarees and chequered shirts is the dress code and the inbreeding situation is so bad there are only a dozen names in the local phone book! This was also Bible-belt country, with churches everywhere. Guys wearing green John Deere baseball caps drove pick-up trucks with stickers on the tailgates proclaiming 'Jesus Lives' and 'God Bless America'. Essentially it was a sleepy town where greyhound breeding was the number one employer. This place was to American greyhounds what Newmarket is to British horses. There were dozens of similar greyhound breeding farms in the area, along with a Greyhound Museum and the National Greyhound Association's offices.

It was in the information area of those offices that I came across a poker magazine featuring 1989 World Series winner Phil Hellmuth on the front. I read that magazine from cover to cover, especially the bits about the big-money wins and glamorous lifestyles. I could easily relate to poker thanks to all those childhood card games at my gran's, but I was so busy working in Abilene that it got put to the back of my mind. Christ, for the first time in my life I wasn't even gambling. I couldn't: there was nowhere to do it. I still have that magazine to this day, and I believe that reading it that day sowed the seed that sat dormant until I took up the game.

Thinking back, it may have been sleepy, but the place did get exciting for a short while. When the bombing of a federal building in neighbouring Oklahoma went down a week after my arrival it transpired that the Ryder truck used to stash the explosives was hired nearby and that one of the suspects, Timothy McVeigh I believe, was held in Abilene's jail. This prompted a serious police presence.

For me, things were going swimmingly, and as a reward for

my efforts Jack Butler drove me down to Florida with him to visit the dogs they had in training at the tracks in Jacksonville, Daytona and St Petersburg. This was heaven to me. Florida – I'd finally got there, courtesy of another awesome drive which took us through Missouri, a memorably lush-green Kentucky, Tennessee and Georgia. Ultimately, during my greyhound days in America I travelled through eighteen states and found myself in some unlikely places such as Waco, Texas, where I also lived and worked for a short while.

During this trip to Florida, a phone call home to my gran resulted in the terrible news that she had been taken poorly and was in hospital. I had three weeks to wait for my flight home. My initial thought was to get back to England immediately, but I decided to wait it out when a message came through that she was resilient, improving, and in no hurry to go anywhere.

I flew home on my twenty-sixth birthday, 10 June 1995, and went directly to Southampton's General Hospital. My gran was clearly very poorly. It was simply lovely to see her and the nurses told me of how she spoke of me, how proud she was of my being in America, and how I was coming home to see her.

Slowly, during the course of the summer, Gran deteriorated. She was allowed to leave hospital and was taken by ambulance to my parents' Boston home some two hundred miles away. Mum nursed her throughout. I drove up with my uncle to visit on a few occasions, but at the very end she had to stay in hospital up there.

That's where I saw her for the final time. I knew the end was coming. I'd accepted it, but when I went into her hospital room I could hardly look at her. At a time when I should have been sat alongside her, telling her how much I loved her, I simply peered out of the window, appearing disinterested, unable to make eye contact with her. It's hard to explain. I think subconsciously I was protecting myself. I've had to live with my stone-faced behaviour ever since. I loved her dearly, but, sad to say, she went to her grave not knowing just how much.

Gran was cremated in Boston, but there was a second ceremony, a memorial service in Southampton, shortly afterwards. It was a nice day as these things go. Plenty of people came to pay their respects. But I found it very tough.

As the autumn approached I made plans to return to America. I'd kept afloat during the summer by working for a job agency, Driver Hire, and had lived in my gran's flat. That job only kept me ticking over, feeding me and funding my weekend bets in Mintrums Betting Office, the one I had cleared out so memorably nearly a decade beforehand. Apart from having television screens installed, it hadn't changed.

Thankfully, and quite remarkably, Jim Cremin at the *Racing Post* loved my stateside contributions, which were part diary and part news, facts and figures. Thrillingly, they were used a lot within the newspaper. It was his £500 cheque which allowed me to purchase another return ticket to Kansas.

I went back on an American Airlines flight, this time via Dallas. (I confess, when I hear that company's name nowadays, I only think of poker and pocket Aces.) Naturally it was nowhere near as comfortable as my first trip in first class, and this time it was also not such an adventure. With my gran gone I felt quite lost in the world; I knew that when I did return to England she would not be there. I felt all alone, and beyond this ten-week live-in position I was also homeless.

My new role was with one of the biggest operations in the

US, Flying Eagles Kennels, also in Abilene but on the other side of town. My brief was to train sixty dogs, young puppies, in preparation for just two big races; afterwards they'd be put through a public auction. Their sale price would depend on their performance and I was promised a share of the revenue made from the sale of the dogs by Vince Berland, owner of the operation. This guy's money had come from the legal pyramid-selling company Amway, and an office adjacent to the kennels displayed pictures of Vince shaking hands with numerous celebrities and politicians including Ronald Reagan, so he must have been very successful.

On arrival I found the Berlands to be decent upstanding God-fearing people. They said grace before dinner (a dinner put on specifically to welcome me to their fold) and had effigies of Jesus all over their house. Strangely, this husband-and-wife team with five children, seemingly with about ten months between each, didn't have a television. It was something I had to enquire about. Just as I got my question out at the dinner table the youngest of the two daughters announced, 'Television is evil. It corrupts the mind and destroys the brain.' It took me back somewhat. The statement came out as if it had been etched into her mind. But each to their own, I suppose. In fact I did kind of chuckle to myself when thinking back to my first flight into Canada, when I'd thought the frozen ice cap was no bigger than Salisbury Plain. Maybe they were on to something.

The Berlands gave me a truck and a motel room in the sleepy town where I was to live for the next ten weeks and thereafter I was ready to get down to work. All sixty of the dogs had a racing name prefixed with the word 'Flying'. There was Flying

Rolex, Flying Seiko, Flying Neptune, Flying Saturn, Flying Mars – the list went on and on. They would pick on a brand and name every dog in a litter after it. You know, like Honda, Suzuki, Kawasaki and Yamaha.

Initially all went well. I gradually got to know the dogs I was working with, and their individual characters, and moved into a regime of nail cutting, worming, grooming and high-protein feeding. After a week or so it was off to the training track, where we would see how the squad was performing by timing their 550-yard lap times. Naturally, Vince was keen to see how they were progressing and he brought along his son Lance and a family friend, Greg. I think they all went well, and everything looked good with them when we returned to the kennels. I mean, I could see no bruised toes, no sand burns, and the dogs lapped up their post-exercise milk and glucose. However, in the room next door, an area where the stud dogs were housed, I could hear a conversation taking place between Vince, Lance and Greg.

'Right, I want you to kill that one and that one there,' Berland was saying, presumably pointing to his clipboard, which he used to write down the dogs' times. 'In fact, get rid of those two too. We need the space and I'm not in the business of keeping slow dogs, so if those two don't improve their times next week you can kill them too.'

'Do you want me to kill [Flying] Seiko too?' Berland junior asked.

'No, he's got one more chance, but if he don't improve, do him next week.'

Moments later the door into my kennelling area opened and in walked Lance and Greg. I looked at them in total shock, the kind of shock that makes you just stare or gives you an urge to run from the scene, like witnessing a nasty car accident. Surely I had got it all wrong. Surely they weren't going to take these animals to the vet to be put to sleep. The word 'kill'. It was so brutal.

The dogs were taken outside and loaded on to the truck. It did not head out towards the main gates and on to the open road but down a dusty trail towards the far reaches of the ranch. I listened intently, wondering where exactly it was headed, and I could still hear the engine noise as it pulled up again and the engine was turned off. I heard a metal door to one of the dog's compartments on the transporter swing open, violently enough to make a clattering noise, and then, BANG! Moments later, BANG! again, and again and again. Never in my life had I experienced first hand such barbaric behaviour. Those loving, adoring animals had been slaughtered by gunshot.

Somehow I did not want to believe it, and later in the afternoon, with an aching in my legs and pain in my stomach, the type you normally get after running a marathon but which I had through pure emotion, curiosity took me on a walk down to where I'd heard those gunshots. There was a pit, the size of a small swimming pool, full of dead dogs. A hideous sight: limbs strewn in directions they should not go, cannot go; heads and necks folding back on to themselves; brains and blood splattered everywhere; flies crawling over the melting jellies that were once their eyes. Scores of cartridges, brass casings and blood-stained iron bars littered the rim of the pit along with a few other dogs' corpses which were more decomposed, rib cages breaking through the fur. In places it looked like petrol had also been thrown on to them and their corpses had been set alight.

Here was the brutal truth. Any dog considered incapable of winning races was brought down here to be shot. The stench of death got into my clothes and my hair. I can smell it to this day. And what I saw has haunted me ever since.

I drove back to my motel numbed, and thinking of my pet dog Friendly back with my folks in Lincolnshire. I desperately wanted to be with him, just to make sure he was safe and well, unlike those poor creatures in that death pit at Flying Eagles Kennels.

Unable to sleep – in fact I spent the night with the light on – I called in sick the following morning and went directly to the offices of the National Greyhound Association. Marching in, I asked the registrar bluntly, 'Where do you stand on the slaughter of greyhounds?'

The response was automated, as if it were the sort of thing people normally asked: 'Here at the NGA we are purely a registry organization. We register matings, whelpings and ownership. That is where our function ends.'

'So who do I see about dogs being shot, murdered?' I continued in a voice loud enough that all of her dozen colleagues could hear.

Nonchalant, without emotion, without her tone of voice changing in any way, she replied, 'Well, if you would like to report a case of cruelty you can always go to the sheriff's office.'

Off I stormed, pulling no punches when it came to explaining to the sheriff's assistant what I had witnessed. When I finally paused there was a matter-of-factness about his response. 'Well, you know what,' he slowly replied, deliberately chewing his gum, 'under Kansas state law the shooting of pretty much any animal ain't a crime on private property. It's what people do around these parts. We breed a lot of dogs. It might be a little different in Australia but there is really nothing we can do.'

What an unbelievable place. I'd seen people driving their trucks with shotguns displayed on the back window – they are legally allowed to carry such weapons providing they are on display. In a town where ten thousand dogs a year were bred, I now had some idea what the process was.

So what was I to do? If I left or if I stayed the killings would continue. I now had fifty-five dogs in my care, and if I could make them perform they would be sold at auction to new owners who would, hopefully, give them a life after racing. But if I left . . .

There was a woman who worked at the place and I spoke to her about her experiences there, asking how she felt knowing that puppies she brought into the world would meet a grisly end. She was hesitant to discuss her thoughts on it: the Berlands paid her well and provided her with a house for her young family. But she eventually told me some horror stories. Dogs young and old, healthy and sick, fertile and infertile, had just been killed for not being profitable.

I stayed, but I was a very different person. I was totally fucked up in fact, partly insane. Taking a gun from the cabinet in Berland's office and shooting him, his son and henchman Greg clean in the face became something of a fantasy, and I truly believe if I had witnessed any more killings I could and would easily have done just that.

From this point on, whatever I earned was blood money. I only stayed in order to guarantee that at least my dogs, among the hundreds these people bred each year, would have a chance. The best way I can describe it is like this. Imagine you have been put in charge of a factory at a concentration camp. If you leave the factory it will be shut down and all the workers will go straight to the gas chambers. While the place is open its workers, no matter how atrocious their conditions, have a chance.

But I became dehumanized. Now I treated the dogs in my care kind of how I treated my gran on her dying day. I could not get close to them; I distanced myself. What was once a stroke, a pat on the head and a 'come here, son' was now a grab of the collar and a pull into the direction I wanted him/her to go. I just didn't want to get close to them.

Finally, and thankfully – after the big race meeting during which I looked at the people in the grandstand, other grey-hound owners and breeders, and tried to identify the good from the bad – my time in Kansas came to an end. I cannot account for the pups that did not make the grade or the dogs returning from the tracks, but not another dog from my numbers met a grizzly end during my time there. I have lived every day of my subsequent life fully aware of the day-to-day happenings there but despite subsequent lobbying and work with American television network HBO on the matter I've been unable to change a thing.

Over eleven years on, in the spring of 2007, I read in the *Racing Post* how a greyhound owned and bred by Vince Berland had won the world's first million-dollar race. In an interview he boasted he was the 'luckiest man in the world, owning such a wonderful greyhound and 1,000 other dogs'. If only the readers knew how selective his breeding programme was and what future those thousand dogs had.

11

Straight Wrap

On my return to England I can vividly recall walking out of Gatwick Airport and standing on the pavement where taxis drop off excited holidaymakers. It was a cold, raw, windswept November morning in 1995. I dropped my bags, which contained everything I owned, on the floor either side of me, felt the $3,000 in cash I had come back with in my pocket – my blood money – looked right, looked left, and asked myself, 'Well, Roy, what the fuck are you going to do now?'

I had nowhere to live, no close family to fall back on, no job and no idea what I was going to do for the rest of my life. One thing was certain, it would not involve Abilene, Kansas. I'd already decided never to put a lead around a dog's neck again, not after what I had just witnessed. I couldn't handle it.

Andover seemed the logical choice. There was nothing for me in Southampton any more and I wasn't going to go to Lincolnshire to pick cauliflowers out of the fields either. Things had gone from bad to worse with my father on the back of a heated, grief-stricken row immediately after my gran's funeral.

Above: Mum, Dad and me, four days old.

Above right: A day out in London, October 1972. This is Trafalgar Square.

Right: Going abroad was a luxury in the seventies. Here we are in Spain.

Left: Dressed in Southampton kit on the eve of the 1976 FA Cup Final. It was also the eve of my first winning bet.

Above: Mum, Dad and Gran seeing me off on 28 February 1995 – the morning of my Miami disaster.

Right: Grandad Jack and Gran Nora at a wedding.

Below: Nan. She is now ninety-nine years old and still going strong.

Below: Brother John – the best of the brothers at my school.

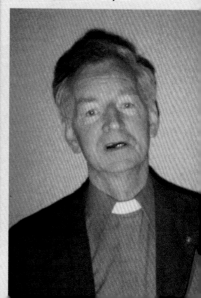

Above: Dad's junk shop, 'Goods and Chattels', in Lodge Road, Southampton.

Right: Here I am aged seventeen. Every teenager goes through an awkward stage, don't they?

Below: Little David, my childhood friend who died tragically young, and his dad, Tom Rolfe (*right*), who later put me up.

Right: Fascination with cars started at an early age.

Below: My £65 Ford Fiesta. It had to be parked on a hill as it would only go if jump-started.

Bottom: The MG bought from the proceeds of a game of three-card-brag at Lingfield races.

Above: I like cars, but what was I thinking? Scores of £50 notes once fluttered out of the roof of this beauty, never to be seen again.

Right: My MG, July 1996. This one got smashed up – I think I was trying to kill myself at the time.

Below: I'm now lucky enough to be the proud owner of this Ferrari.

FENGATE STADIUM
PETERBOROUGH

Above: My first open race winner, Bertie Small – named after the gangster turned supergrass.

Right and below: My beloved pet, Friendly.

Right: My canine win machine, River Ridge, with his teddy bear.

Above: Happier days in the USA with Waltham Abbey, February 1996.

Below: Derby Lane dog track in St Petersburgh, Florida. I went back there ten years later when poker had arrived.

Above: A Kansas breeding farm; each building houses about 200 greyhounds!

Below: Dog days in Dublin. Here I am interviewing Pat Kenny after his greyhound Late Late Show won at Shelbourne Park.

It was over nothing really, but some nasty things were said. Andover it was then.

I took a train to Southampton, bought a blue Ford Sierra for £120 from the 'banger sale' which took place at the car auctions there every Saturday morning, legalized it and drove directly to the William Hill betting shop on Weyhill Road, Andover, in time for the afternoon's racing.

Walking back into a betting shop brought back all kinds of emotions. I had tried to live a dream, get away from all this, but it had gone badly wrong. I felt different watching six dogs scoot around a track; now I wondered where they would end up after their racing days were over. But this was an environment in which I was comfortable. The same old crowd was there. They had no idea of where I had been, or what I had seen. That's the good and the bad. For them, like most people, life just trundled on as normal, day in, day out.

On this day, for once, I spent more time reading the local newspaper, the *Andover Advertiser*, than the *Racing Post*. I was urgently looking for somewhere to live. Then I saw this: 'To rent, room in beautiful farmhouse in rural setting, available immediately'. It sounded ideal, literally in a lovely neck of the woods, Kimpton, a picturesque village on the outskirts of town close to Fyfield, Thruxton and my old stomping grounds of Amport and Monxton.

If the location was nice, the place was a dive. The walls were painted yellow, on top of old paint which was purple, and it was lifting through from damp in some places and flaking off in others. The whole place reminded me of my time in Ranmore, Surrey, eight years earlier. But it was in a lovely country setting with a beautiful view, and I was homeless and desperate, the rent was cheap, and I could move in there and then. A month's rent in advance plus my first week's keep was handed over to the elderly owners, who looked like characters out of *The Munsters*, and I brought my suitcase and bag up from the car.

I shut the door, lay on the bed and thought. I felt like a criminal who had come out of prison after a ten-year stretch, finding that everything had changed and nothing would ever be the same again.

That Sunday evening I went for a drink in the nearby pub, the White Horse in Thruxton. I only vaguely knew one person there, a stable hand from the nearby racehorse stables. He and his friends had a good laugh on discovering where I was living – I learned it was known locally as the Hammer House of Horrors and the Château De'spair.

I spent plenty of time in that room of mine, shut away from the world, watching raindrops run down the windows. I felt safe there, safe from what people would think of me if they had any idea of what I had been involved in. I had plenty of time to think. I was twenty-six and felt as though life was passing me by. I had few real friends in the world. I'd always been a loner, or at least happy with my own company, but now things were changing. I was going through a crisis of confidence. I had no job, no life, no wife, no family, no children, no dogs, no mortgage, no mother-in-law. I was not yet that person and I was feeling like an alien. I was just dossing my time away, not to mention my blood money in the betting office.

I had, however, taken up an opportunity to do a monthly column for a publication called the *Greyhound Advertiser*, earning the princely sum of £30 a month. Added to that,

Jonathan Hobbs, assistant editor at the ever faithful *Racing Post* greyhound desk, instructed me to fax over any news or snippets I had. My copy was still arriving written in freehand on a sheet of lined A4 but it gave me another £150 or so monthly.

In pursuit of what I wanted to be – 'normal' – but, ironically, becoming the epitome of everything I didn't want to be, I took an office job. This was to be a career, not an odd job like van driving for an agency, and as it happens I was good at it as it involved bullshit by the bucket-load.

Tele-sales was the gig – you know, phoning up people, in this case companies, and selling wares over the phone. Now, what's the most boring thing you can imagine trying to sell over the phone? Well, whatever it is doesn't outdo 'mains cord sets', which is plugs and cables in most people's dictionaries. Not just any old plugs and cables, mind. Oh no, these were fully moulded plugs and cables, because thanks to EU legislation you can no longer wire your own plugs on to appliances, they have to come fully moulded. Technical term, an IEC 320.

The job allowed me to move into a tidy, self-contained flat fit for one in the same area, although the cost of my rent was only just covered by my working wage. I needed extra income beyond this sales job and a few greyhound-related stories that went into the newspaper, so I took a second job working in a country pub, the Abbot's Mitre in Chilbolton. My shifts were Friday nights and all day Sunday, noon till eleven p.m.

If that workload was not already enough, I added to it by taking a role as a sports presenter on a regional cable TV station, Town TV. This came about by pure accident – a guy really did walk into the pub one night – but I loved it, despite not knowing the first thing about sport. I interviewed numerous personalities and particularly enjoyed a day at Salisbury races where we did a piece with veteran jockey George Duffield and Desert Orchid's trainer David Elsworth. Now, what more could I do? I had transformed myself from a degenerate gambling bum into a workaholic, and there are few things more legitimate than a television presenter. I did all this for myself for what I thought I wanted in life.

At this time, with my resistance lowered, unsurprisingly I suppose, infatuation with a woman manifested itself. Of course, to develop an infatuation is to develop reason to believe this is exactly the right person for you. In the haze of infatuation you believe this is just what you have been searching for all these years. Like addictive gambling, it's an illness. You can't see straight and you think everyone should see things your way.

Our relationship started off close; it was to end poles apart. I believed that if I could prove to her, and to myself, that I did not have to gamble away every penny I had the moment I got it, I could be the kind of man for her. But it was a fatal attraction. It was the push-pull effect whereby the more you seem to do for some people the more they pull away, and the more they pull away the more you push.

I paid the price. I was a mess, a zombie, working my fingers to the bone, weighing a little over ten stone, a nervous wreck, drinking heavily. Ultimately the frustration inside me exploded into controlled violence. One day I drove round to my girlfriend's house, took out a heavy piece of wood and proceeded to smash the living daylights out of a van.

To be honest, it was a wonderful sensation, a feeling of relief as a volcano of tension was released. I started with the windscreen, which exploded into a million fractured pieces, then walked round the entire van not missing a single piece of glass. Seven windows, two wing mirrors, two headlights and the rearlight lenses. Having got rid of the tension, I calmly got back into my car, cried like a baby listening to an Elton John song, and returned home to make a cup of tea and prepare for my inevitable arrest and night in the police cells.

I don't know how many criminals answer the front door when the police are trying to bang it down but I did just that, explaining, 'I'm ready to go,' as I held my hands out to be cuffed and asking if I was allowed to bring a book and washbag. I'm sure they were bemused. I was, after all, a face that appeared on their television screens each and every week. At the police station they sat me down and asked all the questions they wanted. I gave them all the answers, every single detail. I never told a hint of a lie.

A court appearance some two months later followed. There I chose not to take legal representation. I held my hands high and asked for a little understanding, some leniency, considering the circumstances, which I can assure you were considerable. They did go lightly on me. I was ordered to pay for the repairs to the damaged Transit van and given a conditional discharge. The conditions were simple: pay for the damages and don't get into trouble again. If I did, I was surely going to jail.

Away from all this mess, things were happening aplenty. Comedian Richard Digance had come into the pub where I worked and a chance conversation with him led him to pass on details of producers who would consider scripts for televised comedy (I'd always fancied myself as a funny man). At my first attempt I got a reply saying one of my spoof scripts was being considered by Hale and Pace, the top comedy act at the time.

While this was going on, sales of plugs and cables rocketed. I was on the verge of earning some great commission as well as my fixed wage. Then Town TV lost its contract with Comtel, the regional cable television operator, and there was a chance a group of presenters and researchers, myself included, could take it over. Town TV had been run by Tony Murray, a former member of The Troggs, an Andover band which had a huge number one hit in the sixties with 'Wild Thing', and Al Grindley, who fronted some band or other in the seventies. Anyway, to cut a long story short, we got together to talk about the prospect of taking over the contract with Comtel, who had to produce a one-hour regional news show each week as part of an agreement which got them the regional franchise, stretching between Oxford, Winchester, Salisbury and Andover.

After two hours in this meeting there was a big personality clash between me and another guy, whose name I cannot recall, only that he had a beard and an attitude (they seem to go hand-in-glove). As a result I was voted 'out'. My parting question to the room as I walked out, humiliated, was this: 'Let me ask you, does any single one of you have a penny to get this proposed project of yours off the ground?' There was no reply, just a sea of shaking heads.

This to me was like a red rag to a bull – ambition is a virtue when it drives to excel – and by the end of the week, with no experience in the field I was supposedly going to enter and no experience in such matters, I had a business plan compiled and on a director's desk at Comtel.

Jock Scott, my old mentor from Nazeing, got the first call. His company had something to do with something or other in the television business and he provided me with a letter, a statement of intent, for financial backing. I pulled together the cameramen I used to work with who gave me their prices and indications of the cost of hiring equipment. I contacted Soho editing facilities, who gave me prices for using their suites in order to transform footage into a television show – it was cheapest during 'down-time', which meant two a.m. until six a.m. on a Sunday morning – and I tracked down a host of presenters, top-class presenters with national television experience, who sent letters confirming they would be interested in presenting the show.

With all the figures thrashed out and the set-up money guaranteed I had a first-class package at a competitive price on offer to the cable provider. Within days I was called in for a meeting. I hired a suit for the afternoon, and such was the success of the get-together that we were due to sign a contract within the week. Not bad for a greyhound trainer.

Then, as it seemed to do for me at the time no matter what I did, the brown stuff hit the whirly thing. Forty-eight hours later the *Andover Advertiser* carried two stories with my name in them. One was a back-page feature on how I, with Jock's company as backers, was set to relaunch a regional news round-up and diary programme on television. The second, in the 'Court Round Up' section, was not so good: 'Roy Brindley, of Littleton Manor, Kimpton, was ordered to pay a fine of £700 and given a conditional discharge when pleading guilty to criminal damage before Andover magistrates this week . . .' By noon that day I'd taken a call at my plugs and cables company. It was short and sweet: 'We are not in the habit of employing criminals or having them represent our organization. Negotiations with yourself in regards to a regional TV programme are now closed.'

I was in pieces. That night I drank until I was nearly unconscious in the Amport Inn, my old local when I used to train dogs. I made a right show of myself. I decided to tell the live-in manageress about the whole deal, from my failed shot at running a television station through to my love life, which was tearing holes into me. In sympathy she gave me one of the rooms for the night and was very supportive during this time.

Over the following weeks I went crazy in every sense of the word. I became aggressive, madly aggressive. I don't know what was happening to me, to my body, but I would guess it was related to an imbalance of hormones. I would go jogging; I would do hundreds of press-ups; I'd fantasize once more about killing the Berland family in Kansas and then come up with this crazy idea of having a vasectomy.

Mad things were going on all around me, too. For the second time in my life armed men tracked me down and were on my front door. This time it was all to do with a massive scandal that happened at Epsom racecourse on Derby day.

A fraudster had turned up at the racecourse with false documentation, in this case a permit, showing he was a bookmaker. He set up his pitch at the centre of the racecourse and offered his prices on the big race and the big race only. For hours people placed their bets with the bogus bookmaker, who called himself 'John Batten'. They did so as he was offering better prices about all the runners than any other bookmaker.

Now, somewhere between the last horse entering the stalls and Benny The Dip crossing the line a narrow winner of the Derby, Mr Batten, who ironically had the code word 'Fagan' on the tickets he was handing out to his punters, pulled a stunt on the general public by closing his satchel and making his way off through the crowd to his car and out of the county. It was huge news, not just within the racing world but on national television. It eventually turned up on BBC's *Crimewatch*. It was estimated that £40,000 of the racing public's money was stolen.

Now, hand on heart, I don't know who it was standing up as a bookmaker that day, or who his clerk was, but I was pretty certain I knew what part of the world he was from, who taught him how to stand there and take bets like an old hand and, likewise, knew what a permit looked like and got one reproduced. There was a huge reward for simply supplying information that led to a conviction of this guy, but I saw breaking the story as an opportunity to make a name for myself. Not quite on a par with Carl Bernstein or Bob Woodward (who brought down a president with their Watergate investigations), but unmasking such a huge fraudster who was the subject of a national manhunt, plus his accomplices who were all but forgotten by the police, and telling the story serialized in a national newspaper would surely do something for my long-term future, not to mention the immediate financial gain.

Scraping around in betting shops and doing the rounds at dog tracks and the like had led me to meet a lot of the type of characters that would get mixed up in this. Like me, they were always looking for an edge, and once they could not find one they would cross the narrow line that divides skilful punting and the identification of probability outweighing the odds on offer from plain old criminality.

I got on the telephone and started my attempts to track down the people involved with this huge scam. I began with the people I believed coached the bogus Mr Batten, whose face had appeared in national newspapers and on television screens. One thing was certain: he was not a bookmaker of any kind, otherwise he would have been recognized.

In next to no time I knew I was on the right track, but no sooner had I gathered the workings of the scam, the boys were on the door threatening to do me over. Funny as it sounds, when it happened before, I owed money; this time the stakes were higher. These guys were not worried about a grand in winnings being paid to them, they were worried about the prospect of doing ten years in the slammer. It showed, and they scared me shitless. I took it no further.

Things seemed only to worsen. Still in pain from my on/off relationship, I was still drinking, and one night I drove home from the pub not caring if I lived or died. I lived, but the car, and the wall I ploughed it into, did not fare as well. It was an MGB GT with chrome bumpers, the best car I had ever owned.

More devastation followed when my father phoned to tell me that Friendly, my dear loyal dog whom I'd had with me through all those years of working in kennels and living in caravans, had slipped in the garden and broken his back. He had to be put to sleep.

I now took every penny I earned directly to the betting shop. What did I need money for? I had never had it, and with no one to share it with, what use was it to me?

I knew something crazy was going on inside me so I went to

see a doctor, explaining that I could not cope with what life was throwing at me. I was depressed, I was a mess. He told me to go home and take some rest; he offered to give me a sick note so I could relax. What a load of bollix. A man who was supposed to be helping me told me to go home and sit in a chair or stay in bed. I stood up, picked up my chair and screamed, 'I don't think you understand! Something is happening to me here and if you don't help me I'm going to throw this chair through this fucking window!' If only he knew how out of character that was he would have surely sent me away with something more than a prescription for anti-depressants like he did.

Soon enough I fell to pieces again and had another emotional outburst. On this day I got into my car, my new car, a £200 Fiat Punto, backed it up and drove straight into the front door of a house. I reversed and did it again – not violently, I mean, it was a nudge, but enough to force the door open by breaking the door frame. I'm not sure what I was thinking; I just wanted to prove a point to someone, I suppose. The door was a barrier in every sense. It was a breakthrough and a breaking point.

I didn't think I was mad, but I knew I was frustrated, and now I was on the run from the law. This time there was no returning to my flat to wait for the police to arrive. I went to the pub in which I worked at weekends and drank myself into oblivion. Late that night I drove back to my place seeing double. I knew I was in a serious amount of trouble and it was my intention to pack my worldly possessions into my Fiat Punto and disappear. But as I came down the hill that over-looked the property, I spotted four police cars around my place driving across the fields and along tracks, plus there were other officers walking around with torches. They obviously wanted me badly.

If I was caught by the police this time, the charges would include being drunk and disorderly, drunk-driving and driving a car while uninsured, and that was before taking into consideration the criminal damage to the door, threatening behaviour, and God only knows what else they could dream up. They'd throw the book at me and then throw away the key. Not knowing what to do, I turned up on the doorstep of a woman who worked in a nearby betting shop. I knew where she lived as I had given her lifts home. She was a friend, and she helped me out. No one would come looking for me there.

The next day I woke disappointed to find it was not all a drunken nightmare. Racking my brains, I decided to call up an old mate, Charlie. Separated, thickset and bespectacled, he was from the same mould as all of us. He'd gambled all his life, lost money he could not afford to, even got sacked from a bookie's where he was working as a manager because of fiddling (that was only to feed his habit). He was actually one of my dad's friends from back in the eighties when they both owned dogs running at Portsmouth, but latterly he'd had a dog in training with me. Once, when I was a child, both our families (he had four kids) took a holiday to Spain, where I had got on really well with his eldest son, Steven, who was about a year older than me. We lost touch afterwards and I'd not seen him in a good ten years or so.

'What you been up to, sunshine?' Charlie asked when I met him in a pub in Portsmouth. I didn't tell him the whole story. How could I? I just explained I was in the shit and I was stuck.

Charlie offered to let me stay in his rented flat in Ashburton Road, Southsea, the seafront district of Portsmouth. He was working and living in Surrey on a contract at the time and the place was empty for most of the week anyway.

He took me to the flat, gave me £40 and left me there. He was not coming back for two weeks. I went straight to bed and stayed there for the best part of a week. I could not face the world. I tried to get out and about, walking down the seafront and pavilion a few times, but the faces and gazes of people just went through me. It was as if everyone knew about me, what I had done, what I had seen and how I was on the run.

I made Charlie's £40 last nearly a fortnight. At the time the supermarkets were at war and you could buy a loaf of bread for 9p in one store, a tin of baked beans for 6p at another; a cheap packet of own-brand biscuits cost 15p and a dozen sausages 22p. I could feed myself for a whole day on a pound, and I did.

Charlie's son Steven arrived at the flat one day looking for his dad, unaware I was there. It was great seeing him after so many years. We talked about his life, and about my problems. His tale was so similar: he had been messed up by a number of factors, and he too had taken a live-in kennel-hand job in grey-hound kennels during his teens.

Still shell-shocked and broke, I dared not phone up my friends at the *Racing Post* and offer them a snippet of news from nearby Portsmouth dog track. Similarly, I simply left the Abbot's Mitre pub and never returned to my full-time tele-sales job. Doubtless, judging by the number of cars they had out looking for me that night, the police would have been in touch with all of them trying to track me down.

But I needed clothes, I needed vital personal possessions – I needed to get back to my flat. It was about three weeks later, after a lot of time spent sleeping – I'm talking about eighteen hours a day, all depression-induced – that I ventured back to Andover by thumbing three lifts. I had to as I'd sold the Fiat for £90, desperate for money. I went back to my flat at three in the morning to get my stuff. The lock hadn't been changed. I stripped it clean of everything and crammed it all into my MG, which was still parked outside with massive front-end damage and a flat tyre. I had to do all of this silently as mine was one of four flats on the back of the landowner's house and the walls were paper thin.

A tin of tyre-weld helped inflate the tyre, and thankfully the car started up first time. I say thankfully as there was a police car parked on a nearby hill throughout, clearly looking out for me or the flat's light to be turned on. Therefore I had to make off quickly before the landowner alerted them, and I also had to drive across ploughed fields for the best part of two miles with my lights turned off.

Back in Southsea with a change of clothes and a wash-bag, things were slightly better, but I was in a state of total melancholy, hidden away as a fugitive, unable to work because of the fear of being traced by the police's computer systems. I was a wanted man.

The MGB was sold for £100; it was the only thing of value I owned and it had cost me considerably more. Sadly, that money went into a betting shop in the continuing stupid belief that I could win a fortune.

As it was, Charlie didn't come back to his flat for about a month, but Steven visited most days, and eventually moved in.

His worldly possessions filled a black dustbin bag – we were so alike. Steven kept and carried me for a long while. He was driving a taxi. He loved the cash-in-hand lifestyle. It bought him a curry, a packet of fags and a bet. When that was gone he would go out and work some more and then repeat the cycle again.

He was a big help, slipping me tens and twenties; he even picked me up and took me out. City life and nightclubs were something I was not accustomed to, but Steven had it down to a tee. Every night of the week we would hit somewhere different. He had it all sorted out: Route 66 offered drinks for 66p apiece on a Sunday night; Zoom gave you two drinks for the price of one on another night; Joanna's was a regular haunt with beer at 80p a pint every Thursday night.

Still not daring to take work, I took to going to Portsmouth dog track a fair bit, the place where my dogs raced when I was training. Few of the people I believed to be friends were interested in my plight. I was wonderful when they were getting something from me, information and tips. However, one, a guy called Terry, who I didn't really know that well apart from the fact he was a good race reader and worked in a supermarket collecting trolleys, gave me £40 with instructions to 'use it to get yourself back on your feet'. Funny what you can remember, isn't it? I'd love to catch up with him again and repay him in some serious way now, with an outrageous holiday or a new car or something. If I ever track him down I'll do just that. You can certainly work out who your real friends are when your back is up against the wall.

Talking of memories, I was dossing in this flat with Steven when Diana, Princess of Wales, died. Everyone knows where they were when that happened, don't they?

Trouble was looming large, though. Charlie had lost his job in Surrey and he was coming back to his Southsea flat. He was really hoping I had sorted myself out and had moved on. It had been several months after all.

Charlie had no real idea of what bother I was in, and when he said I had to go, I had to go. It was abrupt, and there was a small argument, but, of course, I was in the wrong. I had abused his generosity. But I had nowhere to go, nowhere. I shut the door to his terraced ground-floor flat, walked a hundred yards down the paved road, sat on my old-fashioned tin suitcase containing my belongings and once again posed myself the question, 'What the fuck are you going to do now, Roy Brindley?'

To use a poker term, I had no outs, I was drawing dead. My parents were out of the question: the police had been in contact and my father was so moralistic he could turn me in if I went there. Beyond that there was no one to ask, nowhere to go. I could hand myself in, face the music, but prison?

Once again I began to dream of a big win at the bookie's which this time would mean I could leave the country, maybe get myself to the south of France, work in a bar and enjoy the sunshine. It was all a sad desperate fantasy. I was rapidly losing all sense of reality.

12

Down and Outs

That first day, I had no idea I was going to end up sleeping on a park bench. I walked the streets for hours on end, wrestling with my heavy tin case, somehow believing I would come up with a plan; but as the night drew in and the streets grew quieter, I found myself on the seafront park, near the skatepark, laid out on a bench.

That first night under the stars was strange, especially because the only noise I heard on that park bench was from the nightclubs as people left at kicking-out time. A few nights earlier it might have been me stumbling drunkenly and noisily out of one of those very same clubs; but now I was a tramp, a meaningless specimen of a human being in the eyes of most people.

I didn't sleep a wink, and I realized for the first time why people live in a drunken state out on the road. You cannot sit there sober for hours on end as people step over you in disgust, uninterested in and unsympathetic to the circumstances that put you there. I can also tell you this: the one thing you do when living and sleeping rough is contemplate life, and you come to absolutely no conclusions.

The following morning I made it to the nearest bookmaker's. There it was warm, comfortable and, more important than anything else, familiar. I didn't have any money to place bets but it was better than sitting on a bench. I stayed for the best part of the day. I left after the last race and aimlessly wandered once more through the grey, monotonous streets. I walked with my head down, scanning the pavement, living in hope of finding a coin sparkling in the gutter. It felt as if time was standing still – not helped by the fact that I didn't own a watch (I never have). My feet hurt like hell because I was wearing black leather lace-up dress shoes. I'd had a pair of trainers but they'd been stolen a few days before I was evicted from my flat, having been left outside on the doormat.

Years earlier I'd seen a TV documentary about a homeless guy who said it was always better to find somewhere to sleep near a launderette or hotel because they constantly pump warm air through outlet vents. We all know tramps sleep in cardboard boxes because they fend off the draught and keep some heat in, so I found myself a cardboard box in a metal crate outside the tradesman's entrance to a supermarket and headed for the rear of the Queen's Hotel, again right on the seafront.

There I came across three homeless blokes bedding down. It was only two hundred yards from where I'd lived in a flat just a few days earlier. The casino, once one of my favourite hang-outs, was also a stone's throw away. I exchanged a brief nod with my new pals, hardened tramps who looked like they were tuned into a different planet, and settled down on the pavement. There was no warm vent but it was quiet and I managed to sleep.

Disturbing images of past incidents flashed through my dreams, and when I awoke with a jolt next morning, the stark reality of my situation hit home. I really was completely and utterly alone in this world.

Now I had a momentous decision to make. I had the princely sum of £1.79 left in my building society book. There was no shame in walking into the branch and asking for it – by now I was almost beyond shame – but what should I buy with it, a packet of Bic razors and a cheap deodorant stick or some biscuits and a carton of milk? I settled for the food because I felt the need to fill my stomach even though I wasn't actually hungry. I just knew I should eat something. That said, I remember ducking down a side street, opening the packet and, after my first bite, manically cramming biscuits and milk down my throat.

A few hours later I overcame my pride, sat outside a corner shop and started begging. I promised myself I'd only do it for as long as I really needed to. It wasn't as if I needed to buy a bottle of sherry or meths and Ribena like the other guys who lived down the alleyway behind the hotel.

In the beginning it was hard work, and there was a definite pattern to it. People would do things like buy a bar of chocolate and then drop the spare 7p change into my cup. Begging felt a bit like gambling: I lived in hope that I'd get a big win (which would be represented by a pound coin being dropped in my cup) and that would feed me for the day. I even put imaginary odds on how much would be dropped in my cup each time. The biggest fantasy of all was a £2 coin. That was the equivalent of winning the Grand National, but the odds were longer on that happening than on any of the runners at

Aintree. Two quid would feed me and pay for a bet. I had it figured out too: five selections, all 10/1, 10p trebles. If I had three winners it would be over £100 back; four winners would be over £400, which would soon get me back on my feet; all five winning and I'd be on a beach in the south of France in no time.

Eventually I managed to get that packet of disposable Bics I needed so badly, but with no shaving foam I had to find a public toilet with some hand soap so that I could lather up. With that in mind I walked through one of the several slot-machine arcades on Southsea's seafront, passing banks of push-a-penny machines, the ones with hundreds of coins on moving steps being pushed into a 'winner's tray' at the bottom, although the majority fall to the side and into the arcade's profits box.

As I passed by, I heard coins falling into the tray at the bottom of one machine and stopped in my tracks. Looking in both directions to see if anyone was watching, I quickly moved over to the machine and scraped out about 20p. What a money maker, with no humiliation! It soon became an obsession of mine. It was my working day, walking around arcades looking for money in pay trays which had either fallen from the pushy machines or been accidentally left by the players. I soon realized the odd coin would also roll underneath the machines, so when the arcade staff weren't looking and punters were scarce, I got down on all fours and used a discarded candy floss stick to scrape the floor beneath the machines. Chewing gum, condom packets, ring-pulls and cigarette butts came out aplenty, but so did a coin or two.

To think how my life had changed. One moment I was going

to be a television executive, the next . . . My priorities had been thrown upside down. Now, while most people worried about what to watch on telly of an evening, my main concern was finding a half-decent, dry cardboard box to sleep in, acquire enough change for a pie, a pint of milk and a packet of biscuits, and pray that it wouldn't rain.

With all that said and done, it's important for me to make sure you, the reader, know that despite all this desperation I never once did drugs – never have, never will. As it stands, gambling is the only addiction and the only vice I've ever had. But I've had that badly.

This lifestyle continued for a week. Then I encountered a very big turning point, a lesson in life, something I would never forget, something that helps me to this day, especially when I'm in a poker tournament and start to lose focus.

I had found some newspapers, needed to keep me warm. It was a trick I picked up from some of the other guys: placing a few flat pages underneath you will soak up any dampness, and screwing the remainder into loose balls and pushing them into the bottom of your box will keep your feet warm. So there I was, merrily scrunching up the pages, when I came across a story about well-known people who, it was believed, had attempted, and in some cases succeeded, to commit suicide. Bjorn Borg led the cast of the unsuccessful candidates, closely followed by Billy Joel in their top ten, while Kurt Cobain had the distinction of being at the top of the successful list. I later discovered that Borg denies the story altogether, but seeing his name in that newspaper made one hell of an impression on me at that particular moment.

It struck me, how could things get so bad for these

multi-millionaires with countless houses, cars and stunning wives? I'd like to challenge any one of them to spend a night in my shoes, in the gutter, I thought. It would sober anyone up, no matter how drunk they were on life. But this 'newspaper experience' was sobering for me, in many ways. It gave me a fresh view on life. Maybe we were all insane and simply didn't know it. It's certainly true to say I'd lost my mind now. I wasn't sure if the accepted definition of normality – mundane nine-to-five work, two package holidays a year, a mortgage and a car loan – was for me. But certainly living on the streets wasn't either, and the following morning I made the decision to return to my roots in Southampton, the place where I'd been born, bred and educated.

People looked at me strangely in the crowded streets that morning as I lugged my tin trunk five long miles to the edge of the M27 motorway. The trunk was so heavy I switched it from my right to left hand and back again constantly. I felt very uneasy, concerned that a police car might stop and question me as to its contents. Then they'd call in my name and discover I was on the run. But nobody took a blind bit of notice of me, and after what seemed like hours of waiting and desperate thumb waving on the edge of the motorway slip road, I finally got a lift all the way to the turn-off for Southampton's Eastleigh Airport.

My other gran, Nan Happy, my dad's mum, lived nearby, just opposite the house I spent my childhood in. I set off by foot in that direction. Soon my wrists, arms and shoulders were all aching with the weight of my possessions but I shuffled on uphill and an hour later I was knocking on her front door. OK, I didn't exactly look my best, exhausted, hungry, unshaven and smelly, when she opened it, but her reaction was just to stare at me, as if to confirm who I was. She then looked at my tin suitcase, looked back up at me and exclaimed, 'You can't stay here,' before closing the door right in my face.

Like the opening scene from the Bob Hoskins film *Mona Lisa*, word for word, I clattered the letterbox again and shouted, 'I've only come to say hello. HELLO!'

Nan Happy eventually reopened the door. 'You can stay here tonight, and one night only, then you have to go,' was her next statement. She was a fiercely independent woman, Nan Happy, and I think she feared that if I stayed one night I might expect a second, and a third . . .

We talked about the horses and the successful bets she'd recently had, but it was nothing more than small talk. She didn't ask why I was there so I guess she really didn't want to know. Next morning, Nan Happy started pulling the covers off me at seven a.m. and said it was time to go. Less than an hour later her front door slammed shut behind me and I was back where I'd started.

I closed the metal gate at the end of her small garden and within seconds I was passing my old home in Binstead Close. Seeing the family house sparked a lot of memories. The hedge around the back garden, now six feet high, was planted by me; the shoots were ten inches tall at the time. I looked up at the bedroom where I'd played with my Scalextric and once stashed bundles of notes. But mostly I stared at the stretch of road where my half-brother so angrily told me I was 'not a Brindley', I was 'nothing but shit', that I wasn't wanted and never would be. As I stood there with nothing in the world but my tin trunk, it would have been easy to concede he was right.

I mean, just look at me. But, just like the newspaper suicide story, this flashback inspired me.

I eventually reached the bottom of the street where Bassett Green Road met Stoneham Lane. At the traffic lights I took a right and then another right, walking directly past where my nan Nora used to live. Two doors up from there, at 137 Carnation Road, were Tom and Greta, the parents of a childhood pal, Little David, who'd died aged just twenty-one. He was a 'blue baby', born with a defective heart. I poured out most of my troubles to Tom, who offered to put me up on the understanding I'd get a job and pay a nominal rent. Tom and Greta, retired and both hard of hearing, were salt-of-the-earth simplistic people. They had a soft spot for me as years beforehand my mum would be in and out of their house skiving off from school, and I spent a lot of time there with their precious son. In fact, I'd be living in David's old room. Tom reminded me it was ten years to the very week that David had died.

Driver Hire, the agency I'd worked for when my gran was so poorly, was the logical place for me to find work. I got on well with the people there and they already had all my details on file, which hopefully meant no alarm bells would ring in relation to that police bounty still on my head.

I worked flat out throughout December, which helped me avoid the local bookies. I was determined, focused and hungry to get my life back on track. With my first week's wages I bought a T-reg 1979 Ford Fiesta, brown with a blue door and a lot of blue smoke coming out of it. It had three months' tax and one month's MOT. Well, what do you expect for £60? The second week I got a mobile phone, and through that the agency work came flooding in. I took a night job as a barman at the

Dolphin Hotel, in Lower Bar Gate, Southampton, and even did silver service waitering for Christmas parties at the city's five-star Grand Harbour Hotel. By the end of the festive period I had worked my fingers to the bone, delivering packages all over housing estates in Bournemouth, Salisbury, Portsmouth and Reading during the day – I once had the misfortune to reverse a 7.5-ton lorry into a Cash Converters shop window – and working in the hotel at night, but in the process I'd earned enough money to take up residence in a shared house in Dunbridge, near Romsey, north of Southampton, with two housemates.

There was one small problem: one had a friend who just happened to be a woman police constable. The first time she knocked on the door of the house, on a breezy but otherwise normal evening, I nearly died, but thereafter I kind of enjoyed the buzz and irony of having a police officer in my house drinking coffee at the kitchen table.

This, and the fact that 'wanted by the police' alarm bells had not yet gone off on some tax or national insurance computer somewhere or other, led me to question if the police really were looking for me after all. Perhaps they weren't. Maybe they simply hadn't entered me into the computer system. Maybe once I didn't turn up that fateful week they'd just closed the case.

From rock bottom, life was moving on apace. The agency even offered me a 'special assignment' as a driver for the crew and presenters on a live BBC TV daytime series called *The General*, which followed the day-to-day life at Southampton's General Hospital. Chris Searle, formerly of *That's Life*, was the lead presenter, with Yvette Fielding of *Blue*

Peter fame and a certain Heather Mills, who later found fame through her stormy marriage to Paul McCartney, also on board. I drove Heather to various assignments and had no idea she was a limb short until she took off her fake leg to parasail down the side of the hospital one day for charity. For me it was remarkable getting close to these people you only ever see on your television screen. But I was still basically an odd-job driver.

Once, after a day's filming, I took Heather home to Stockbridge, which is on the outskirts of Andover. We had a long discussion about greyhound racing. She insisted it was cruel and brutal. I fought my corner and told her about all the dogs I'd once trained and how I loved them, though I couldn't tell her of my part in the Kansas killing fields.

My confidence was growing. It could just be possible that I had lived a miserable existence needlessly. In fact, so carefree was I feeling that when I bumped into my old drinking mate Simon Cornelius I took him up on his offer of visiting him in Andover the coming Saturday afternoon. We spent the day punting on horses and drinking in the town. It was the nicest time I'd had in at least a year. There's a lot to be said for the term 'carefree'. I repeated the trick the following weekend and started regularly to drive the fifteen miles to Andover from my lodgings using a quiet back road, the B3084, in order to avoid the police.

In hindsight, I'm guessing deep down I was either enjoying flirting with danger or I wanted to get caught. I suspect it was the latter. It was, after all, only a matter of time before the police stopped me, and it happened on a Friday evening. Firing on only three cylinders, I was happily spluttering down the road in my 1,100cc Fiesta on my way to Simon's when, bingo, a policeman stepped out into the middle of the country road and flagged me down. Immediately I protested I was not speeding, after which the officer announced he was simply checking tax discs. Mine had just one week left on it, and on seeing that it was just about valid the copper then asked for my licence. It still had my old Andover address on it, but nevertheless I willingly handed it over.

Initially it seemed he was only going to browse over the details, but when he took it off to his car and got on the radio I knew this was the moment I'd know one way or the other if I was home free or going to jail. He spent an age on his radio before coming back, impassively handing it back and wishing me a safe trip.

Christ, the car wasn't even MOT'd! But I wasn't feeling joyful about avoiding this misdemeanour, it was the relief of discovering that Roy Brindley was not the on-the-run offender he thought he was. All these months, those days of living on the streets, the despair and desperation – all for nothing!

Feeling as free as a bird, Simon and I drank and gambled hard that weekend, and on my drive home I was still laughing to myself. The nightmare was over, I was free. There was no stopping me now. I'd get a real job, a career – any number of options were available to me. I was a sixteen-year-old school leaver all over again, my whole life before me.

As I rounded the very same bend on the B3084 where my credentials had been put through the police's computer two days earlier, still chuckling to myself, I saw that the police were out in force again.

'Hi there,' I opened. 'I was actually stopped at this very same point coming in the opposite direction two days ago, so I'm guessing you'd like to see this.' I handed over my driving licence. This time the officer simply glanced over it, smiled, took a note of my name and returned it to me, sending me on my way.

I drove on for a mile or so, then I looked in my mirror and it was full of a BMW police patrol car with flashing headlights and roof-mounted blue lights revolving. Moments later I got a blast of their siren before being gestured to pull over.

'Out of the car, please, sir. You're under arrest.'

That was it. Cuffs were slapped on my wrists and I was placed in the back of their cruiser.

I tried to pretend I didn't know why I'd just been arrested. 'What have I done?' I asked from the back seat.

'You're nicked for an incident that took place last year.'

It turned out they had given me a background check on another computer and this time it had flagged up a 'wanted' status.

On arrival at the station I had my fingerprints taken and was then put in a cell to await questioning. An hour later two coppers sat me in an interview room and tried to find out what I'd been up to while on the run. The two officers employed a good cop/bad cop routine which involved firing questions at me and then hinting at certain scenarios and claims about what had taken place that day; then they would say 'We only want to know the truth!'

I told them I had absolutely no recollection of the incident. It was a long time ago and it was not a good period of my life. I'd held my hands straight up last time, but this time was different. I knew if I started talking they'd add more and more charges. All I'd done was break a doorframe but I had to be careful not to confess to it being 'with intent', or that it was accompanied by 'threatening behaviour' or even that it happened as a result of being 'drunk and disorderly'. Thanks to this self-imposed amnesia, all they could charge me with was criminal damage. They looked disappointed. Unfortunately there was also a warrant out for my arrest for non-payment of fines relating to the original criminal damages court appearance. The fine was being paid off and was up to date; I'd just missed a few of the weekly £4 payments when I was on the streets. It gave the police grounds to keep me locked up until an appearance in front of the magistrates, who were not sitting again for another two days.

So I was locked up in a cell with bare cream-coloured walls and a floor made of a black, non-slip material like the surface of a nail file. A mattress wrapped in blue PVC lay on top of a stone bench with wooden boards on top of it. There was a tin toilet and a sink, and the windows were made of thick frosted glass you couldn't see through. Yet I slept more comfortably and soundly there than I had done on any night out on the streets, in the Southsea flat, at Tom and Greta's, even in my own shared house. The chase was over. I was so relieved.

Two days later a chunky white security van – the sort of vehicle you usually see transporting suspected killers to the Old Bailey – took me to Andover Magistrates Court. There I was bailed to reappear before the court to answer those charges of criminal damage to the door, and warned about the consequences of not keeping my fine payments up to date. Then I was sent on my way, a free man.

I only had a couple of pounds on me, I was miles away from

my home, and it was pouring with rain. I walked to the factory where my friend Simon worked and borrowed a few quid from him before walking several more miles back to the train station and on to my digs.

It was raining heavier than ever as I got to the door mid-afternoon and was dismayed to find my key would not work. I tried my back-door key but that too was not working. I must have tried both half a dozen times before it sunk in: the locks had been changed. I'd been locked out and I was getting drenched on what was one of the best days I'd had in the past year. I just laughed and laughed and laughed. I couldn't believe what was happening, and at the same time I didn't care.

During my time in the cells the police had asked where I was living and who with. They must have then phoned up my housemates, who'd taken it upon themselves to banish me without a chance to explain what I was in trouble for and why I had done what I had done.

One neighbour, a woman in her late twenties who must have been watching me, came out to ask me if I was all right. 'Have you lost your keys?' she asked.

I told her the truth. I told her the locks had been changed, that my housemates clearly no longer wanted me there, and that it must have been because the police phoned them over the weekend when I was arrested. God bless this woman, she invited me into her house for a coffee, gave me a towel to dry myself off, and allowed me to borrow a tool-kit to get in through the window.

I looked at her, then at her modest but spotless front room, the pictures of her husband and children on the sideboard. I was envious, but at the same time encouraged that there were some good people out there. Here was one who was not judging me, despite my confession that I had just come out of police cells. It was another of those unforgettable turning point moments.

Keen to be out before five when the first of my housemates returned from work, I got to work on the window. It was a tough job, though it shouldn't have been: they were only old-fashioned sash windows with a single latch after all. I could not believe the pair had gone to the effort of screwing wooden blocks on to the runners of these windows. I mean, how badly did they not want me to get in? Didn't they simply want me to move out? But in order to move out I had to get in. I don't know what the story was but I guess they were pretty intent on something and they were clearly not for talking to.

I finally got in, and filled up my Fiesta with all my possessions. It was still pouring down, a dreadful day. I fried up some sausages that were in the fridge and gave them to the resident Alsatian, a pet belonging to one of the housemates. It may sound daft but I felt for this dog, as he was only ever fed dry food, his owner believing some crap about meat being unsuitable and potentially poisonous for him. Poor thing, he could not believe his luck, eating meat for the first time. I also gave the neighbour a tub of ice-cream and some unopened bottles of pop from my fridge-freezer for her kids, and thanked her for her understanding and help.

Broke, with my possessions in the back of an illegal £60 car, with the rain lashing down, with nowhere to stay and nowhere to sleep again, I kind of laughed. I may have cried. No one said winning was easy.

13

On a Rush

I drove in the general direction of Southampton, eventually going to see my childhood friend Phil Rowles, who was still working at the same place he'd been at since leaving school. He'd just bought a new house in Chandlers Ford on the outskirts of the city.

I hadn't gone to them before. I couldn't, what with them having two young children. Now, though, Phil and his wife kindly agreed to let me stay in their new house while it was being renovated (they weren't yet living in it). Phil didn't need to know my woes; he couldn't relate to them anyway. All he kept harping on about was the time when we were fourteen, returning home from a BMX meeting, and I lost our train fare in a fruit machine in the café at Fareham train station. It meant we had to ride home more than fifteen miles, and he never forgave me. You see, Phil is one of those people who believes that gambling is a mugs' game. It's not, it's a game that attracts mugs.

The following morning, with my wages through from the

previous week's work, I sat in one of the house's empty rooms – the floorboards were up and wires were coming out of the light and plug sockets – and made my selections for the afternoon's racing from the *Post*.

Just then I heard voices in the street. I looked through the window and watched as a wedding procession floated by. The bride was none other than a girl I'd had a teenage crush on back in my college days a decade earlier. I knew it was her as I once gave her a lift home and recalled that she lived just two doors away. It was another example of how everyone's life but mine had seemed to go on as scripted in that playbook titled 'normality'.

That afternoon I managed a half-decent win on the horses – not a life changer, not even four figures, but enough cash to buy a golden-coloured Vauxhall Cavalier. It had a faulty alternator, which meant I had to put a new battery in it every fortnight. I got them from a local scrap yard but they put me back a fiver apiece. One knock-on effect was that the headlights would burn brighter than a lighthouse. I nicknamed it the Golden Shiny Chariot.

I rekindled my connections with the *Racing Post* and the *Greyhound Advertiser*, and a week or two on, with the slow climb out of the gutter continuing, I moved back to Andover. Simon had just bought a flat and I was his lodger. It was a good fit as we had a lot in common: he was sympathetic to my situation and I was understanding about his ups and downs in life. We drank together and placed bets together, although I could not bring myself to watch the days and days of monotonous cricket on the box which he enjoyed so much!

With a car that was slightly more reliable than my old Fiesta

I was able to make it to the dog tracks, and I quickly picked up work as a racecourse commentator at Portsmouth and Wimbledon. It was only £50 a night, but allied to the odd day here and there working for driving agencies and the odd cheque from the *Racing Post*, it all made up into a wage. I had no problems with British greyhound racing. I had been around it all my life and I'd certainly not come across any atrocities such as those secrets Abilene held.

That *Racing Post* number took me to Swindon Stadium one midweek afternoon where I was to report on a major competition final, the Guineas. Now far more upstanding than I had been in years, I approached the winning owners after the race to ask the usual questions – Did you back your dog? Where is he going to run next? – in order to get a quote from them which would complete my report. The race was sponsored by the British Greyhound Racing Board and their chief executive, Geoffrey Thomas, was there to present the winner's trophy. I didn't know him from Adam, but he listened in when I spoke to the winning owners and took note. Little did I know he was about to offer me a four-month contract to work for his organization.

The BGRB had reintroduced a competition called the Supertrack, which involved every stadium in the country, and Thomas asked me to prepare and unearth stories from it which could go into the trade papers and the national press. I embraced the idea, installing a telephone line and buying a fax machine and a second-hand PC in order to set up an office. I was earning £750 a month for the next four months, a price which I quoted. It was pitifully low for the late nineties, but I wanted the job. There was also an expense account paying 30p per mile that I drove; suffice to say I travelled the length and breadth of the country in my Golden Chariot, which had set me back £250.

This is it. Do a good job here, Roy, and you'll be set. There could even be the chance of full-time employment with the BGRB, or possibly something with the *Racing Post*. Maybe you can become a real journalist despite your lack of experience and qualifications.

There was one small problem. Before the Supertrack came to an end and before my contractual period was up I had that appearance at court to decide my fate. There was a chance, a very good chance, that I would be sent to jail. Breaching a conditional discharge was serious stuff. I'd had plenty of meetings with my solicitor – provided for me, of course – and he did not want to make any predictions about the penalty. He did, however, instruct the court that I intended to plead guilty and there was no need for a trial.

If I was sentenced to prison, my future, my possible career in greyhound racing journalism, would be over. The truth was bound to come out. I took yet more solace in gambling – rarely on the greyhounds at the countless tracks I was visiting almost every night of the week up and down the country, but in betting shops in the afternoon. I had more cash coming in now than I had ever had, after all.

The big day, 23 September 1998, finally arrived. It's one of those days you just cannot forget because, as crazily as these things seem to work themselves out, should I walk free from the courtroom with something like community service, I would be heading straight to the House of Commons later that day for a gathering of the World Greyhound Racing Conference. If I was detained . . . once again the consequences did not bear thinking about.

My solicitor met me at the courthouse and explained there had been a problem: the court had not received his notification that we were pleading guilty and that a trial was not necessary. My guy used this mix-up to strengthen our position in some way or other. If the prosecution dropped something they were pushing for then we would spare their witnesses questions in the dock, even though they were never going to be put in the dock.

My solicitor said the most notable thing was that the offence had taken place over a year ago. He also pointed to a letter from the doctor confirming that I had gone to him seeking help and was put on anti-depressants. He produced a second letter showing my invitation to the House of Commons that afternoon, 'an indication of how my client's life has changed for the better'.

Ultimately it was left to me to address the magistrates, and I offered up a letter that I had written for my mitigation. Naturally I had been advised to be remorseful and apologetic, but deep down I wasn't. So much depended on the impression that my story had on the magistrates. If they could begin to know the truth, the endless misery endured, how I was forced to live, to survive, these past fifteen months, and simply why I committed the crime, they would concede that a fair sentence had already been served. Of course, they were duty bound to depend on the bare jagged facts that had been delivered to them, but I believed that I deserved to walk from this cold room a free and dignified man.

The three magistrates, all men in their late fifties, stared intently as the usher took the plain envelope from me and in turn passed it to the front of the court. It was given to the largest one, sat in the centre, the one who was hard of hearing and who constantly asked the prosecuting solicitor to repeat the torrid facts. The three no longer looked at me, instead acknowledging each other with a simple stare and shake of the head, before gathering their notes and my letter and easing themselves out of their seats.

'All rise,' said a voice as they made their way to a door behind them.

There was a sense of silence when they left the courtroom, despite the numerous people who were there muttering among themselves; curiosity had brought them along, I suppose. I was left feeling alienated, scrutinized like a tiny organism out of its environment, being prepared for dissection under a microscope.

How stupid of me, I now thought, believing that I could portray over a year of my life in a simple note, full of excuses in the face of hard truths. I sat back down, gently sighed, covered my eyes, slumped my head forward and went back through it all just one more time.

Behind me another defendant or witness from an upcoming case tapped me on the shoulder and said loudly enough for the entire courtroom to hear, 'House of Commons, mate? You'll be all right there, you'll fit in, don't worry, the place is already full of criminals!' As the gallery fell about I could not argue that his statement was not funny, and it did ease the tension.

The magistrates returned, and the chief magistrate coughed lightly before addressing the court. I struggled to look directly at him as I rose to my feet. I heard him say calmly and in a virtual whisper that my punishment was a fine for the value of the damage. I can't recall anything else he said.

It was like the weight of the world had been lifted from my shoulders.

I celebrated the end of my life as a fugitive in some style by keeping that appointment at the House of Commons. No one there knew I'd been in court a few hours earlier and might well have ended up in a prison cell. Now here I was sipping Bucks Fizz, shaking hands and talking la-de-dah with some of the most powerful politicians in the country.

Soon the Supertrack came to an end and I got the reward I was looking for: the appointment as deputy editor of the *Greyhound Advertiser* magazine. It sounded far more glamorous than it was, but who was to know? Basically I would compile news, views and interviews either written by me or by contributors, and then, once a month, take a train to the publisher's Newcastle offices to put the thing together. I put my heart and soul into that publication and within three months had helped transform it from a twenty-page mono-coloured giveaway into a sixty-four-page full-gloss magazine on sale at WHSmith.

The magazine seemed to be going well, but when the owner, a printer, announced he was shutting it down with immediate effect because of spiralling costs, I was once again out of a job. It was back to supplying the odd snippet for the *Post*, a little warehouse work on night shifts for an agency, and some driving work I picked up for a character I knew from the local William Hill betting shop. We called him 'Ben the Pen' because he always used his own gold pen to write out his bets. He was about fifty-five, thickset with curly hair and a scar on his face. He only ever bet in crisp £50 notes, of which he seemed to have thousands – my kind of guy. When he lost his driving licence he hired me to drive him around in his brand-new Merc for £50 cash a day, and all we did was go horseracing. It was my dream job!

The Pen lost £12,000 at Ascot the day Daylami, ridden by Frankie Dettori, won the King George. Afterwards he directed me to the Waterside Inn, a fabulous restaurant in nearby Bray, where Richard Burton, Liz Taylor and hosts of other celebs have eaten down the years. I'd never had a £200 meal before, or sipped glasses of Cristal champagne. This was the life. It was a lifestyle I so desperately wanted for myself. On another occasion I drove Ben the Pen to Chester races, where he blew £7,000 on a horse trained by Peter Chapple-Hyam that finished nowhere. We got straight back in the car without seeing another race and drove home as if nothing had happened.

I'd made no firm plans for the future, I was just content with freedom, a slow upward trend in life, and the ability to chase big wins. That was until I read the editor's page in the *Greyhound Star*, a monthly newspaper and, essentially, my rival when I was working at the *Greyhound Advertiser*. The text read, 'I never shed a tear on hearing the *Greyhound Advertiser* had closed. It was often tatty, unprofessional, run by amateurs. No doubt someone will come along full of good intentions of starting it or another publication back up, but they will only be throwing their money away as the *Greyhound Star* is unrivalled and always will be!'

If you know the first thing about me, bulls and red rags, you will know how I felt about reading this. Despite having no intention or money to start up something afresh, I was determined to do so. One of the *Advertiser*'s contributors, Russ Watkin, was thinking the same, and he had contacted printers in his local area, Coventry, asking about prices for printing a new publication. Apparently, during one of those conversations it was put to him by the printer, whom Russ had never met, that 'you sound a little desperate'. He conceded that he was, and told him the full story about the *Advertiser's* sudden demise. When the printer said he might 'be interested in helping out' we were there, Nuneaton in Warwickshire, for a meeting the following day. A first-class guy, Ian Naylor, and his brother Neil, of Wilkinson Printers, listened to our predicament and mashed through some figures on projected sales and advertising revenue. We didn't bother stating that between us we could raise no more than a few hundred quid. I think Ian guessed, and by the end of the week he had come back with an offer to print, publish and distribute a new magazine, the *Greyhound Monthly*, of which I would be the full-time salaried editor.

July 1999 was the first month the magazine hit the shops, with Derby winner Chart King on the cover. I had little real idea of what I was doing. I just compiled everything and anything I could, then banged it over to the publishers for laying out creatively on pages. I put my heart and soul into it, determined to succeed. I had, after all, been gifted the kind of position I had dreamt of, and all because of a nasty jibe.

On our launch I got a spot on Sky Sports' greyhound show. I went on as Jeff Stelling's guest to announce that the magazine was here and here to stay. We did a deal with Sky whereby six annual subscriptions could be won each show. It was great PR for us, what with a picture of the colour magazine's cover going on screen three times a night.

Next up we got Jenny Pitman on the cover, when she was due to be guest of honour at an Injured Jockeys charity meeting at Walthamstow, and John McCririck waved a copy of the *Monthly* around for the Channel 4 TV cameras on the *Morning Line* programme, giving us yet more publicity. Even if we were selling just a few hundred copies, we were well known, and that meant I could approach the all-important bookmaking industry for advertising. This was a great time for it, too. I mean, all the bookmakers were launching their online gambling sites and they needed to advertise. Once we'd got our third edition knocked out, with Vinnie Jones on the cover alongside one of his greyhounds, we had enough history to put out media packs and launch a website.

Websites were still something very new to me. I didn't even possess a computer with internet ability at this stage. Neil did an excellent job on this side of the business. The result, following a lot of telephone calls and begging, was an advert from Ladbrokes, the world's biggest bookmakers. Once they came on board, William Hill followed, then Coral's, Stan James, Victor Chandler, Bet365 and Paddy Power. Spread betting firm Sporting Index were then encouraged to give us a try. The following month all the other spread betting firms were on board.

It was amazing, and all a result of ambition, determination and a challenge. From a standing start to a sixty-eight-page full-colour full-gloss magazine with every major bookmaking organization advertising inside, all within six months.

Sadly, the editor of the *Greyhound Star*, a former policeman, with none of the above advertising within his newspaper, somehow discovered my history and went around telling people about it. I heard about it first from a track's marketing manager whom I'd had a brief relationship with. His

allegations, no matter how true, made me yet more determined. I even contemplated going to night school to learn
formally about journalism. Induction day would have been
funny.

'So what is your name and what do you do for a living?'

'My name's Roy and I'm a magazine editor.'

The *Greyhound Monthly* also helped get me a starring role
on TV soap *Coronation Street*. Issue number four featured an
article about a storyline in *Coronation Street* where the cast
went dog racing to see Tyrone's greyhound run. I was recruited
to commentate on the race, which went out on the soap opera.
It was watched by thirteen million people – that's more people
than tune into the Grand National.

The magazine made me affluent, and I was starting to fulfil
my dream of betting for serious stakes. OK, I wasn't quite
there yet, but I could, for the first time, bet in the hundreds
regularly. As I said before, it's all about staking as much as you
can afford to lose and a little more.

My biggest ever win was still £3,700, from a time when
legally I was too young to gamble, but that was about to
change. The big night happened at the last ever greyhound
meeting at Wembley Stadium. There was a fantastic gathering
of greyhound fans there to see the old place off and that meant
a good old drink after the hare had spun its way around the
fabled pitch for the final time. And I had more reason to drink
than many: I'd parlayed £250 into a grand by backing my
selections fearlessly for ever-increasing stakes. I was rightly
proud of myself as I stood there drinking with the journalists
from the *Racing Post* and also those formerly of the *Sporting
Life*, which had closed a year beforehand.

We went on to Leicester Square, where the lads piled into Napoleons Casino and drank some more. There I played blackjack seriously for the first time in a decade, eventually pulling stumps with £4,200. It was a casino game though, so there was no huge buzz involved; my winnings were in chips, not in notes. I was as drunk as a skunk too, so the enormity of what I had achieved did not sink in.

I made my way home, some fifty miles away from the capital's centre down the M3, at about three in the morning – idiotically, because I really had drunk too much. I started to feel the effects when joining the A303 dual carriageway on the outskirts of Andover. I'm sure you know that point when you feel sick; you kind of want to be but decide to fight it. I was at the wheel of a car. I simply could not pull over to throw up on the hard shoulder. I'd be nicked for sure. I had a great idea: I'd unleash the fold-back soft top of my car (a rust-eaten MG Midget at that time) and let in plenty of fresh air. That would come to my rescue and sober me up.

I gotta tell you, I sobered up double quick when the piles of £50 notes which were sat alongside me on the passenger seat lifted up and flew out of the car like confetti. They just shot straight up into the sky, and in my rearview mirror I could see them fluttering back down again into the path of lorries which dispersed them in any and every direction. All but £700, lost for ever! All that time waiting for a big win and it was lost in the most unlikely of circumstances!

On with the magazine, and a new frontier, Ireland. I took a two-week trip to the place, during which I visited every greyhound track in the land – twenty in total. At each I sought advertising and got the *Monthly* on sale.

Next the Continent, with a trip to the European Greyhound Championship in Turku, Finland. It was the first time I had set foot on continental Europe as an adult and I had no idea what to expect. In fact, what with Finland being so notoriously cold, I took a case full of coats and jumpers. When I arrived, in the middle of July 2000, it was eighty degrees, warmer than England. It was an experience all right, and I had a great old time, picking up a new advertiser and a bunch of new subscribers. The people, camped out in the dog track's car park, were brilliant. I danced over a fire with the Russians, had a sauna with the Finns, and sang all night with the Dutch.

But I'd really fallen in love with Ireland. I realized I could run the magazine from there and increase its circulation in the process. I also saw the country as a beautiful place for a completely fresh start.

It was at the Greyhound Trainers Championship at Hove, another big meeting, that I got the money together for the move. Once again a number of the *Racing Post*'s staff – Paul Millward, Jim Austin and Jonathan Kay, to name a few – were around and after racing we got together to play that maniac card game three-card brag. The game got out of control at the hotel bar so a bunch of us went up to a hotel room to play. Jonathan lent me the money (£200) to get into the game and I got stuck into my first card school in years. I proceeded to clean up and, once in control of the game with a pile of cash in front of me, I rocked right up, played only premium hands and didn't jeopardize a penny. I stayed only to be polite.

Some of us have different ideas about being polite, however, and one guy certainly did not take kindly to me hoovering up all the dough and refusing to put it back in play. A small ruck followed, one we laugh about between ourselves these days, and I was ejected from both the game and the room. Now, some people would be very upset about that, but I was delighted! When I got back to my room there was over £3,000 in cash wedged in my pockets, ranging from £1 coins to £50 notes.

This win should have given me enough money to get to Ireland and rent a place all of my own. However, the following day I was sucked in like a paper clip to a high-powered magnet by the nearest racecourse, Lingfield, with more cash on me than I knew what to do with burning, as it always did, a hole in my pocket. By the fifth race I was absolutely stuffed, having backed loser after loser. I placed my last £200 on a 14/1 shot simply because, if it did win, I would get all my losses back. Crazy stuff, hey? It won, and I got that adrenalin shot I needed, from risking everything in the pursuit of winning nothing. I simply could not learn.

Alanis Morissette once recorded a song called 'Hand in My Pocket' in which the lyrics go 'I'm broke but I'm happy'. I understand that line better than most. All through my life, when I had money I was dangerous. I could not sleep at night, I had to find a place to gamble, and when the money was finally gone the craving disappeared as well. If there was no money, there was no urge to bet. What a fucking stupid way to lead your life.

On my way back from Lingfield races I tracked down Charlie, who I heard had hit hard times. I found him in a Portsmouth bedsit and I felt good about giving him cash for the time he let me use his flat.

Quickly, before jeopardizing my cash again, I made plans for

Ireland, agreeing to take a place sight unseen in Kilpedder, County Wicklow, about thirty minutes south of Dublin city. I just had a good vibe about the place, and the woman who recommended it to me – Imelda Grauer, the track photographer at Shelbourne Park dog track – seemed a good old stick.

14

The Turn

It was 2 January 2001 when I once again crammed my possessions into my car and found myself on the road. Things were a little different this time: this time I had somewhere to go, and life was good.

The new house in Kilpedder, all mine, was pleasantly tidy, and I cannot tell you how proud I felt to have my own place. Ireland was an adventure too, and in no time I'd made friends with Imelda's two sons and a daughter, all of whom were around my age. Plus, unsurprisingly, I soon became a regular at Dublin's two dog tracks, Shelbourne Park and Harolds Cross.

I'd bang away on the keyboard with a phone next to my ear all day long, and at night I'd be at the tracks. It was not the worst life imaginable, although the prospects of my keeping money remained as likely as filling a pierced bucket with a hosepipe. And it was flowing in: at the time I was also supplying a betting guide and tips for a few races from Wimbledon each night for a gambling company in Sweden that was now using the races to make up part of their national lottery; additionally, I wrote for an Irish publication, the *Sporting Press* newspaper. In fact, I was working so hard I couldn't get to a betting shop to squander it. I ordered a Sky package, which allowed me to watch all the horseracing at home, while I could now bet via the internet.

When the racing was over there was time for some conventional TV. One evening, flicking through the abundance of tat which infects our televisual airwaves as I ironed a shirt ready for a night out in Dublin, I paused on hearing the name Noel Furlong. Furlong had landed one of the biggest horseracing gambles in history when his horse, Destriero, won the 1991 Supreme Novices Hurdle at Cheltenham. That win cost bookmakers a reputed £1 million as the owner/trainer had got his money on all over the place just moments before the off, meaning the bookmakers were unable to contract the horse's starting price. The programme was a documentary about the 1999 World Series of Poker, and Furlong, who went on to land the million-dollar first prize, was the star of the show. I watched every second and thought to myself, 'That's fuckin' brilliant. I've got to get myself some of this.' Seconds after it finished I scanned the TV listings and found it was repeated six hours later. I set up the video recorder and must have watched that documentary at least half a dozen times over the following twenty-four hours.

Later that same week, a Spike Lee-directed movie called *Clockers*, about inner-city gangland crime, was due to be screened. I'd caught a trailer for the film and thought it was worth a watch. However, as the movie started I realized I'd made a mistake and I was about to see a flick called *Rounders*.

I decided to watch the film all the same. Five minutes into it I had already concluded that *Rounders* was the finest gambling film ever made, and during the ninety minutes it took to run its course I became hooked on poker.

The opening featured a lead character called Mike McDermott, played by Matt Damon, gathering his gambling stash, which was scattered all over his flat, including inside books, behind picture frames, in video cases and the like – that was me. He was mathematically astute – that was me. He'd lost everything – that was me. And, as the film drew to a close, he was embarking on a journey to find his destiny – that was me.

This double dose of televised poker reignited a fuse which had been quietly smouldering for twenty years. Suddenly, memories of those nights sat around my grandparents' front room playing Nomination and the barring from Southampton's Tiberius Casino for winning at blackjack seemed as vivid and exciting as ever.

If television rekindled the romance of card playing, the internet was my vehicle for tracking down a game, and when I Googled 'Poker Ireland' just one thing came up: the Jackpot Card Club in Montague Street, Dublin. (Try that trick these days and the Jackpot Card Club lists as the five thousandth suggested site among a million 'poker' alternatives!) Mid-morning I telephoned the club seeking information, only to be told they were not open until late evening. I was talking to a guy who was restocking the kitchen. Nevertheless I pressed him for details and urged him to find a leaflet; I had no wish to phone back in the evening. By then, in my excited mindset, I had to be playing. 'It says here nine p.m. three nights a week, Tuesday, Wednesday and Friday,' he explained in a disinterested tone, obviously keen to get back to his work.

With the passion of a teenager granted an all-areas pass at the Playboy Mansion I left home at six that evening for the thirty-minute drive to the city. I did not even know where Montague Street was. I simply could not wait to get started.

There is a nervousness associated with doing something for the first time. I used to see it in novice racegoers at the dog tracks, shy and apprehensive as they attempted to place a bet with the bookmakers, concerned about doing or saying something inappropriate or foolish. Driving into Dublin that evening I was starting to feel similarly uncomfortable. It was uncharacteristic. I was confident of ultimately being successful – this Texas Hold'em looked tailor-made for me – but I was concerned about being mocked for making a silly mistake or being the butt of a joke because of my greenhorn status.

Since my time on the streets, life had been a series of small forward steps gradually returning me to the accepted definition of a normal person. Such was my state at the time even a rebuff in a card game could and would knock my confidence. Therefore, ironically, the back alleyway on which I parked just behind the Jackpot had a kind of 'my territory' feel about it. Make no mistake, even a sewer rat would have been uncomfortable walking down it at night, but the oil-stained tarmac and the smell of urine at every drainpipe reminded me of where I had lived rough just a few years earlier. You may struggle to make sense of that, but let me ask you, where would you feel more comfortable on a Saturday evening: your local boozer followed by a meal in a nearby Chinese restaurant, or the Ritz for tea followed by a night at the opera?

The front door of the Jackpot Card Club really was like a scene from Teddy KGB's place in *Rounders*. The big heavy blue door took me into a small single room featuring nothing modern and nothing more than five blue-baize kidney-shaped poker tables and fifty sturdy red chairs, ten around each. There were no pictures, no televisions, no posters, no decorations. It was clear that poker was all that mattered here.

Thankfully there were no people either. What a relief. My fear of a gaggle of punters all sat at poker tables busily doing their thing who would descend into silence and then stare as I walked in was not realized. It was something to do with my arrival being a full two hours early, which gave me an opportunity to acquaint myself with the setting.

I strolled around the tables silently, like a tourist in a museum, considering how this place would look in a few hours' time when the action was underway. I heard a noise coming from below a counter and coughed to allow whoever was there to know that I was in the building.

'Jesus, you nearly gave me a heart attack,' exclaimed the lofty middle-aged man who appeared from underneath it.

'I'd like to play in your poker competition tonight,' I explained.

'Well, we don't start till nine o'clock, but I can take your entry fee and name and you could come back,' replied the man, who I could now see was dressed in a well-worn white shirt, black trousers and a dickie-bow.

'Yeah, that sounds great, but I've never played before and I'm slightly unsure of how things are done.'

He looked bemused, and shaking his balding head he replied, 'It shouldn't be a problem. You need to know the rules of poker, you need to know the hands: a pair is almost at the bottom of the ladder, better than that is two pairs—'

I interrupted him, explaining that I knew poker's ranking of hands, I just didn't know some of the nitty gritty: the blinds, the antes, dealing, where I bought my chips from.

'Ah, you'll be fine then,' he said. 'Just sit back and watch at the start and you'll soon pick it up, in minutes.' He passed me a pile of poker magazines from under his desk. 'Here, you might find these interesting. You have a long wait until we will be starting.'

Accepting his magazines, and happy to be staying as opposed to being forced to leave and, later, face that potentially embarrassing entrance I feared so much, I sat in the corner of the room, at a poker table for the first time. There I read each and every copy of *Poker Europa* magazine from front to back, engrossed and becoming more excited than ever. The results section at the back of the magazines showed that huge cash prizes were being won every month, up to £20,000 in some cases, and I discovered that poker was being played in exotic locations all around Europe.

Gradually, people began to arrive. They gave their name to the man in the bow-tie, who I discovered was called Bernard, and paid their tournament entry fee of £20, with another £5 for a registration fee. Thankfully I heard two guys, in their late twenties I guessed, talking about horseracing and I used the opportunity to butt into their conversation and introduce myself. I didn't know if that was the done thing, but making conversation with someone about a subject I understood certainly helped ease my apprehension.

As more and more people shuffled through the door I realized the average age had risen to about fifty, although thinking back to my grandparents' game I didn't feel out of place.

Suddenly there was a roll-call. 'OK, listen up. Christy 7-2, Bernie 1-2, Alex 2-3,' said Bernard. I had no idea what it was all about. I must have been looking bemused because he explained to me that the first figure was my seat number, the second the table number.

I sat at my seat and immediately asked them all to go gently on me, telling them that I'd not played before. 'Oh yeah,' said one player in an affable tone, 'we've heard that one before.'

As I glanced around the table at my rivals the fear of God shot through me. I hadn't seen a ghost, but I was looking at Noel Furlong. That's right, the legendary gambler, the man I had seen on my television just days earlier collecting a million dollars for winning the World Series of Poker. How could I beat this guy? He was the best in the world. He could probably tell me what cards I had in my hand the moment I looked at them. I could not have been further out of my depth if I'd been making a personal inspection of the hull of the *Titanic*. Seriously, what chance did I have against him?

His presence was the most memorable part of that first night for me, although the silver-haired thickset man did not distinguish himself by being loud or arrogant, or by making predictions about the outcome of certain hands. He sat and played his game silently, as did his opponents, whom I later discovered to be Harold Hubberman, an English-born pipe smoker, bald, in his fifties, quietly spoken; Pat Crowe, lofty, burly, chirpy, in his late forties; Vernon Clay, another

Englishman, happy-go-lucky, fifties, bad teeth; and Bernie McMahon, black leather jacket, static, in her fifties.

Perhaps if I had covered myself in a veil of glory I'd've remembered more of the cards I played. No doubt if you were reading a glamorized novel I'd be telling you all about how I won the tournament that night. The truth was I was woefully outclassed and quite clueless. That's fact, not fiction. I had no idea about what was considered a playable hand and what wasn't. I'd picked up on the lead character in *Rounders* saying something like 'you only play wired Jacks, Queens and better'. I'd taken this to mean that should one of my two hole cards be a Queen, it was a playable hand. Suffice to say I was getting some funny looks when the likes of my Queen-6 was dogging pocket Aces, but still the ambiance was laid back and the game both friendly and enjoyable. I felt robbed when I was eventually eliminated. It didn't seem fair. I wanted to stay and play all night. I was enjoying myself so much, it was an absolute buzz. I left after taking down details of when the tournaments were: Tuesday, with a £100 entry fee, Wednesday (£15) and Friday (£20). I could not wait until the next tournament.

I barely slept a wink that night. In a dreamlike state I just kept seeing cards flashing in front of me. Two cards in my hand and five on the table being turned over one at a time; stacks of chips being pushed in my direction with every full house and flush I made. Under my bed were all the *Poker Europa* magazines Bernard had given me, which once more I read from front to back and back again in the days leading up to my second visit to the Jackpot.

Among the characters I read about was a lady in her

seventies called Jenny Hegarty who had won the Irish Poker Open just a few months before my debut. Lo and behold, who was I sat alongside on that second visit? Jenny looked a bit like my nan Nora so I warmed to her immediately. She smoked like a chimney, as had my gran. Despite my dislike of the dreaded nicotine, I found her great company.

It was all so different from betting shops, where I'd often come across manic, unpleasant characters who looked as if they were on a day release from an asylum. The card club did not have that heady scent of desperation about it which you found in a betting office; there was no sense of people going broke around you; it was like playing with family: everyone was being nice to you, losing was not a monumental catastrophe, and tea, coffee and sandwiches were free for everyone.

On this occasion I sat back in my chair and barely played a hand for the first hour. This was my opportunity to sit and learn, just like all those years ago when I watched my family in Gran's front parlour. It led me to wonder why such legendary faces were playing in relatively low-stakes games. I also stopped to consider whether the people sat around me were actually enjoying the card playing as opposed to the social get-together – I mean, you could hear a pin drop they were so quiet. I soon learned that the enjoyment comes from the reward of intense concentration, deliberation and out-thinking people.

Once again I was all done and dusted in no time, and on thanking everyone for the game the response was a resounding 'please come again'. That night my attendance had swelled the numbers to a record-breaking twenty-nine entries.

Despite no success, I was hooked. A lifetime spent trying to turn fivers and tenners into thousands in betting shops, and I now appreciated the difference between poker and the horses. One was completely out of my control. I've backed horses that have taken the wrong course when in an unassailable lead and others whose jockeys have fallen off thanks to a riderless horse running head on into them while going down the course in the wrong direction just yards from the winning line. But in a poker game your destiny is in your own hands. Back in those early days in the Jackpot people walked away from tournaments with £750 winnings in their pocket parlayed up from a £20 stake. Such wins relative to a small starting stake were as rare as a summertime snowflake in a betting shop environment.

Additionally, all my life I'd been useless at anything sporting. I could never kick a football, catch a cricket ball or play tennis. I wasn't any good at the straightforward ones either, like pool or darts. Now, suddenly, I knew I'd found something I could be good at.

'Could' is the operative word here. I was anything other than an accomplished poker player, but I had self-belief in abundance and a desire to succeed. To aid my progress I bought and watched a host of poker videos, including the classic *Million Dollar Deal* documentary and final tables from the World Series of Poker throughout the nineties, although they featured no under-table camera shots. I was still working flat out with anything greyhound racing-related, but any spare moment was spent dreaming about poker, and nothing got in the way of my tournaments three nights a week. I was determined to crack the knack of winning at the game, because poker had quickly become an obsession.

The breakthrough came early in September 2001. By now the local players knew my name and greeted me like an old friend. On this occasion I went head-to-head, meaning there were just two of us left, me and Harold Hubberman. I found myself looking down at a pair of Jacks, with Harold announcing 'raise' before I'd had a chance to make my own betting decision. I was about to push all my chips into the middle and announce 'all-in' with my monster hand when I paused to consider that Harold had not raised a single pot during our heads-up battle, or at any stage during the game. I thought on. I could not remember an occasion when he had raised a pot pre-flop, ever. Tossing my pretty hand of Jacks into the middle face up, I announced 'pass'. Harold looked dismayed as he showed a pair of Aces and drew in his winning pot. My correct pass gave me supreme confidence. Now I was a poker player, not just smashing my chips into battle with any big hand but capable of passing a big hand. It was a key piece to the jigsaw puzzle.

I went on to win that tournament, my first ever. It was the first time I could call myself a winner in any sphere, and I loved it. You just don't forget such monumental things. The £1,000 winner's purse was almost irrelevant, despite it being a winning sum I'd reached on only a handful of occasions in a life spent in the dog and horseracing games.

If I'd had trouble sleeping at night beforehand, now I was a near insomniac. I was a winner. I'd learned the winning formula and I dreamt of big pots, big hands and big show-downs. Dog racing was out the window; the prestige of being a magazine editor and a 'someone' was all but forgotten. Poker was all that mattered.

Actually, just days after this first win I had to take a flight back to the UK to appear before the Sky Sports cameras and talk about the forthcoming Irish Greyhound Derby. I had no real interest in the task but I flew over, landed at Bournemouth and then drove to Andover with a friend. We stopped at the Abbot's Mitre, the pub I'd worked in five years earlier, where we watched live pictures of the second plane hitting the Twin Towers. Later that day I appeared on TV from Wimbledon Stadium singing the praises of the coming greyhound competition with little genuine enthusiasm. The fact that the biggest terrorist attack in American history had just occurred was on everyone's mind. Naturally I was shocked and horrified like the rest of the world, but I was also concerned about how it might affect my ability to return home for the next game.

It was nowhere near as difficult as I thought it was going to be. I was on my way back to Ireland within a couple of days, and I was straight back into the poker swing. I spent my 'off nights', when there was no tournament, alone with a deck of cards going through various scenarios like Ace-King versus a pair of 7s. I'd deal out a five-card flop hundreds of times over, writing down and recording the results. I was like a man possessed. I wanted to know all the permutations. It was a bit like Granddad going through the form book each night before he went to sleep. I was using my own mathematical prowess to calculate the probability of hands prevailing, mixing it with 'reality situations' and likely betting patterns. These days there are a host of websites that will spill out the figures for you, but I maintain it does not give you the same understanding. It definitely proved valuable to me because following that initial win at the Jackpot I landed thirteen out of the next nineteen tournaments at the club and managed three other prominent finishes.

That hot streak was just perfect as the Irish Winter Poker Festival, which attracted a host of travelling pros, was about to kick off. It was staged in a Georgian terraced house otherwise known as the plush Merrion Casino, in Dublin's city centre. It was to be my first major tournament, with a £600 entry fee, and I spent weeks planning and dreaming about winning it. Can you imagine? Eighty top players including Simon Trumper, the reigning champion of TV's *Late Night Poker* programme, and the unknown Roy Brindley takes it down?

With wily determination I waited for my spots, played superb poker, watched every opponent intently, did nothing wrong, and subsequently found myself among a final field of fourteen players. I was so close to the hallowed final table I simply had to jeopardize nothing and play only premium hands.

Dare I say it, skilfully I managed to manipulate my opponent, John Walsh, to move all his chips forward with just one pair in a hand while I held the stone-cold nuts, Ace-Jack with the board showing 10-Queen-King. I was set to make it through to the final as the chip leader. That was until Walsh, who had stood and tapped the table in submission while preparing to leave, saw a diamond fall on the turn, giving him a glimmer of hope. Then another diamond landed on the river, giving him an unlikely flush for victory.

The net result was total devastation. I left the building feeling wretched, utterly deflated. Despite a torrential downpour, I simply walked the streets of Dublin for hours on end during the small hours. I was numb, and drenched. I could not come to terms with the defeat. It should not have happened. Surely it could not happen like it did. I believed I should have been at that final table as chip leader.

I was actually looking for a tramp on a street corner. If I had found one I'd have given him the contents of my pockets – which were considerable, considering my tournament wins – plus the keys to my car and house too.

I once read a story about the original Fleetwood Mac member Peter Green, who went out to the shops one day and didn't return for two years having met a cult member on a street corner. It read so stupidly, it was simply not plausible. But now I could see it was. I too would have joined a cult there and then if they'd promised to take away the pain of that defeat. Little did I know, but my obsession with poker success was already coming dangerously close to its workable limit.

15

All-in

That disastrous beat in the Irish Open hit me hard. I'd never been competitive before but I had installed a work ethic into my subconscious which dictated that defeat was simply unacceptable. It took a few weeks, which were filled with sixteen-hour days running my magazine, analysing races for the Swedes and contributing to various newspapers, but I eventually came to terms with the elimination and returned to the Jackpot, both playing and winning.

There was one last hurrah of the year, the Helsinki Freezout, where the last major tournament of the season was staged and where the European Poker Awards were to be distributed. With a double issue of *Greyhound Monthly* at Christmas and no January edition, plus a drawer full of cash as a result of my tournament wins, allied to no desire to take my bounty to a betting shop, this festival was within my grasp.

Christmas in Helsinki is magical: cobbled streets, tram bells ringing, roast chestnut vendors on street corners, crisp snow, and children scrambling to look at the festive displays in department store windows. Poker was my ticket to enjoying this lovely city, and the four-star hotel accommodation in which I stayed was a far cry from the antiquated terraces of Henlow dog track – the kind of riches that greyhound racing magazine editorship brought me. Yet, to think, just a short while earlier it was everything I had ever wanted.

As it happened I did not land a tournament at this festival – a string of four competitions including a 'main event', all boasting European ranking points – or even make a final table, but, thankfully, I didn't crack up like I had following the Irish Open. In fact I learned a lot, and I looked on enviously as the European Poker Awards were handed out at a lavish ceremony. I vowed I would be back the following year to collect an award for myself, be it Player of the Year, Tournament Performance of the Year or, more realistically, Rookie of the Year.

My enthusiasm burned brightly as 2001 drew to a close. Life could not be any better, what with the discovery of a pastime which I loved and the knowledge, at the age of thirty-two, that there was something out there in which I believed I had natural talent. I constantly thought back to my time on the streets but purely for inspiration at the poker table. While in a predicament over whether to pass, call or raise in a situation where the outcome of a tournament, sometimes worth £1,000, was on the line, I would pause to consider the times when I had spent an entire embarrassing day gathering coppers in order to buy a packet of biscuits. The value of money would strike home and this, allied to an unwavering determination, meant that mistakes were few and far between.

Among my new circle of friends and associates was Ken Robertson, marketing manager of Paddy Power, the Irish bookmakers. Originally Ken had taken advertising within the *Monthly* and then awarded me a small contract to promote the Irish Greyhound Derby, which they sponsored. One evening, while in the midst of enthusiastically telling him of my new-found passion, Ken divulged that his company had been approached to sponsor a televised poker tournament.

If it went ahead, I simply had to play in it. I mean, poker was the future; I could see where it was going and where it would end up. I realized that winning a televised event at a time when poker was at an embryonic stage would be my ticket, the catalyst to a full-time high-profile sportsman's career. At this time Channel 4's groundbreaking *Late Night Poker* was the only televised poker. It had created some sizeable ripples among the television companies and broadcasters – the under-table cameras were the key to its success – and I realized that not only did the game have the prospect of being bigger, in terms of viewership and popularity, than darts in the seventies and snooker in the eighties, but, as an industry, poker could conceivably generate more money than bookmaking, bingo and fruit machines all rolled into one.

This was all in the future. For now, the Paddy Power-sponsored event went ahead, promoting only the company's online betting service (online poker had not been considered by them or any other bookmaker at the time). The game was to be played early in January 2002, and through Ken I got myself one of the twenty-seven seats in the tournament, which would be broadcast on Sky Sports. It was the network's first toe-in-the-water with serialized poker, and the winner of this event would gain a ticket for the forthcoming Poker Million, which would also be televised. If I could win it, then I would be showcased in the Million, meaning I could secure pretty much enough airtime to become one of Europe's best-known poker players.

During that first year living in Dublin, with the magazine doing so well, I returned to the UK quite often, where I would do the occasional guest appearance on SIS (the betting shop channel) and Sky Sports for the big greyhound meetings they covered. If poker became what I thought it would, the plan was simply to transfer this line of work, plus the magazine and newspaper columns, from greyhound racing to poker. So everything hinged on winning that televised tournament, and I had a little over three weeks to prepare for it.

Preparation in poker is so important; don't let anyone tell you otherwise. I think most folks out there think you turn up on the day, sit down at a table and wait for a good hand to put your chips in with. If only it was as simple as that.

I spent the two-week period over Christmas and New Year thinking about nothing other than poker, fearing defeat and what a loss in the tournament would mean to my sanity. The wait alone was nearly driving me demented, so, equipped with my new-found wealth, which was only a couple of grand but more money than I'd ever held for more than a few days, I booked a holiday to Madeira. It was just me (albeit surrounded by hordes of pensioners), a deck of cards and a pocket poker diary which I'd got for Christmas. In the back of that diary was a chart showing probability of outs arriving. I memorized it. I must have worked through another eighty hours of poker theory during this 'break'.

The ninth of January 2002 was the big day – it's funny how you remember key dates with remarkable accuracy, isn't it? (Of

Above: Early days on the poker circuit; this was at a tournament in Brighton in 2004.

Right: William Hill Grand Prix 2005.

Below: At the final table of the Poker Masters of Europe 2007.

fair.com

Above: Sebastian is as keen as I am to get hold of the Poker Masters trophy.

Above: Sebastian with an appropriate T-shirt!

Right: Our latest arrival, Elise.

Above and left: Meeting Mags turned my life around. On a poker cruise (*above*) and (*left*) on holiday in St Moritz.

Above and below: Proof that poker can take you around the world. This was in Lithuania, where I later held court (*below*).

Above: My Aces stood up in Amsterdam's Masterclassics Omaha event, November 2006.

Right: Copenhagen's EPT, 2007. I had another huge stack but the final table eluded me.

ROY THE BOY

Above: Being a sponsored pro has its benefits.

Above: And proof that being a well-known player is tough …

Above: Jimmy White won the Poker Million in 2003, helping to boost the game's popularity. We were drawn alongside each other in the 2004 edition.

Above: In 2003 I faced off heads-up against another snooker legend, Steve Davis, and came second. The guy is an absolute gentleman.

Above: Me with (*from left to right*) the former Mayor of Dublin Royston Brady, Liverpool legend Ian Rush, a drinking companion, Bryan Coleman, and my friend Nick Leeson, at a corporate event.

Above: Working for Sky has been a great experience; here I am with *Soccer AM*'s Helen Chamberlain.

Above: Jesse May on MC duties during a poker cruise around the Mediterranean.

Below: Trophies, once the be-all and end-all, but these days it's about the money!

course, others you quickly forget.) The setting for Paddy Power's poker tournament was a sports hall within a Catholic priest's teaching college, a seminary, in Maynooth, County Kildare, where, after stepping over camera cables at a doorway, I asked a bemused resident priest where the poker tournament was being filmed. 'This is not the first time a game of cards has been played here and it won't be the last,' he preached, while pointing me in the right direction.

Naturally, just like for that debut at the Jackpot, I had arrived extremely early. As a result, after I'd wandered down the darkened hallways of the seminary and was eventually led to the tables and their cameras I found everything sat dormant like a game-show set without any contestants. It was quite a strange sight.

One by one the players arrived and handed over their entry fee. By the standards of the day it was sizeable enough at £500 – now, of course, converted into the newfangled week-old Euro currency. These days you can safely multiply that figure by ten or even twenty, and the field sizes . . . instead of the twenty-six players I had to overcome, try up to fifty times that number, often more in America.

I sized up my opponents before a card was even dealt. None scared me, but I was facing one of the biggest battles tournament poker players have to combat: impatience. Tournament director Liam 'Gentleman' Flood added to my anguish by announcing delays due to faulty lighting, unfocused cameras and dodgy microphones.

This was a time for gritty, uncompromising determination and intense focus on the mission that lay ahead. As they say in dog and horseracing, I was 'trained to the minute' – in other words, all the preparation I'd put in was focused on this precise time. I'd lived the Hold'em obsession over and over when I was in Madeira. OK, I never read a book on poker strategy, and I never will. I did, however, spend many solid hours with a pocket diary, fifty-two cards and a piece of paper working through a boundless number of incidents and situations, normally five hundred times apiece to get a fair idea of the mathematical probability of each occurrence.

I'd even bought myself a new suit specifically for this day. Everyone else was dressed casual, but I wanted to be different, upstanding and distinguished. However, I'd given no thought to being 'made up' for the cameras, and no consideration to a pre-match interview.

A microphone was shoved under my nose and some obvious questions – 'Where are you from?' 'How long have you been playing poker?' – were posed. These were followed by 'What are your hopes for today?' I naturally replied from the heart: 'I've come to win, with no exceptions!' It may have sounded incredibly arrogant, but if I didn't carry that kind of attitude around with me, what realistic chance did I have? The words just came out.

Tennis champ John McEnroe was a true champion with a clear desire to win. The 1989 World Series of Poker winner Phil Hellmuth, whom I'd been studying in poker documentaries and first seen in a poker magazine seven years earlier, also had it. I respected their mindset, their determination. You know, arrogance and a desire to win can easily be confused. Endear yourself to people by all means, but the cold, hard truth is this: nice guys usually lose.

As a tiny microphone was fed up my shirt and clipped close

to my chest, the order to 'take your seats' was finally given. As I mentioned, I'd trained myself 'to the minute', and thankfully that minute had now arrived. Twenty-seven players sat down, attentively, as the cards were dealt for hand number one.

Yes, you could argue there were no superstars among us, but what constitutes a superstar? At the time, those who played on TV's *Late Night Poker*, still being re-run now years after its debut, were considered stars, though in truth many of them were no more than enthusiastic club players. The bottom line, as I said, was that winning this tournament would catapult me into the public eye, even if I hadn't quite overcome the poker equivalent of a Davis, a Hendry, a White, a Doherty or an O'Sullivan. (As it happens, in time I was to play poker with all of these cue-men.)

As the cards landed I had a chuckle with Derek Williams, one of the characters who made up the Jackpot's faithful and one of the people I could now call a friend. I had told the person interviewing the players to look out for Derek. He was nicknamed 'The Clamper' as that was his job. 'Make sure you give him a good grilling about his nickname and ask why he has it,' I told the interviewer.

'So, did you have a good interview, Derek?' I asked in such a way that he was sure to know I had set him up.

'No problems,' he replied. 'You can watch it on TV soon enough.'

When the show did finally go on air, sure enough Derek reported that he was called 'The Clamper' because he put a stranglehold on his opponents and his profession was 'a road traffic management consultant'. What a bluff!

I was not feeling nervous. This was my stage; it was where I had always wanted to be. I felt very confident around the cameras, under the spotlight. I had always craved attention. Maybe it was because I was an only child, possibly because I was never good at anything sporting and always wanted to be. When I think of it, I loved seeing my name on the race-card when I trained greyhounds, or next to a story in the *Racing Post*.

I soon had my personal CD player plugged in. It was quite novel at the time, not just because iPods and MP3 players did not yet exist but, most notably, because listening to music while playing was not the done thing. When you listen to music it lessens some of your senses, but the perception of what you see is massively enhanced, of that I am convinced. Have you not heard of the saying 'the eyes believe themselves, the ears believe other people'? I needed to rely on what I saw with my own eyes, and music helped me concentrate on that. I was the only person with headphones on. They're not allowed in televised events these days.

Naturally I had some good luck along the way. In one hand I had a pair of Aces and only called with them looking for someone to raise. The raise did not come and my opponent, Dave Cleary, flopped a full house; I luckily rivered an Ace and won a monster pot, which put me in a great spot. From that point on, at no stage was I in any danger of getting knocked out before making the final table.

With the live recorded version of Hans Zimmer's classics – the music from *Rain Man*, *Gladiator*, *Driving Miss Daisy* and *Thelma and Louise* – filling my head, a suit and silver tie dazzling people like a peacock showing his feathers, and my relentless raising, I arrived at that hallowed final table as chip leader. Zimmer's music is so uplifting yet so very relaxing, and with its help plus, possibly, new glasses – I'd only realized I needed them a little over a year before when calling a host of dog races completely wrong at Wimbledon over the PA – I felt invincible at that final table.

This really was my opportunity to land on the big screen in front of an unassuming public and stake a claim in poker which I remained convinced was to become a revolution the like of which we had not seen since the Rubik's Cube.

I knew all the players there except one, a character called Alan Betson. He had the right name for a poker player and a pile of chips almost as impressive as my own. He also grinned like a Cheshire Cat. My friends, the likes of youngster Conor Doyle and Michael Frisby, both of whom I'd go on the road with in months and years to come, told me this guy was the dog's bollocks, a recent winner of the European Championship and the most accomplished player in Ireland and possibly Europe.

I cared not. I had everyone else sussed and I just went about my business and played my game. It was a fatal mistake. The hand that did all the damage was about to happen against him through a lack of understanding and knowledge about Betson's game.

Looking down at a pair of Jacks, I simply flat-called. It was a ploy that had served me well throughout the day. You see, I'd re-raise when someone bumped the pot up with a raise themselves. Right on cue, the Cheshire Cat raised. Brilliant, he had fallen into my trap. Music to my ears, even better than Hans Zimmer.

I moved all-in. He couldn't call unless he had one of the

three hands I was losing to. Sure enough, he made an immediate call and turned over the best of them, a pair of Aces.

As the realization hit that I did not need to commit every single chip in front of me to discover I was losing this hand, more than three-quarters of them were being scooped away. I'd messed it all up. I'd had the chance of glory within my grasp, I could taste it, but now I had nothing more than a few chips and a story.

The temptation to lash them into the next pot in desperation was there. Kind of like going for a match-winning black when you know the white is going to go in-off in pool. The technical poker term is 'to go on tilt'.

But I stopped. I recalled how it had felt walking the Dublin streets at two a.m. in the pouring rain as a loser, a dejected, eliminated player from the Irish Winter Poker Festival just weeks earlier. Then I thought some more. About the times I walked the streets without enough money for food, without a roof over my head. I didn't give in then, why should I now? If I did, all those hard times were for nothing.

There was no smashing my chips in until I had a fighting chance, a chance of making my opponent pass or getting a much-needed double-up. Impatience has no place at a poker table. Well, maybe it does, but once I pass a threshold, usually around six hours of play, I can hang around for longer than a tortoise on EPO. So I dug in and indeed fought my way right back into the fray.

Cheshire Cat Betson may have picked up an abundance of big starting hands and hoovered up every chip, but his luck was about to run out. Three of us remained – Daisy O'Grady was still with us. When the fourth person was eliminated Daisy had gone to war, moving 'all-in' each and every hand. He was gambling on the fact that we didn't have a hand good enough to call him. It was a fantastic bit of play at the perfect time. With the blinds high the wily, grey-haired, bespectacled craftsman soon pushed himself into the argument, and there was nothing between the three of us.

I knew I had to get involved in this raising business for myself, and when Betson announced 'raise' I pushed my entire stack of chips into the middle, holding nothing more than 7-6. It was my turn to gamble, to gamble that this audacious play would work, that he did not have a hand good enough to call with. I knew full well he had enough chips to pass and stay in the hunt, so it all depended on his cards.

As he immediately announced 'call' I pulled my earpieces out and prepared to leave the room. Last time it was Aces, this time I expected to see something ranging from a pair of 8s to an Ace-King, Ace-Queen or Ace-Jack. To my, and everyone's, amazement he flipped over a 7-4!

With low cards arriving on the board there was that terrible moment poker players often have when their money is in and adrenalin is pumping. I could not quite figure out quickly enough that my 6 played and I had eliminated him with 7-high and that 6 kicker.

It was not a case of me eliminating him, actually, but him going through meltdown and eliminating himself. Afterwards, in his post-match interview, he declared, 'I looked at him and I thought he wasn't that strong, and I was right. But he thought he was, so all's well and good!' I could never quite figure that out as he was the one who made a horrific call of an all-in to eliminate himself!

I was now heads-up with Daisy, who had so brilliantly taken to steamrollering us, raising every pot, just at the right time. I knew he was going to attempt it again with me, the chip leader, having everything to lose, and him, with the chip deficit, little to lose. It was either the first or second hand when, having not looked at my cards, he raised me. Now, listening to what should have been a mellowing 'Annie's Song' by John Denver, I confidently announced 're-raise' – playing blind allows you to do that: what you don't know cannot scare you – and before I knew it I had so many chips committed to the pot I could not pass when he announced 'all-in'.

My heart sank as he turned over an Ace-Queen. I flipped over a defenceless 5-8 – it was the first time I had seen my cards. I was destined to give him the clear chip lead. That was until a miracle 8 appeared on the table and it was all over. I'd done it, I was champ.

I don't think Daisy would mind me telling you there was a tear in his eye as he left the studio behind curtains and a heavy door, leaving me there all alone with just cameras and silent cameramen following my every move. I was expecting some kind of celebration, confetti falling from the ceiling maybe, but there was nothing. Deep down I knew I'd done something special, and I knew I was now made. I was going to enjoy all this exposure on Sky Sports. It wasn't the prize, the ticket to the forthcoming Poker Million, it was the ability to call myself a winner before an audience of thousands, some of whom might well have walked over me in a Southsea side-street just a few years earlier.

There was no trophy for this tournament – that got over-looked by the organizers – so I was presented with an empty envelope which was supposed to contain my Golden Willy Wonka ticket . . . to the Poker Million.

What struck me, though, was that every eliminated player stayed behind to see the conclusion of the event. They gave me a rapturous round of applause and there was a wealth of hand-shaking. It was conclusive evidence that I had found myself in the right country among the nicest people. I was accepted within the Irish poker community. That was important to me.

When it was time to leave the priests in peace and go home, Daisy, Pat Crowe, three staff members and I went for a Chinese meal. I was buzzing. I offered to treat everyone to drinks and dinner and I attempted an appreciation speech. I loved this attention. I was James Bond after all, and I was going to go to the Poker Million in the firm belief that I could win it. I was never going to get beat, and the money I had become so used to over the past few months was never going to dry up. I had found my niche.

16

2002: A Poker Odyssey

Within twenty-four hours of my televised win I was back in the Jackpot. I loved poker, I wanted to play every second of every day. I'd have walked over red-hot coals or broken glass to get to a game. I'd have played for peanuts, shirt buttons or matchsticks. The stakes didn't matter.

There was plenty of back patting in the card room from people who were genuinely happy for me. This included a set who resided in the far corner, cash game players whom I'd had no dealings with. They arrived midway through the nightly tournaments, at about eleven p.m., and played until nine a.m. These were a hardcore, oh-so-serious bunch of people who never played tournaments. They put their cash on the line each and every hand they played.

I'd never played a cash game before and I didn't really understand the game they were playing, called Omaha. The hand rankings were exactly the same as any poker game but they started with four cards in their hand instead of the two I was used to in Hold'em. Massive sums would be bet with just three cards face up on the table. It was so different from the game I had spent months perfecting and, to be honest, it didn't make much sense to me, although I watched it for hours on end, intrigued.

Like I say, they were decent enough to offer their congratulations. Of their number, one, Scott Gray, later claimed to have given me the stage name 'Roy the Boy'. (Scott went on to make the final table of the World Series of Poker a few months later, further endorsing the quality of player that called the Jackpot either their home or their workplace.) I'm not sure if that was the case as in weeks to come Liam Flood, who commentated on that Paddy Power Poker Tournament, used the phrase repeatedly during each episode and it stuck thereafter.

Most, if not all, of the poker players on the circuit have appointed themselves a nickname or alias, and to be honest, most are woeful. In my book there is something wrong with grown men calling themselves 'The Elegance' or 'The Iceman'.

With this televised win under my belt I believed I was set and I contacted each and every marketing manager at every bookmaker and spread betting firm I had dealt with through the *Greyhound Monthly* with an angle to work poker into their product base and to work myself into an enviable position. When you have lived on the streets and woken up to find yourself transformed into a respectable magazine editor, journalist and commentator, you might well argue that throwing the lot away to play cards and hopefully convince someone that poker is going to be one of the fastest-growing crazes of the century is a mightily stupid decision. But I was convinced that poker was going places, and as for the greyhounds, the real buzzes, like getting Vinnie Jones to come along to the Irish Greyhound Derby final and bring along his mates Ronnie Wood and

Frankie Dettori, along with earnings that I had never enjoyed before, were always tempered by the memories of the atrocities in Abilene.

Around this time, the BBC broadcast an episode of *Kenyon Confronts* called 'From the Cradle to the Grave'. It was billed as a secret look at the greyhound underworld and was, for the best part, a lot of nonsense, but there was no denying that they had unearthed a Swindon trainer who was shooting unwanted greyhounds. It was a guy called Steve Davis, a former jockey and a guy I had drunk with on several occasions. I believed him to be a very sound fella – some judge I am. I had no idea such things were happening, or even could happen, on our shores. I hadn't even considered it.

Thankfully, like a jailed murderer on Death Row finding Jesus, I had found poker, and I decided to leave greyhound racing after spending my whole life in and around it. In the following month's edition of *Greyhound Monthly*, in my 'Editor's Views' column, I wrote my own obituary, announcing that poker would attain more television airtime than grey-hound racing. It was the future without a shadow of doubt, and possibly dog racing should take a look at itself.

I was burning some bridges. I mean, there was no turning back now. If I failed in my quest to make a go of poker, well, I could end up back in a factory or warehouse. Not much of a back-up plan, but life's a gamble not a destination.

Maybe it was a typical Brindley gamble, the type that had cost me so dearly down the years, as it only took a few weeks for almost every bookmaker to come back to me and express their disinterest in my plans for poker and my belief that it would be the next big thing. Most had launched their online betting sites amid much pomp and ceremony a year or so before and all were extremely disappointed with the business, or lack of it, they were generating. Budgets for promoting their sites had been slashed, and none had faith in the concept of online poker.

There was one exception: Betfair.com, a betting exchange, a completely new concept and a new player in the gambling market. I had phoned them the day they launched their site asking if they would consider advertising within the *Greyhound Monthly*. In those early days they declined, but I made follow-up calls every two months and they eventually joined us. With more television coverage from Sky Sports during the Poker Million guaranteed, their marketing manager Jojo Primrose liked the idea of their logo being slapped on my attire and we soon agreed on a deal that would give me £10,000 a year.

I cannot begin to describe the enormity of this. I was to become the first commercially sponsored poker player in Europe, and one of the first in the world.

Delighted, I went off to chase my dream . . . doing the European poker circuit. The first stop was the 'North of England Open' in Salford, Manchester. I was totally new to the scene. Dublin and a trip to Helsinki apart, I'd never seen another card room and had no idea what to expect. I knew next to nobody and had that feeling about me, that nervous feeling I had when going into the Jackpot for the very first time. Nevertheless, just like the Dublin players, these ones would get to know me in time, of that I was sure, especially after I finished sixth in the main event in Manchester. I should have been happy, considering I flew in on the day and by the time we sat down for the final table I had been awake for over twenty-four hours. But, driven like I was at the time, I was disappointed. The winner was Julian Gardner, who, just over three months later, finished second to Robert Varkonyi in the World Series of Poker, earning himself $1 million, so the form was strong.

When I returned from this Manchester trip there was a letter on my doormat. It was from promoters Matchroom Sports explaining that, for reasons beyond their control, Poker Million 2002 was being cancelled. It turned out they wanted to stage the event in a London hotel but the police could not confirm they would not raid the place and close it down on the grounds that the event would be, in essence, illegal gambling.

In one sense it was so disappointing as I firmly believed I could overcome an estimated field of three hundred players to win it, but in another I was going to take a $10,000 cash alternative, and that would boost my bankroll and allow me, along with the £10,000 Betfair cheque, to do pretty much all of the European events. But that, too, was about to be curtailed. An e-mail from Jojo arrived later that evening saying that 'as the Poker Million was not being broadcast she could not justify such a large outlay for my sponsorship' and it would now have to be cut. Ultimately I don't think they did too badly out of their eventual £1,000 sponsorship as, during a drunken conversation in Clonmel, Co. Tipperary, Ireland, I was to put a punter on to Betfair and he, Harry Findlay, has doubtlessly earned the company a healthy sum in commission since.

As spring 2002 dawned, the setbacks made me more determined to make a mark. Stumbling blocks like these inspired me to perform all the more, to attain a better sponsorship deal and show everyone that my faith in the future of poker was not misplaced.

I had continued to play in Dublin most nights of the week and my friendship with fellow player Michael Frisby had become quite firm. I just thought the guy was a great character and a fine drinking companion. The nights when there was no poker, I'd often go drinking with him in the Irish capital. It was a lot livelier than Andover.

With the seven-week run of the Paddy Power Poker Tournament now coming to an end on Sky Sports, together we set off for Birmingham and the 'Great British Hold'em Festival' at the Rainbow Casino. The Rainbow was a right old gambling den, slap bang in the middle of Birmingham's red-light district, with hookers on every corner. However, it was well known in poker circles and the turnout was incredible.

We'd been in the place for about three minutes when a well-spoken character approached me and said, 'You're that chappy who won that tournament on telly, aren't you?'

'Yes, yes, I am,' I proudly said, enjoying the recognition.

'Well, old boy, you're playing with the big boys now and you don't have much chance here.'

What a tosser! What's wrong with a conventional 'well done, good luck today'? Of course, I was back in England, which I found irksome and hostile.

His comments riled me, and I immediately entered the opening tournament of the series, which was Hold'em/Omaha, a round of each. In short, that meant we played nine hands of Texas Hold'em followed by nine of Omaha throughout the competition. The problem was, I'd never played Omaha in my life, only watched it in the Jackpot on the odd occasion. And if that wasn't enough of a handicap, there was also a field of a hundred players to overcome. Still . . . I won it. My first European ranking tournament, £4,000, a first trophy, and a picture wearing a Betfair T-shirt accepting it. It was so sweet.

That trophy was so important to me. I mean, I'd never won anything more than an empty envelope, and before that Paddy Power event, among a host of things I tried, nothing whatsoever.

That night Michael and I celebrated in style. This was the dream, and only champagne would do. I suppose once upon a time with four grand in my pocket in cash a bookmaker's would have been my first port of call. It struck me that I'd never won such a sum in a betting shop but I'd sure as hell lost a lot more than that in each and every year of the past decade. What was the point? If I could turn a £50 poker tournament entry into £4,000, what could I do in a big tournament with a £500 entry fee? I could win the kind of sum I had tried to achieve in years of betting shop gambling. I'd grown up, progressed from being a gambling degenerate, and poker had played its part in the process.

This was the point where all the fun began, the hedonistic rock 'n' roll lifestyle. I was in my thirties, but the best way I can describe it is like this: imagine a seventeen-year-old lad whose school band has just secured itself a record contract, a number one song and a sell-out tour. This was the best time of my life – flights, hotels, bundles of cash, birds, and the recognition my personality had secretly craved. Soon I was out of control. It's addictive stuff, you know.

The next major tournament was in Dundee, Scotland. I had no idea what part of the country it was in or how to get there, but Michael and I were keeping to our pledge to travel together around Europe and do it on the back of poker. We flew into Edinburgh, took a train to Dundee and stayed at the Hilton Hotel. OK, that chain may not quite have the prestige it once did, but it was a world away from a caravan, toilet or cardboard box. Here I found the locals far more affable than those I'd encountered in Birmingham. They were genuinely appreciative that we had come to their casino and made us feel very welcome. That kind of approach made it far harder to take their money from them, but I wasn't about to go soft. Poker was the way forward and I wanted to be at the cutting edge of its development.

The opening tournament was a Pot Limit Hold'em competition. I'd never played this before either. It wasn't a world apart from No Limit Hold'em though, and I finished fourth in a field of seventy-six players. Days later I took down the feature event, earning £8,500 and another all-important trophy. Add to that the first ever cash game I'd played – I was dealt three Kings in seven-card stud, probably played the hand terribly yet won a £5,000 pot – and I'd cleared £15,000 in three days. The money was in sealed bags worth a grand apiece, all in fifties from the casino's cash desk.

With fifteen of them bulging out of my pockets I made my way to the local branch of my building society – the same organization I'd once made that £1.79 cash withdrawal from. On the way I walked past an estate agent's window and saw flats for sale in the local area for less money than I had in my pockets! Possibly I should have walked in and bought one, just like someone picking up a bar of chocolate in a shop. But maybe I was suffering from a guilt trip, a belief that this money was not really mine; I had come to possess it too easily. Gamblers, as I mentioned, often suffer from that syndrome. If you win, the money is not yours; if you lose, it hurts like hell.

Anyway, Michael and I continued to drink and play hard. We made friends everywhere we went, be it in the casinos or at local bars and clubs after the poker. How could you not like us? We were having a ball and throwing around £50 notes – £100 notes in Scotland as it happens, legal tender there – like they were confetti. Want a drink? Here, have a bottle of Bollinger. Fancy a night out? Good, fill a suitcase, grab your passport, we're off to Paris tomorrow.

Back home, in between these trips, I had way too much time on my hands. In these days there was just one major tournament festival a month, and with no magazine to worry about I was often at a loose end.

One sad and sorry day I suffered a 'betting shop incident' of the very worst kind. I suppose it was inevitable, like a reformed alcoholic having one drink and then going on a full-scale bender, not wanting to sober up, knowing it would bring home just how catastrophically bad the decision to have that first drink was. I'd collected another wedge from the Jackpot, and the following afternoon I was on my way to my local bank in Greystones to deposit the loot (by this time I had already been called in by the manager, who was concerned about possible money laundering and asked me to explain where these bundles of cash were coming from). Somewhere between the car park and the bank lurked a betting office, and as another dejected losing punter made his way out of the shop I caught the sound of an excited racecourse commentator calling the horses home inside the final furlong of a thrilling finish.

Some kind of chemical must have been spontaneously released in my brain as I was sucked in like dirty bath water to a plughole.

I'm guessing I went fifteen races without backing a winner. It all started off as some fun bets to fill my afternoon – you know, €20s and €30s. But before long the grand in my pocket was eroded away by my ever-increasing stakes. The cash-point was then hit for the maximum €600, which went on to a selection at a big enough price to get me out of jail. When that went awry I dashed home to pull my stash out of every nook and cranny – another couple of grand. Suffice to say I still could not find a winner. Funny as it sounds, that wasn't a major worry. Nor was the thought of what I had lost. Getting more money together for my next bet, to get back my losses, was my only concern.

I went straight to the bank and pleaded with the manager to allow me an instant €10,000 cash withdrawal. Considering the cash lump sums I had been depositing, they agreed.

My next bet was €4,000. That too was money burned. My final hurrah, to get back every penny I had lost during the day, was for €6,000. In one of the finest exhibitions of irony imaginable, my selection was running in a race worth £1,356 to the winner and that eventual winner was sold for £3,000 after the race.

Betting can be like sex: it's best just before the end. For the first six furlongs of this mile race it would be impossible to explain the buzz of watching everything on the line, with adrenalin pumping around my body. The final two furlongs, however, was the start of the unimaginable deflation as my selection, worth less than I had placed on it, tamely faded out of contention.

After the race I walked back to my car knowing there was no more money. I'd lost the best part of a working man's take-home wage for a year in a single afternoon on a day when I'd had no intention of placing a bet. To add insult to injury, there was no petrol in my car, the warning light was on, and all I had left in the world was a jar full of coins alongside my bed. By the time I'd got some petrol, every penny had gone. The champagne lifestyle was over. I struggled to scrape together the entry fees for the €25 nightly tournaments now being played in the plush Merrion Casino, as the operation had been transferred there from the Jackpot.

No one could understand how it felt or why I did it. Or could they? A chance depressing discussion with one of the local poker players reassured me I was not alone.

Jim Delaney was a guy I could communicate with as his gambling exploits are legendary in local parts. His most famous foray came at a blackjack table at what was the Griffin Club in Merrion Square (it later became the Merrion). In those days the gaming tables within 'private members clubs' were actually rented by people, punters, who either took the profits or sustained the losses. On this day, 'Big Jim', trying to ease my pain, told me the full story.

'I'm not sure who owned the table at the time but I was having the night of all nights and near emptied the dealer's cash tray' – which is known as a 'fill', meaning he was £5,000 in front. 'The table owner went to the cash cage and ordered a fresh fill' – a selection of chips ranging from £1 to £500 – 'which I promptly won. At this stage I was £10,000 in front – some spin up for a traditional £5 and £10 player.'

Some may ask why he didn't quit when so far in front. Those

are the same people who would claim he should have left when winning £200, £500 and £1,000. They will never get the point, and they will never win big.

Regardless, Jim was on a roll, and was soon another £5,000 in front.

'Dismayed, the table owner came down with another fresh fill of £5,000 and told me, "This is it, Jim. If you clear us out of this lot the table is closed for the night!" An hour later I had a mountain of chips in front of me, a profit of £20,000, and as I landed the last winning hand, the dealer said, "'That's it, Jim, you've cleared us out. We're closed for the night."

'However, I saw there were still thirty or so £5 chips in the dealer's tray.

'"What are those in there?" I enquired.

'"Those are the dealer's tips," said the croupier.

' "I'll play you for them," I said. Winning £20,000 and wanting the last £150 is indeed greedy, but I had a crowd of people around me all in awe at this spectacle and I wanted to boast I had wiped the house out of every last penny.

'It was the worst single statement of my life because, despite my £20,000 plus in chips dwarfing the dealer's £150 in tips, the house went on a winning streak and I left the building six hours later with not so much as a taxi fare in my pocket.'

Sick gamblers like me are everywhere, I know that. I had to get back on the wagon, remind myself how easy winning was – at card tables, not in betting shops.

It was now the third week in May. The next tournament of any note on the calendar was the World Heads-Up Championship in Vienna, Austria, in a fortnight's time. I didn't even know where Austria was on the map, but I knew I had to be there. I knew I had to get back into the groove and I still believed in poker and its potential growth, if not in myself so much.

The entry fee for the World Heads-Up, which was also going to be televised, was a whopping €3,000. I had two weeks to scrape it together, plus €900 or so for flights and a hotel. By hook, crook and three tournament wins in the Merrion I reached the magic figure by the skin of my teeth. After my flights were booked and the hotel paid for I had €3,380 to take with me in cash, for food, spending money and the all-important €3,000 entry fee. This was my biggest ever tournament, a world championship event. I had to perform. I needed a result or that warehouse job could once again become a reality.

The tournament was held in the Concorde Casino Club, which to my surprise was situated in an industrial area and was open twenty-four hours a day. It had no roulette wheels, just dozens of card tables – poker and poker only. I went there straight from the airport, keen to make sure I was registered and all paid up before going on to my hotel, the cheapest one I could find on the internet. It was miles away from the venue. As I proudly smacked my €3,000 on the counter I was told that I needed to pay another €270 in registration fees. I could not believe my ears. That would leave me with just €70 in cash, as I had just paid my taxi driver €40.

What should I do in this spot? Well, I had come this far and there was no turning back now, but I simply could not make my money stretch, what with taxi fares and food costs. I know that in betting shop mode I'd have plonked €100 on something or other, hoping to bolster my funds. But if that had got beat my next bet would have been €300, and then €900, until it was all gone, along with my chances of competing in the World Heads-Up. I could, in the same way, have tried a cash game, but I was still sore after my €24,000 betting shop loss and had vowed never to chase money again, no matter how valid the reasoning. So I signed up and took the decision to walk to and from my hotel every day while retaining the €70 to feed myself. I needed nothing else – well, maybe a taxi back to the airport five days later, but that was a bridge I could cross at the time. Once that €3,270 was taken from me I knew I had to get a result from this competition.

Heads-Up poker is like chess, and I fancied my chances at being good at it. The game-plan was simple: if I had a big hand I'd check to induce a bluff or betting action; if I had no hand I'd bet to prevent my opponent making a play. In short, hopefully I'd win with the best hands and also with the worst. Simple, isn't it?

What I clarified from the outset was that I'd need to make the final sixteen players of this knock-out event to get any money back – and I needed that €1,500 badly.

When the draw was made I got the absolute worst of it. For starters, most of the field got a bye in the opening round; I didn't. Secondly, my opening match was against Pascal Perrault, whom I had looked up to as a face on *Late Night Poker* and who was the reigning European champion, having won a bundle of tournaments throughout 2001. Still, I had to win three matches to get half of my entry fee back and I had a determination to do so about me which cannot be measured, in the way experience, knowledge and know-how also can't. It's invaluable.

This was major league, and when the remainder of the draw was announced, I realized I was playing in the Premiership. With everything considered – this was a world championship being televised around the globe, vital to the CV of a person who saw the 'bigger poker picture' – I wanted to win this so badly I could taste it.

I won my first game the following day all right; it took ninety minutes. I walked back to the hotel, which had no internet connection and no English TV channels, clutching a McDonald's and thinking about nothing more than my second-round match against Hans Pfister. Twenty hours later I was walking again, back to the Concorde Casino, mentally preparing for the clash with the player who was leading the 2002 rankings at the time. I had to win this match and the next round, otherwise I'd be hitch-hiking to the airport twenty miles away at the end of the week. In the same way as I did with Perrault, I slow-played big hands into Pfister and showed him the door within two hours.

And so on to the crunch match, round three, where I could win my taxi fare to the airport. It was against no less a player than the defending World Heads-Up champion, Bruno Fitoussi.

It's safe to say I had gone unnoticed until this point, distinguished only by the Betfair T-shirt I was wearing. I was the only person in the room with sponsor's attire, something that is commonplace these days but barely conceived of at the time. Unsurprisingly, the players who were laying odds on the game made me the big outsider, but in my own mind I was a clear favourite. It's that kind of self-belief you need, I tell ya.

Bruno arrived late, eating his croissants and drinking

thimble-sized cups of coffee, as calm as any Frenchman gets, yet I'd been waiting fifteen minutes for him to arrive. In fact I'd protested to the organizers, who agreed that he should be penalized. He would have been if he'd been just a few more minutes late.

'What is the problem?' Bruno questioned as he got comfortable in his seat. 'We could be playing for hours. What difference does fifteen minutes make?'

It made a lot of difference to me. Just like for the Paddy Power event, I was trained and focused to the minute.

Understanding that he did not like this rush-rush approach, I played fast and loose, throwing chips in a pot to make a call before his bet had even hit the table. He didn't like it.

Make no mistake, I was concentrating intently, and I soon realized that he was playing a basic Hold'em tournament strategy of raising with any two big hole cards. I went on the theory that his two big cards would flop a pair very rarely and I could bluff him off a lot of pots on the flop instead of pre-flop.

Betting and raising with no hand, unlike the previous games where I had the benefit of good hands and took to making them get genuinely paid, I soon had Bruno on the ropes. The death knell for him came when he typically raised with something along the lines of King-10. When the flop came down Queen-9-4 he moved all-in, knowing I would struggle to call with anything other than top-pair, and if I did call he could still get a King or Jack on the turn or river to win. Calling immediately, I unveiled my 2-9, and after the requisite handshake he stormed off in disgust, claiming to anyone and everyone who would listen that I was an idiot who called raises with any two cards. I cared not. I'd taken down three big scalps, and the organizers gracefully paid me my minimum return of €1,500 immediately, which allowed me to take a taxi back to my hotel and enjoy a steak dinner.

Now the goalposts had moved. Gritty determination had led me to win three successive heads-up games but now I was hell bent on glory. All the desire was there, that desperation to be a winner, to gain household recognition courtesy of more television coverage, still convinced that poker was the new snooker in terms of rapid acceptance and popularity among the general public.

The third day of play, and my fourth match, was against a character called Chris Bigler. The Swiss player was in that 1999 documentary about the World Series of Poker, where he finished fifth, which was so instrumental in me taking up the game. This time we were on the feature table, the one with cameras all around and underneath. This was, after all, the quarter-finals – some way to celebrate my thirty-third birthday.

We were both asked to do a pre-match interview for the cameras. I listened to his intently. He didn't strike me as a particularly nice person, and when I got my turn I took great satisfaction in saying it as I saw it. 'He looks like a big baby,' I remarked. 'I'll soon have him on tilt, throwing his toys out of the pram!'

His toys were indeed off in every direction a few hours later. I mean, fair play to him, my policy of betting no hand and checking with made hands didn't work with this fella. If he bet or even called a bet you were in trouble. At the same time he so rarely paid you off, he was hard to overcome. But, as the blinds got bigger and bigger and being out-chipped, I took to simply raising every pot pre-flop. This way he allowed me to get right back into the mix while he was waiting to find Aces, Kings, Queens and the odd Ace-King. Ultimately I collected a mountain of chips, and, after losing a fifty-fifty situation for the remainder of his decimated stack, he gave one of the best post-match interviews ever recorded. 'I can play good players, I just cannot play bad ones, that's why I lost,' he protested to the cameras. Not a way to endear the viewing public to you, methinks.

I now had €10,000 in guaranteed winnings, and from now on further wins would give me an almighty profit. I had only a few hours to spare before my semifinal match against the little-known local Mark Duran. Victory would put me in the final and give me a minimum €24,000 payday. Defeat, with my driven mindset . . . that was unthinkable.

The key hand against Mark was my 78 versus his 89 on a flop that came down 6-7-8. He had top-pair and a straight draw; I had two pairs which became a full house following a Queen on the turn and an 8 on the river. Mark was unable to pass his three-of-a-kind following my bet, his raise and my re-raise all-in, and suddenly I was at the final of a world championship event which was just twenty-four hours away.

I didn't sleep a wink that night. I replayed each and every match I'd contested in my head over and over as I prepared either to bully or manipulate a winning advantage over my opponent in the final. I was convinced the determination I took to the Paddy Power event, to the Rainbow, to Dundee, and to every match I'd played here in Vienna, was the key to my success. I had even taken with me a piece of paper with 'he cannot win, I can only lose' printed on one side and 'remember the pain of defeat' written on the other. It was placed within eyeshot, next to my chips on the table, throughout every heads-up game.

The day of the final it was hot – I mean just short of a hundred degrees. Thank God I didn't have to walk to the venue. I decided, as I did in the Paddy Power event, to wear a suit and tie; it's about being as distinctive as you can be. When I got to the card room I found my opponent, Russian Kirill Gerasimov, dressed up like something from a KGB movie: a grey jacket zipped up to the very top, a baseball cap pulled low down over his face and the darkest pair of sunglasses imaginable.

After some fine fanfares, playing of national anthems and an introduction over the PA, we took our seats. It was like the footage at the end of a Rocky film, two gladiators preparing to square off. It all looked superb for the cameras, and I realized that no matter what happened next I was going to get another three weeks' coverage on Sky Sports and this tournament, like the last, was sponsored by a bookmaking organization, Ladbrokes.

Now, I'm not going to lay out elaborate reasons for my defeat as, truth be known, in time I came to appreciate I was totally outplayed, from flag-fall in fact. In mitigation, the hand I was eliminated with was an Ace-Queen against his Ace-2, but even then he got his money in once making two pairs – hitting a 2 on the turn – and to this day I cannot say Kirill was anything other than a worthy winner.

The trouble is, I never took defeat anything like as well at the time. Gracefully maybe, but once I'd left the casino and got back into my hotel room I head-butted the first thing I could find – the bathroom door – which left bruising all over my face. I threw my winnings – €34,000 in crisp purple €500 notes, owing to an agreement between Kirill and me to refine the prize-money structure from €60,000 to the winner and €24,000 to the runner-up to €50,000 and €34,000 respectively – on the bed and paced around the room while looking at it in disgust. It was more money than I had ever seen or had, yet in a moment of madness I bundled the whole lot together and went to lash the lot out of my twenty-fourth-floor room window.

The determination factor had driven me mad. The money did not matter. The thought of being a loser in this game when I was convinced I was a winner caused immeasurable pain, and the dirty evidence was laid out before me. I'd had a chance to be the best in the world and I'd blown it. Nothing else mattered, not even a lot of money in compensation for being runner-up. I really wanted to watch it float down to the pavement three hundred feet below, to see people scrambling to grab the five hundred notes as they dropped out of the sky. It would mean more to them than me because I felt like the ultimate loser. Unable to stop thinking this way, I was overcome with a form of guilt and remorse at my own failings. Somehow I felt violated. When I think about it, the reasoning behind people inflicting pain, usually cuts, on themselves is understandable to me.

The windows would not open – the joys of air-conditioning. I kept my money, only giving away €500, to my taxi driver, who was an immigrant and who told me – not, I believe, looking for an outrageous tip – that he sent all his money home to his family in a war-torn country. I took him as a decent guy, the type who earlier in the week would have taken me to the airport for €25 despite the true cost being €40 if I'd explained my problems to him. It could have happened too.

On returning to Dublin I drove directly home and went straight to bed. I did not come out of my room for eighteen hours. After filling a glass with fresh water, I returned, forced a blanket over my curtain rail in order to blank out any light, and went back to sleep for another eighteen hours.

Little did I know, I was in a clinical depression. It was over a week before I got out of the house, and then it was only for bread and milk. Of course I did try to get up. I'd occasionally turn on the telly but soon give up on it and go back to bed. This went on for two weeks. I lost several stone in weight. I had mentally driven myself to a point where defeat was unacceptable. But I had lost. I'd lost my mind.

And I'd never had so much money in my life. After I stashed some of the €34,000 around the house I had €20,000 remaining which needed to be banked. Thankfully, this time I did so without being lured by the betting office.

Remaining anything other than, well, sane or normal, eventually I realized the only way back for me was to start playing cards again. I went to the Merrion, where the congratulations on the result was once again overwhelming. But, like someone who finds themselves on a fairground ride who is actually scared of them, I soon jumped off and asked for my tournament entry fee to be returned. I did hang around to drink with some of the local lads, though, urgently trying to reintroduce myself to society, and after the benefit of several beers I returned to the club to deal some hands of poker for the regulars, who were in need of a dealer.

After some time, using the softly-softly approach on myself, starting with dealing, I decided to go back on the road playing ranking events again. By the end of the following month I was in the winner's enclosure once more with victory in Southampton's 'Hold'em Double' festival. This was my third European ranking tournament win and there wasn't a betting shop or a hint of depression in my mind.

It was nice doing the business in my home town, which I'd left fifteen years earlier and never returned to. This time I was old enough to be in the casino legally, although this venue was new. The Tiberius, which had barred me for card counting, had long since closed.

Some very good news was waiting on my e-mail when I returned from Southampton. One of the marketing managers I'd sent my original sponsorship proposal to, Ian Williams at Victor Chandler, had bumped into an interesting guy in Gibraltar while out drinking. He was no Joe Soap: it was a person hired by Ladbrokes to head up their about-to-launch online poker site. The pair had got chatting and Ian explained to the Ladbrokes guy, Tony Ure, who formerly managed casinos in Egypt, that he knew me, a poker player who was looking for sponsorship. Tony was reportedly excited by this as he had seen plenty of me on Sky Sports, not least in Ladbrokes' World Heads-Up Championship. Days later he was in touch, and my proposal compared favourably with his needs.

Now, fair play to this guy, when he joined the company he could barely turn a computer on, but he had foresight beyond comprehension. I'd say he was a genius. We were very much on the same wavelength with our beliefs about poker's future prosperity. He spoke about tournament reports, blogs, diary pieces, tutorials and strategy pieces, 'Play the Pro' online for cash prizes and bounties, all for the Ladbrokes site. It was cutting edge. No one had done this stuff before – no one, including me, had even thought of this stuff before – but Tony put it in place for me to execute.

This was it, this was the big break I'd been looking for. At the time things were happening so fast, though. Nic Szeremeta had also been on to me about the possibility of my taking over the editorship of his *Poker Europa* magazine. To think, the poker explosion was yet to happen.

But a high-profile player with a slice of an embryonic industry is what I wanted to be so I flew straight to Barcelona to meet Tony Ure and a Ladbrokes director, Martin Saunders. Overlooking Port Olympic, opposite the Grand Casino, which was yet to stage a poker tournament of any description, we agreed on what I could do for their company and how and when they wanted it delivered. Wearing a T-shirt was just a small part of what the contract stated.

But, in my anxiety and enthusiasm, I probably sold myself a little short. I was asked how much I was looking for for what they were expecting from me. We agreed on a retainer, but playing the game is what it's all about and I therefore added, 'I'd like to play a major tournament somewhere in Europe each and every month.' They were agreeable and keen for me to do so, and together we looked at what that would mean financially. Well, with main events at most festivals costing £500, we agreed on what would now be thought a minuscule retainer/agreement. Unfortunately, as you will discover, poker tournament entry fees were about to go stratospheric.

It would become a problem in years to come, but for now I

had what I wanted: recognition, a trophy cabinet that was starting to fill up nicely, and enough cash to do pretty much anything I wanted. Just take this Spanish trip. I stayed at the Hotel Juan Carlos, one of the finest hotels in Europe. A quartet of violinists permanently plays at the hotel's reception alongside a breathtaking water cascade. It was all a million miles away from the flats, sheds and caravans I'd lived in for much of my life, not to mention the streets of Southsea.

The next poker stop was Salford, where I'd been earlier in the year – possibly not as glamorous as Spain, but I could still make an impression, and I did so, at the 'Northern Challenge Festival'. With friend Michael Frisby in tow, a Ladbrokes T-shirt on my back and just two of us left in a tournament, I took a brilliant deal offered by Gareth Jones which gave me the majority of the money but technical second spot in the opening competition in the series.

Afterwards, not knowing the area's reputation or taking any notice of the twenty-five-foot-tall barbed-wire fences which surrounded the hotel opposite the casino, I decided to walk home at four a.m. with bundles of £1,000 cash bags in my pocket. The following night someone was reportedly mugged for their personal stereo on the same stretch of road!

My third piece of luck – added to the second-placed effort and not getting banged over the head with a brick for my money – was a win in the concluding tournament of the festival four days later. European ranking tournament win number four was on the board, and another trophy was in the cabinet.

Winning poker tournaments just seemed so easy. I was ticking these things off my list like people put a line through days on their diary. That may sound arrogant, but I can assure you I was not acting that way. Or maybe I was, as I was starting to get a slating from some quarters.

Firstly, Tony Ure at Ladbrokes fielded a call from a North London player representing himself and some colleagues in a collective saying that my sponsorship was an absolute joke and they should never have been overlooked for such support. When Tony took no interest, the caller moved up the chain of command and protested to similarly uninterested directors.

Next up someone started peddling a story that my sponsorship had only come about because I was the favourite (on betting exchange Betfair) to win the Masterclassics of Poker in Amsterdam and I had backed myself into favouritism for that event specifically to impress Ladbrokes as potential sponsors. An absolute load of shit. There were bundles of money for me to win this event, but it had come from a bunch of Premiership footballers I had met in Paddy Power's box at the Irish Greyhound Derby final. They were all poker fans and knew me through the TV exposure. When they asked where I was playing next I told them and said that, considering recent triumphs, I hoped to win. Interestingly, when I asked them where they were playing next they told me Middlesbrough, and the following weekend I found myself on the back of their team bus for the coach ride north (from London), teaching them how to play Hold'em and watching aghast as thousands of pounds were won and lost before we had passed Newport Pagnell Services.

Anyway, the story was rubbish. My deal with Laddies had been signed long before betting opened on the Masterclassics.

Just as well, as Amsterdam was an absolute *nul points*.

It was back to the happy hunting ground which was Dundee. Here came a fourth-placed effort and a win – a win in an Omaha competition, my first. More cash-laden plastic bags were deposited in the local bank and more glassware was collected for the cabinet.

Helsinki was now looming once again, and that meant European Poker Awards time. The kind folks in Dublin had given me a nomination for 'Rookie of the Year' and I was more than hopeful I could win the award. Still, I didn't stop and rest on my laurels, I wanted to enhance my chances, so in November I went back to Southampton for their second festival of the year, the Southampton Poker Championship, and landed their feature tournament for good measure.

In fewer than twelve months I'd landed six European ranking tournaments, come second in the World Heads-Up Championship, won a televised event and got sponsored by a plc. So rarely in life do you get everything you ask for, and I had for an entire year. I had one last wish: to collect that award I had promised myself twelve months earlier.

As the fine people of Casino Ray in Helsinki gave award-nominated players free accommodation, I brought my parents over to watch the spectacle (my relationship with my father had improved over the last few years). I could not help thinking how proud my grandparents would have been to see me on stage. I'd thought of them throughout this successful year. Granddad Jack would have loved it.

Amid a jazzy presentation ceremony I and the other two candidates for Rookie of the Year made our way on to the stage. It looked a straight match-up between myself and Kirill

219

Gerasimov, the Russian who had won the Heads-Up Championship. Suffice to say I was disappointed when the judging panel, consisting of the likes of Marcel Luske (ironically Kirill's mentor) and Alex Kravchenko, gave it to him. But, as the saying goes, that's poker!

Was it really poker? Did I really have such a sentiment? Not at all. I remained driven and determined, desperate to prove those judges wrong. And there was only one way to do that. Later that night I played in the €500 tournament like a man inspired, like a man prepared to go through weeks of depression if he got beat, like a man who remembered his roots. Sure enough, in front of his peers and parents, this man landed a seventh European ranking event of the year, finishing at the head of the finest field assembled in Europe at the time.

With 2003 only a few weeks away I asked myself if things could get any better. They couldn't. They didn't. As far as poker went, the twelve months ahead were about to be my annus horribilis.

17

Cashing Out

A lull in the poker calendar at the start of 2003 allowed me to get busy with traditional work, like writing news, stories and strategy pieces for my sponsor's website. Naturally I'd done most of the things they'd asked, but I had not yet played poker on their site. In fact, I'd never played poker on the internet, only read about it.

Tony Ure had set up the first in a series of 'Play the Pro' promotions where people could play me online and earn enhanced prize-money for eliminating me or taking my chips. At the same time people could pose questions and have a natter in the onscreen chat-box. Sounds mundane if you're an online poker player these days, but I assure you this was novel, ground-breaking stuff at the time.

In preparation for this I downloaded the software and was totally amazed by what I saw – fully interactive online poker. Again, it may be commonplace now, but when I saw it for the first time I realized it was the missing link, the thing that would fill the void between popularity and mass appeal. It was the place where fortunes were to be made by a select few players and the corporations running online poker.

On that first occasion, I was given $2,000 to play with; anything I lost would be given to the customers and anything I won would be given back to them. I was a little apprehensive. I mean, I had no idea what to expect, what kind of questions would come in from players active in the chat-box, or if I would have all the answers. But it went swimmingly. The action came thick and fast and the questions were mainly harmless banter. One player, using the alias 'JOanne', did make some strange enquiries though, initially asking things like who I thought the best players were and going on to ask my thoughts on a certain group of players. In time I was to discover that this alias belonged to one of the players of whom my opinion had been asked. It was bizarre; it smacked of insecurity. But, as I was about to discover, there are two types of poker player: the salt of the earth and the scum of the earth!

I'd also been tipped off that I had been the subject of abuse on a poker forum. Now, I had no idea what a forum was and had never read one, so my tipster sent me a copy of what had been posted. There were two nasty enough postings. One said I had won the Paddy Power tournament by 'cheating and looking at my opponents' cards when calling "that all-in" with 7-6 knowing he had 7-4'. It was, of course, utter nonsense. As I stated before, I moved all-in and was called; I never called the all-in. It went on to say that my sponsorship was a joke.

The other piece, again posted by someone using a self-appointed alias, was far more hateful. There was a lot of name calling, abuse directed at me and my family, and a declaration that my sponsorship was making a mockery of my sponsors.

More adolescent jealous stuff, I suppose, but being so insecure at the time I was really rocked.

I'd never taken criticism very well, and what was appearing on the internet was personal and untrue. Was this what people really thought of me? Was I really a joke, an impostor? People were probably talking about me behind my back, calling me names, laughing at me. I felt like I was being scrutinized, and as a result I lost all confidence in myself. These incidents really shook me. The internet is not just hearsay after all; thousands of people who read these things will believe it all.

With my self-confidence in tatters, my first excursion of the year was to Brighton, and there something else novel happened: I caught a player cheating against me. The move was kiddies' stuff, but when you are playing for thousands of pounds it's a lot more than that. The game in question cost £100 to enter and had a sizeable field. In fact, because of the numbers the casino did not have enough dealers to go round so on some tables the players were forced to deal for themselves.

I was doing quite nicely and took my turn to deal out the cards and control the action. As it happened I made a big bet, was raised all-in, and I called. Both my hand and that of my opponent were the same so it was a 'split pot', meaning the chips in the middle of the table had to be counted out and shared equally. He leaned over the table to view the situation and confirm the community cards on the table meant we both had the same hand, then chirpily announced himself in a squeaky voice, 'It's a split pot.' However, in doing so I noticed he placed his hands over the chips in the middle of the table, the pot, and drew a large number of them back towards himself under his arms. Possibly I should have got him ejected; as it was, I made a show of him before the other seven players at the table by lifting up his arms, and left it at that. But the damage was done. It was becoming clear to me that not everyone in poker was that nice, and I took this incident as a personal insult.

During the early months of 2003 I was unable to make a final table, let alone win a tournament, despite travelling all over Europe. It was clear that my confidence had gone completely. I lost thousands travelling far and wide, believing that if I kept playing eventually I would recapture the winning thread. The truth was, I couldn't win a ten-seater €10 comp in Dublin. I had lost faith in myself. I had a complex, brought on by these malevolent occurrences.

The strange thing was, I had no idea what I was doing wrong, no inkling as to why things were going so badly. I just couldn't see it. Certainly at home things continued as normal. I loved being a man about town in the polished vintage MG, equipped with shiny chrome bumpers and a sun roof, I'd bought with my winnings. But my lifestyle, allied to so much failure in tournaments, drained away most of my money. On the plus side, at least it hadn't been lost in an afternoon in a betting shop.

The World Series, that once-a-year $10,000-entry championship event in Las Vegas, beckoned. If I was to truly call myself a professional, I had to go there and make a prominent prize-paying finishing position. It would, of course, cost money, so to that end I resorted to playing on the internet in an attempt to raise the money stake to make the pilgrimage.

Now, imagine this for a Saturday afternoon. I cranked up my

computer and, after wading through a pile of jokes, special offers from AOL and cut-price Viagra offers, I paid special attention to the numerous e-mails from poker sites and information pages which I had subscribed to during this honeymoon period with poker. 'Don't forget our $10,000 freerole tonight at 9 p.m.,' said one above a picture that made its players look like an undertakers' convention. Another claimed 'Time is running out for qualification into our $25,000 giveaway' alongside a picture of a Porsche Carrera GT – a connection I could not fathom as this set of wheels was a £100,000 job. Still, I must confess, I've always seen myself in a Porsche, although, being practical, a 924 version (that is, the Volkswagen in drag) or a 944 would be the most likely candidate.

Somewhere in between the 3.25 p.m. at Newbury and the 4.15 p.m. at Doncaster, with the first leg of my imaginary 50p Yankee already down, I did the decent thing by downloading both lots of software and depositing the princely sum of £25 into each of these poker sites. Come five p.m. I found myself in a ninety-runner tournament which offered the first three finishers a place in the semifinals of some event worth some part of $25,000, less all applicable skim-offs, taxes and VAT. Don't knock it until you've tried it, thought I, sitting back with a tin of Fosters and a lasagne straight from the microwave.

Well, bugger me, by 6.30 I had 125,000 of the 180,000 chips in play and there were still twelve players, all sitting on futile stacks that barely covered the next round of blinds, remaining. Four tins of Fosters went as quickly as ten other players, but I managed to get beaten heads-up, meaning I got something like $50.

I took the opportunity to start on the box of six Millers that were left over from Christmas before taking my chances in the nine p.m. 'undertakers' freebie comp which offered a weekend in Dublin along with a meal in the Merrion Casino. It was simply irresistible. There was also $10,000 in prize-money, although it was spread thinner than bird-seed in Trafalgar Square, and wouldn't last much longer!

Around 370 of us all sat tight and played well until the antes went stratospheric, meaning any two cards suddenly looked attractive. I was on Miller bottle number five and couldn't find the bottle opener for number six when I realized that things were not really happening for me, so I carefully picked my moment before going 'all-in'.

That moment came when a player moved his lot in and was promptly called, re-raised, called 'all-in' and got another caller 'all-in'. With four huge stacks all pushed in I figured my 2-9 off-suit was a monster and would be getting paid off at around 9/2.

I'm a genius. The cards were turned over and my opponents were only playing a pair of Kings, pair of Queens, Jacks and 10s. The flop came 2-7-9 and I was the clear leader with two pairs. The next card was a 3, but the final was a 10 and I shit the bed big time.

Gutted and out of beer, I made a coffee, although it was laced with vodka and Bailey's. Lovely, I'll have another, another and another while waiting for a cash game on this site. Checking the 'cashier', I saw that I had in excess of $100 in my account. I don't know how it happened but it was there, so I played a $109 'heads-up' game. Thirteen undefeated heads-up games later, I called for some more refreshments, meaning my friend John Jameson joined me along with his associate Diet Coke. Despite John's help I could not handle the next customer and I lost a single $109 match, much to my disgust. That was quite enough of all that. The cashier said I had in excess of $1,000 and I didn't hesitate pressing the 'cash-out' button for the entire amount as the site, with its undertakers, gave me the creeps and I would not be coming back in a hurry.

Starting with around £50, this had not been a bad night. The rent was all but sorted, plus I could replace those beers, Bailey's and vodka bottles and order in a celebratory curry with some of the proceeds prior to the restaurant's two a.m. closing time. But I was buzzing and I decided to play with that bit of change I had won on the earlier site, Victor Chandler's site, the one with the Porsche.

Munching through a Peshwari naan, the essential compliment to any chicken korma, while busily searching for a game, I stumbled across a $1-$2 cash game that was worthy of a $50 investment. I should have lost this stake within twenty minutes and gone to bed, but on the big blind with 2-6 I received a 6-6-2 flop! My check was followed by bet, call, call and call.

I'd better just call this, thought I, because I thought I could be winning! The next card was a King. I could conceivably have gone behind but I doubted it, and another bet received three callers again. As the river card came down a 6, giving me four-of-a-kind, I bravely put in my final $15, which was called, called and called! Excellent stuff. I was up to $250-plus here, and that called for yet another drink.

My run of form continued and I got to $2,200 as quickly as my bottle of JJ went down. I was probably playing looser than its cap but, pissed or not, I planned to take this and run because I'd just won enough to pay for a flight to Vegas and a fortnight in a hotel.

OK, it's not that easy to leave on a winning streak, and it may have been four a.m. but I simply could not miss, so I pressed up the odd $200 in a shit-or-bust campaign that would have made Nick Leeson proud. I found a lively table with some real loose-playing nutters on it. Once again I could not stop winning. Within minutes that $200 had been turned into $2,000, $4,000, and doubled through again to $8,000, and on to $12,000. Jesus, I could now see a Porsche in my driveway! Not a 924, not a 944, but a 911!

For the first and what was going to be the only time in my life, I came to the conclusion that internet poker could not and would not be a success; nor would it last. I mean, people were throwing thousands of dollars into pots they could not possibly win. The world was going to go skint, and I was going to be the beneficiary. What a fantastic thought that was.

That's it, I'm out of here with a cool $14,000 profit, thought I. But no, no, I had picked up pocket Kings. I really didn't want to see them. Shit, a guy raised $3,000 into me despite the blinds being just $2.50/$5. Where was this bloke from? How big is his palace? He must go through banknotes like I go through toilet paper, and probably uses them for the job. But I could not call. I'd won a fortune in one night; drunk and happy, I didn't want to call. I consulted John Jameson. Alas, he soon talked me into an all-in move.

A silence that seemed to last an eternity ensued before the dreaded call was made. There was another long pause before a flop was created from the wonderful random-number-generating machine. It displayed an Ace, Queen and Jack all in hearts; another Queen followed, and then another Jack. I was dead if this rich Arabian prince, which he surely must have been, had two hearts, a single Ace, Queen or Jack. The lot had surely gone. I was sick, and it wasn't even alcohol-induced – well, not just yet.

Suddenly $24,000 slid its way across the screen to me. In an ecstatic state I ran a lap of honour around the front room and through to what had become a bottle bank of a kitchen wearing nothing more than a pair of Y-fronts.

I phoned a friend back in England who was not disgruntled about being woken so early with the news that a year's take-home pay would be in her bank account the following week (meaning $22,000; I was going to leave two grand in there to play with later). It was, after all, her credit card I was using. I promised her a holiday to the most exotic place in existence, and that 911, albeit a second-hand one, was going to have a turbo-charger attached to it.

I'd done it, I'd managed to quit when ahead – and ahead by some considerable way. All that was left for me to do was navigate my way around the cashier section and send that money home.

Unsurprisingly, considering my delirious drunken state and the size of my withdrawal, the cashier section of the site seemed to be a little disagreeable about my request. It probably had limits on daily withdrawals, thought I, or was I simply too slaughtered to see straight?

The phone then rang, to interrupt my efforts. It was my friend. Christ, it didn't take her long to find a holiday – a ring too, probably!

'Um, why are you crying?' I asked.

'I have just had a man on the phone from Gibraltar, a Mr Chandler,' she explained. 'He says he is very sorry but you can't withdraw twenty grand back to the credit card because there is some kind of problem. He is adamant you will not be paid.'

Angrily, I jotted down the number of this imbecile at Victor Chandler's who was going to claim that collusion had taken place: I was playing against a player using a stolen credit card or had in some way hacked into their system and manipulated the cards. I dare not tell you the details of our ensuing conversation as it was more of a verbal barrage using the maxim 'attack is the best form of attack'. Eventually, when I had ran out of expletives, I gave the young customer services representative a brief respite in order for him to explain how he would get my winnings to me in double-quick time.

His response? 'Sir, you have been playing on a play money table for the past five hours and the $22,000 is not withdrawable from your play bank, it is fun money. What I would say is no one has ever had such a win on the practice tables and here we are most impressed. Congratulations!'

As I slumped back in my chair to contemplate my faux pas, the rep added, 'Incidentally, while you are on the phone, a customer of ours has been on the phone complaining that you have been abusing him in the chat-box.' When he told me the alias of the player I exploded: it was the very same person who had been dishing out personal insults on the poker forum. So I did the decent thing: I phoned him up and left a verbal torrent on his answer-phone. This foolish drunken outburst would come back to haunt me.

Mentally destroyed and exhausted, after winning and losing

a fortune – though I did actually clear $2,000 by the end of the session in real money – not to mention threatening someone's health and a whole lot more, I went to bed. If I was starting to feel unwell now, how was I going to feel when I woke up with a hangover to face the sober reality of my dashed hopes, dreams and aspirations?

Sleep failed to disentangle my emotions. It was to be the most painful of hangovers, the type that sends people teetotal or suicidal. My initial £50 deposit was like a distant memory, the Arabian prince and his $12,000 all-in on nothing a total fairytale turned nightmare. The hard truth was that no Porsche would be sitting in my driveway any time soon and the girl-friend's bank balance remained overdrawn.

This kind of stuff happens to us poker players periodically. A few years later a Dublin-based poker dealer with aspirations of being an online poker pro did something similar. Dedicated, and totally professional, this character successfully mixed both work and poker playing, parlaying up an impressive €3,000 in two months from a €100 standing start. His hours of grinding certainly paid off, but there was one hitch: the high-rolling wannabe was not quite as good at setting up a dial-up connection as he was at playing online poker. In fact, he had chosen an internet service provider that was UK-based, meaning every minute spent playing online poker came at the cost of an international phone call. The telephone bill encompassing his €2,900 winning period exceeded €5,000!

For myself, a week later, with internet poker avoided like the plague, I went on a thirty-six-hour session playing poker with Tarot cards; when I eventually flopped a full house, four people died! But that's another story, a real fairytale, already claimed by someone else.

It was May already, the World Series was now upon us, and I didn't have the money to go, plain and simple. Instead I took the consolation prize of a trip to Estonia. Hey, I'd seen plenty of America as it was, and I didn't like the place or the people, for obvious reasons. But a former communist state? An interesting journey was guaranteed.

Although the country and Tallinn, its capital, had not been under Soviet rule for well over a decade, reminders of old hardships were still evident, such as shops selling just one brand of washing powder or breakfast cereal. I stayed in a hotel which was more like student accommodation, apartments or dormitories. Unsurprisingly, it turned out the place had been built for the 1980 Olympics. Taxi drivers worked in clapped-out vehicles that in one afternoon spewed into the atmosphere the equivalent of a power station's annual waste. What more could you expect when £4 took you any and everywhere for the entire day?

This also meant there was no real money in the casinos or card rooms. It mattered little, as I was playing so badly. My only result was a fourth place in a small Omaha tournament for the princely sum of €470 – my first final table or cash-paying finish of the year.

I had entered a cycle, a pessimistic cycle. What that forum said was true. I was a joke. It was ridiculous that the world's biggest bookmaking organization was sponsoring me. How could I, with such dire results, represent such a company? The more I thought about it the worse I played. It was clear now that the poker division of Ladbrokes had stolen a march on their rivals and pretty much owned the rapidly growing European online poker market. And I was their front-man, the only sponsored poker player in Europe. How could that be justified?

As Chris Moneymaker – the man with the name often credited with fanning the poker craze flames – overcame 838 opponents to win the World Series of Poker, I packed up my bags in Estonia and started to prepare for the biggest tournament of my life, the Ladbrokes Poker Million.

The 2003 rendition of the Poker Million was to be filmed in a studio and restricted to thirty-six entrants. It wasn't actually worth a million so it was branded 'Poker Million – The Masters'. I'd be back in front of the cameras, once again eager to impress, to win. Some sort of success would put me back on the poker circuit and impress Ladbrokes, otherwise I could be washed up and finished. This time the money meant something too: I had to stump up a fortune from my own pocket to enter.

At the reception party and draw the ever-faithful Tony Ure asked the Sky Sports directors if I could try my hand at co-commentating alongside Jesse May. Jesse was a legend, known to millions from *Late Night Poker*, which was now being re-run throughout the world. After a shaky introduction to commentary work I soon realized that two genuinely big hands clashed rarely. All six players normally held absolute junk.

Therefore, in my heat, which was sure to be showcased as it contained Bruno Fitoussi, Dave Ulliott and snooker legend Steve Davis, I decided to employ a mad, aggressive style, the like of which you normally see in a £10 home game. It worked a treat, move making on any and everybody, feeding off tight players such as Davis and Dave Cleary. We were soon down to three and then two – myself and Davis – after I called an 'all-in' announced by Mike Magee holding no more than 2-6! I was, as was the norm, annihilated for this call on the poker forums, which I had become so familiar with. For me, however, it was simply a mathematical deduction that made perfect sense.

The average stack was 200,000, the blinds were 20,000 and 40,000. I was on the big blind for 40,000 (holding 220,000) and Mike, who moved his 110,000 chips all-in, on the small blind for 20,000. What was I supposed to do? Pass my 2-6 because I knew it was losing? That would have pushed me down to 180,000 and him up to 150,000. If I called and lost I would be down to 110,000 but still alive and capable of moving all-in myself the following hand and getting straight back up to 150,000.

The key to it was equity and probability. He had two cards higher than a 6 or, as I suspected, one higher than a 6, probably an Ace or King. In any scenario the probability of me prevailing hovered around 34 to 37 per cent. So, by investing 70,000 more (added to my 40,000 equity, which would be lost if I passed) I would get a return of 222,000 if successful. That's odds of over 2/1 when I knew I was not a 2/1 underdog to prevail.

Well, we all play differently, and that's the glory of poker. Regardless, he flipped over Queen-3 and I spiked a 2 on the river to send him packing.

I was now heads-up with a snooker legend my dear old Aunty May adored and watched on television for weeks on end. The cards did not fall kindly for me, and with the blinds going stratospheric I was forced to push my chips in blind and lost out to Steve's Ace-Queen. There was nothing I could do. It was devastating, and more slander in the forums followed. 'What a muppet, moving all-in with junk. All he had to do was wait his man out' – that was the general theme. That's easy to say from the comfort of a front room, but for me, when the blinds are costing you 90,000 chips every two hands and I only have 270,000 . . . I don't think so.

Summer passed. I was an outcast in the poker community and was left to play nightly tournaments in Dublin, which I still loved and won with embarrassing regularity. The Winter Festival in Dublin soon came round once more. It was my third, and thank God I got myself on the scoreboard for the year by winning the Omaha tournament, banking a desperately needed €24,000. I'm convinced the victory could not have come anywhere other than on home soil. I simply felt so at home, so comfortable. It felt like the light at the end of the tunnel.

But before any more poker I had the unexpected pleasure of commentating on the 'live' Poker Million final. Jimmy White, the snooker player, won that final at the head of a field which naturally included Steve Davis. It may not have been classic poker playing but two snooker stars excelling was a shot in the arm for the game and another contributory factor in its exponential growth in popularity.

After the game, after the cameras had stopped rolling and Jimmy was ready to pop the champagne corks, we all set off for the Victoria Casino on Edgware Road. However, as one by one our posse signed the guest book, I was refused entry. It must have been some kind of mistake; I was a member and had been in once before. No mistake: my membership had been revoked, I was barred. I was left out on the pavement while everyone else was at the bar enjoying themselves. Worst of all, I had absolutely no idea what I had done wrong or what grounds they had for my exclusion.

Following some detective work in later weeks, the reason was unearthed. A poker player with a less than flattering telephone message on his mobile had played it to the management, who, oblivious to the circumstances, identified my voice. I was not welcome there.

This barring was another blow to my confidence. By now I could not wait to see the end of 2003. But yet more shit was on its way to the whirly thing.

On the domestic front I was still loving the trappings of being a poker player. OK, I couldn't hit a barn door from ten paces on the European circuit, but cash game and tournament wins in the Merrion and another new card club in Dublin, the Fitzwilliam, were giving me enough ready cash so that each and every day was my own. Furthermore, each and every one of the cities on the European circuit seemed to offer something exciting or completely mad. But it couldn't last. It was time for another meltdown. This time a set of circumstances came together that allowed me to see the error in my wicked, hedonistic ways.

It was a Sunday afternoon when all hell broke loose. I recall it so clearly. I'd done a lot of damage unto others around this time, particularly to women friends. I'd run around like a juiced-up jack rabbit since wiping the slate clean and moving to Ireland almost three years earlier. Ultimately I broke down and cried shamelessly like a baby in public that day.

Meltdown meant reliving emotions from years, even

decades, ago; I could see all my insecurities clearly for the first time. I didn't think I was a bad person, but I had not stopped to consider others for some considerable time. I was not over the greyhound slaughtering in Abilene, and this had been compounded by my gran's passing. Grief, pain and infatuation had combined to provide a cocktail lethal to my sanity. There was chemistry all right, like a slow-cooking pressure cooker that was always going to explode. I'd appeased it, slowed the reaction, for this long by being a single bloody-minded bastard with no thought for anyone apart from myself.

This was, for me, another cardboard box moment, as pivotal as reading that suicide top ten. I grew up there and then. I saw the error of my ways and wanted to change them.

Come 31 December 2003, I wasn't exactly merrily seeing in 2004 but I was happily saying goodbye to 2003 and the preceding years – all those memories, all that mental baggage. The lifestyle had come to an abrupt halt. Now I needed to care less about what people said about me and concentrate on where I was going, not where I had been. Vitally, I needed to start winning poker tournaments again.

18

Fresh Deal

As part of the fresh start I realized I did want everything I'd once wanted, I'd simply lost my way. Phil, my friend from childhood, had two children, a nice home that was nearly paid for and a stable marriage. Now I was ready and keen to share my life with someone. I wanted to love and be loved again. Crucially, I felt ready to trust again. Furthermore, I was now in a position to enter that realm of normality. I was no longer lying in the gutter or sleeping with the dogs. It never bothered me particularly, but it did not endear me to a potential soul mate. I was relatively secure, in the sense that I was no longer a gambling degenerate, and even if I endured another catastrophic year like the one I'd just had, I could fall back on poker as a growing industry which required journalists and commentators – similar to the way former professional snooker player John Virgo edged over from performing to corporate and studio work.

I knew I wouldn't find love in an over-thirties bar in Dublin or in an Estonian lap-dancing club, and I didn't need to. Over a period of weeks and months I developed a thing for the card room manager at the Merrion Casino, and with the powers of persuasion, we got together. She was my first real girlfriend since I was a teenager. We were a proper couple on equal terms.

Now, I know not many women would put up with or understand their partner coming home at all hours, day and night, one day saying he had won a thousand, the next losing three. But Mags understood the lifestyle and the swings that come with this precarious profession. She was one in a million.

Mags and I worked well together, she as the manager and me as the maverick. I almost lived in that card room for a time; I saw it as my own private club. It was the only place in Dublin where you could get a drink or fillet steak at three a.m. As a result a fair few celebs would roll in, such as Rolling Stone Ronnie Wood. He was a gas. One evening I got a call from an associate asking if it was all right for U2 to come in that night. Apparently they were performing live in their studio for a radio special and wanted somewhere to chill out afterwards. Sure enough, a few hours later, there I was trying to teach The Edge the fundamentals of Texas Hold'em while Bono attempted to beat the blackjack table.

Together, at the very end of 2003, Mags and I took a holiday to Vancouver in Canada. I was actually in search of what I had heard to be a 'soft' Omaha game, but when I found the casino where this discipline was supposedly played it transpired the game was 'limit' Omaha not the 'pot limit' version in which I excelled. After that it was simply a case of rest and relaxation, and we discovered we enjoyed each other's company away from the crazy world of poker.

I kicked off 2004 with a prodigious hunger for glory. Well, the results couldn't be any worse than they were in 2003. Brighton was the first port of call, for their January Sales Festival. Immediately I landed the opening tournament, the first ranking tournament of the year, collecting over £7,000 in the process. Just the start I was looking for. Days later, under the most appalling circumstances, I was eliminated in fifth position from their main event. As this game goes, you can do no more than get all your money into a pot, which would doubtless have won me the tournament, as a 1/6 favourite.

Still, I was clearly in good form and I jumped straight on a train to get to Luton for the Grosvenor Grand Challenge the following day. There, gate-crashing a hundred-runner-plus field with enough re-buys to cover the national debt of Chile, my third place bagged another six grand in the opening event of the festival. Happy days were here again, and happier days were about to follow as the main event of this tournament was mine too. It may have taken seventeen hours of play but that equated to a little less than a grand an hour. Not the hardest way to make a living.

Within a week I'd collected two trophies, landed a title, gone directly to the head of the European rankings and cleared over €40,000. I bought myself the Porsche I'd always wanted. This was Shangri-La. The turnaround in fortunes and form was related to my new outlook on life, and a new happiness and support from my partner Mags.

This year I was not going to miss the World Series. I had to go over there and experience it for the first time. Therefore the World Series of Poker Trial in Vienna, run under the same conditions as the World Series and designed to be a warm-up, was the logical next port of call, and I was delighted with a twelfth-place finish. I discovered I could play for two or three days solid, and I knew, granted a few big hands at the right time, I could have won it.

The British Open at the Victoria Casino a week later was obviously out of the question – I was still barred – but the Poker Million wasn't, and in my second shot at that particular title I once again drew a snooker player, this time defending champion Jimmy White. I dodged bullets and won my heat, making it through to the semifinals, which were being played towards the end of the year – something to look forward to.

We were in April already, and the World Series was now underway. I knew nothing of Vegas apart from what everyone had told me. Here's the proof of that statement: I booked accommodation at Circus Circus, one of the few casinos in Vegas that has been around for more than twenty-five years that has not been blown up. It most certainly should have been!

As I'd done in Canada, it was a case of off the flight, into a taxi, into the hotel and straight off to find the action. That action was in Binions Horseshoe Casino, home of the World Series, which consisted of thirty-three tournaments, one a day, plus the feature, the main event, the championship with its $10,000 entry fee. The first tournament I could enter was the $1,500 Pot Limit Hold'em event. I paid up my money and couldn't wait to get stuck in. I had to wait until the following day at noon, though. Really, I'd spent far too long getting there. I should have been in Vegas two years earlier.

Beforehand, though, a little blackjack. Yes, that's gambling, but I was determined not to let it get a grip on me and I was also proven to be very disciplined at this game. What really attracted me was the signpost 'Single-Deck Blackjack' – the biggest give-me of all time. Even a schoolboy couldn't mess this up. Big cards, Aces especially, are good for the player and little cards are bad, or good for the house. You bet bigger when expecting big cards and smaller when expecting small ones. With just fifty-two cards in play you know that when thirty cards have been dealt out and there has been no sign of an Ace and very few 10s, Jacks, Queens and Kings, a gold rush is about to happen. That's all you have to wait for.

Determined not to dent my bankroll, and in a state of disbelief that such a game was on offer, I pulled up a stool, threw $200 on one of the tables and put my brain to work. The cliché of taking candy from a baby could not sufficiently sum this up. Sat there on my own, placing $2 bets and then, once in a blue moon, pushing forward a chunky stack of valuable chips, in no time my $200 had become $700. I thought that $3,000 was a realistic and sensible 'get out' target for day one.

The pit boss, the person in charge of the gaming floor, making sure the dealers are efficiently doing their job, was impressed. He came over for a chat, congratulated me on my winnings, and asked where I was from. I explained I was from Ireland – as I always do: the Irish get a far better welcome overseas than the English – and that this was my first visit to Vegas.

'Excellent, sir,' he replied. 'So would you like a frequent player's card?'

'What will that do for me?'

'It will give you a number of bonuses here, free meals, and possibly the odd hotel room.'

'Sounds good to me. Yes, thanks, I'll have one, please.'

'OK, sir, I will need to see your ID.'

'I'm sorry, I don't . . . where I come from you don't need ID on you in public places. But I can tell you that my name is Roy Brindley and I can give you my date of birth. If you are giving away free hotel rooms, I'm not going to lie to you!'

'No, that's fine,' he said, but his tone had turned nasty. 'We are aware you are a card counter, and all these cameras' – he pointed to three in the ceiling above and to the side of my head – 'have taken pictures of you. You are now barred from this casino and I must tell you we share our pictures with other casinos here in Vegas. Their systems will soon identify you and we will put a name to your face with or without your help. Now, security will escort you to the cash desk where you can collect your winnings, and then they will see you off the premises.'

I could not believe it. I had been barred from a Las Vegas casino for winning $500 and playing blackjack the only way I knew how. If you play cards of any kind there is simply no ignoring the basic instincts, the basic card sense that makes you look out for the small things, like Aces – like it or not. Some achievement, huh? In town a few hours and I was already barred from the home of the World Series! The list of casinos where I was not welcome was growing.

Anyone who has ever played poker at this fabled venue will know that it features several front and back doors. The rear entrances were well away from the gaming tables during the Series and, as it worked out, I had no problems entering by that route the next day. Obviously I shirked the gaming areas, where the roulette and blackjack action was, and the fact that the pit boss concerned believed Roy Brindley was a concocted name helped, but to this day my picture is on a 'rogues gallery' in a Las Vegas computer system, all for $500.

That day I kept my head down in more ways than one. I played a tight-aggressive style in the tournament, my first ever World Series event, and as the early hours beckoned I found myself down to the final forty or so players. So-called big stars were all around, people ESPN focus their cameras on repeatedly, but I have to say I could see nothing out of the ordinary about their game or approach. Certainly nothing I hadn't seen from some of Europe's finest.

With thirty-six people earning prize-money things were a little tense at this stage, but I felt good. No one knew me, and I was on the big stage and doing well. However, I was about to make some enemies. Firstly, Daniel Negreanu raised-up a pot which I called on the big blind. The flop came down, I checked, he checked. The turn arrived, I checked and he bet.

Now, I don't know what the board was showing and I cannot recall what I had, apart from the fact that it amounted to nothing, but poker players will tell you, play with someone for six or seven hours straight and you subconsciously pick things up about them. My subconscious just screamed at me that this was wrong. His bet did not make sense; his demeanour was not right. I immediately reached for my chips and made a re-raise.

Negreanu, not yet the superstar he's become known as today, turned to Howard Lederer, another appointed big-name player, and said, 'I should have known that wouldn't work when I saw the T-shirt,' as he ditched his hand, seeming to me to indicate I was one of the new breed of unwelcome internet qualifiers, who are often forced to wear attire supplied by the poker website they won their trip to Vegas on. I found the jibe offensive. He didn't know me from Adam; this was unnecessary hostility. Where I had learned to play cards, all newcomers were made welcome.

An hour or so later I came over the top of Lederer for all my chips. Once again I held nothing, but the light-bulb lit up in my head and I simply knew he never had a hand good enough to call an 'all-in'. He threw his hand into the muck, announcing, 'I can do most things but I cannot outplay bad players!' Just how he had come to that conclusion I don't know. I'd not shown a hand in four hours. All he really knew was this: he had to pass and he didn't like it.

As I felt hostility grow all around me, my determination increased. T. J. Cloutier, world-renowned for his stunning results, was sat to my left as we reached the final thirty players. I noticed that every time I limped into a pot on the small blind he would either raise pre-flop or bet the flop. He was doubtless playing brilliantly, and I had to pass every time, but I just knew he could not have had a good starting hand or have hit the flop on all these occasions.

I was waiting my spot to exploit this, and it came in the most unlikely situation. Limping in on the small blind with 2h-7s, TJ this time only called. When the flop came down 2d-6d-10c I decided I had flopped a pair and I needed to bet it to find out if it was good. However, my bet was immediately raised by him. Checking his chip stack and comparing it with mine while considering the pot size, I decided he would have to pass anything other than two-pair should I move all-in. With no more than my pair of 2s I did just that, and to my disgust he called the all-in immediately.

It's all about timing, this game of Hold'em, and I'd clearly timed it wrong. Or had I? The former American football pro Cloutier did not turn over two-pair, three-of-a-kind or even a pair. He showed Jack-Queen of diamonds, meaning he could win with a diamond, making a flush, or a Jack or Queen. To the dismay of the host of American players around me, he failed to find one of the cards he was looking for and my 2-7 scooped a monster pot.

As the groans went around the table, bowed, shaking heads universally announced 'Hard luck, TJ', 'What can I say, TJ?', 'That was too bad, TJ', 'TJ, it's been a pleasure playing with you.' Meanwhile, I was deemed to be the absolute illicit player at this table. The very next hand, while stacking up my chips, I passed up my hole cards only to hear Lederer announce, 'Well, I wonder what he has passed. We know it's not the Deuce-Seven.'

I have to tell you, I've never experienced such hostility and resentment at a poker table, and it got worse. On being eliminated under unfortunate circumstances agonizingly close to the hallowed final table in twelfth, I suffered the indignity of four Yanks around me jumping out of their seats and giving each other high-fives. It's not terribly nice having to gather your things together, disappointed, broken and destroyed, while this sort of unwarranted behaviour goes on around you. It was clear to me that poker in America was a game of 'them against us'. Naturally, being American, they believe they are the biggest and the best. I cannot stand that combination of arrogance and xenophobia.

This was my first taste of blackjack and poker Vegas style, and I didn't like it one bit. I was, however, winning, and what caught my attention next was the dog racing being beamed in by satellite from Derby Lane, Florida. A number of the Vegas casinos accepted bets from this track, and the odds of return they gave you reflected the returns from the track. Unlike horse bets, your money would not go into the racetrack's tote pool.

Well, I knew a thing or two about dog racing, not least the American system of grading, which often throws up races in which there are good things surer than a penalty kick. Maiden races, for example, are what they say on the tin: a race for dogs that have never won a race. Often when a young pup with ability makes his debut he is against rivals which could not beat me in a hundred-yard dash. Therefore good things are often 1/12 shots. Only lightning or a strip of quicksand could get them beat. However, as Americans love exotic bets such as trifectas (the first three in correct order) and superfectas (the first four in correct order), the win pools (the conventional pick-a-winner bet) have very little money in them. As a result, dogs that should be clear odds-on favourites, say 1/4, often start at 6/4.

For me, it was just a case of waiting for the right races, laying my money down and picking it back up with interest. Can you imagine tossing a coin with someone and every time it comes in heads they give you £2 while you only have to pay them £1 when it's a tail? Over a period of time I could not lose.

That period of time lasted exactly three races in one casino and two in another. Thereafter I was told the maximum bet they would accept from me was $5. A third casino had received a phone call and been told to both expect and reject me.

Fewer than forty-eight hours in Las Vegas, the gambling

capital of the world, and I'd been branded a cheat and barred from a casino; I'd found 'big-name' American poker players incredibly hostile; and I'd had my bets refused after winning no more than a few hundred dollars. What a place. What a disappointment.

Downhearted, I stayed for the main event of the World Series, which was a wash-out, and that's because somehow I'd let the world of film affect my everyday life. You see, at the start of level five in the championship a guy with ferret-like features was brought to my table. I immediately took a dislike to him but couldn't put my finger on why. We played for a full hour, and then it hit me: Percy Wetmore, the detestable warden who walked around with a chained, shackled and innocent John Coffey declaring 'dead man walking'. Percy Wetmore, who electrocuted Dale (Eduard Delacroix) by deliberately failing to wet the sponge on his head, leading to a horrible death. Percy Wetmore from the film *The Green Mile*.

Unashamedly I wanted to get this guy. He could well have been the actor who played the role or just a look-alike; in either case, in reality he was probably a model citizen of the USA with no malice in him whatsoever. Being an American, with the 'right to arms' written in his country's constitution, the only similarity was probably the .45 he kept under his pillow. But his presence provoked a barrage of emotions in me, and when finding an Ace-King on the big blind, I could not wait to come clean over the top of his raise.

Calling while flipping over Queen-Queen, it was now Roy's turn to suffer a painful, torturous and undignified death.

19

Mixed Game

Vegas does it for a lot of people, but I see it as a neon-lit Sodom and Gomorrah wrapped in glittering lights and plastic signs floating in a nocturnal oasis of indulgence. In other words, it's Blackpool in the desert and a place where you're not allowed to win but welcome to leave your money behind. The corporations, paranoid about anyone having the remotest chance of winning, get it all.

There were, however, two real positives to come out of my visit. Firstly, I teamed up with a researcher from the television network HBO, which was making an undercover programme about greyhound racing in the United States. I'd been working with groups of greyhound-racing campaigners in the States for a couple of years, those who wanted to clean up the sport and account for and provide homes for all retired dogs, not necessarily radically close the sport down. They were in turn lobbying politicians and furnishing journalists with the facts and figures. I was eager and pleased to tell the television executives all I could about the horrors that take place in the

Kansas fields. Sadly they could not go on to any specific properties but I gave them maps and drawings to support my story, and provided an interview.

Secondly, my half-brother, the one who had affected me so badly as a small child when brutally announcing that I was an unwanted bastard, shit not fit for scraping from a shoe, arrived in Vegas. A quarter of a century had passed since that fateful day and I'd probably not seen him in two decades, but I'd often thought of this day, the day I'd see him again.

He immediately embraced me like a brother. I've never had a true brother or sister. I've never so much as slept in the same house as one of my dad's six sons and daughters from his first marriage. I'd spent many years feeling bitter and twisted towards him, planning on exacting revenge. But now here he was, in his fifties, a lifetime of hard work having aged him dramatically. This trip to Vegas was the first time he had left England. I suspected I'd done and seen more in the past twelve months than he had in his lifetime. Like I often say, it's better to be envied than pitied, and I certainly did not envy him. I firmly believe that people change for the better as they age and mellow, and forgiving my half-brother, choosing to pretend that incident never happened, made me feel a better person.

My enthusiasm for poker did not relent. No sooner had I got back from Vegas than I was planning my next trip, to Barcelona, the new venue for the World Heads-Up Championship. I'd played in it the disastrous previous year, but now that I was playing so much better again, with my insecurities behind me, I saw this as unfinished business. Victory was achievable in my mind.

It's the only discipline in poker where you get inside

someone's head. You can often lose a lot of hands but bluff your way through. It's a bit like boxing: you can leave yourself wide open, take a few jabs on the chin, but when he throws the big punch at you, you duck and counter-punch immediately. It's all about lining your man up.

I did well, winning my first three games, but the fourth round . . . well, I've never got my head around it.

A teenaged Swede was my opponent, and he raised up the first fourteen pots on me. I did once get a raise in first, only for him to re-raise me! Totally bemused but already in a spot of bother considering the chips I'd bled off, I was delighted finally to pick up a starting hand of some note – a pair of 9s. Sure enough, Scandi-boy raised into me and I could not wait to shove 'all-in'. This would get me right back into the argument and break his momentum. That was, of course, if he passed or especially called and lost. Well, naturally he called; he turned over pocket Aces! At least I had no complaints, although of all the poker I've ever seen or played, I've never witnessed such a whitewash. After the game my conqueror told the TV cameras he was going to be a millionaire within a year's time. Considering he was eliminated by Dave Ulliott in the next round, taking into account that a friend had sponsored him into this tournament and taken 80 per cent of his winnings, and bearing in mind he's not made a final table of a poker tournament anywhere in Europe since, I'm guessing it's not worked out for him.

I wasn't about to crack a million either. In fact, I was about to go skint. No betting shops were involved in this seismic hiccup this time round, just a huge cash game in Barcelona's Grand Casino.

You may think I was being stupid losing my entire bankroll in a cash game in one sitting, but remember my 2/1 about a head theory in coin tossing? Well, this time they were giving me 3/1 about a head and I was not worth my salt if I didn't put everything on the line in a game which offered so much value.

The game concerned was a high-staked Omaha cash game, and when walking home through Las Ramblas at five a.m. I had none of the gut-wrenching problems I'd had when bombing out of my first Irish Open or leaving Paddy Power's betting shop thousands down. The reason was simple: I would have done nothing differently. Given the opportunity in the same game over again, I'd happily have put a six-figure poker fund on the line once more.

The enormity of my misstep didn't really hit home until the World Poker Championship (WPC) in Dublin. This was one of the biggest events ever staged in Europe and it remains the most elite, select field ever assembled. It was on home soil, I had to play it – I had to be seen to be playing it – but I could not afford it. I'd blown everything. Yes, I had a second-hand Porsche and a pile of trophies to show for all my efforts during a two-and-a-half-year poker-playing career, but that was it. Mags knew of my problems and offered to lend me the money to play and get a bankroll back together. To be honest I had no idea she was in a position to lend me ten grand, or that she trusted and loved me enough to do so. Inspired by the realization that she was as serious about our relationship as I was, we moved in together shortly afterwards. The whole thing was so novel to me.

The WPC, a Pot Limit Hold'em tournament, was televised. Organizer Brian Johnson asked me to do some commentary, which was good for the profile and gave me a few hundred quid. But getting ten grand out of it, to repay Mags, was the priority. I did too, courtesy of the highest hand in the tournament – four Aces. But that monstrous hand did me no good in the long run. I firmly believe I could have done better than fourth place in my heat – two went through to the final from a field of sixteen – and would have done so had the pressure not been off.

Eight months had now passed since my last tournament win. It didn't feel like I'd been playing badly, though, and I'd got over my massive cash game loss remarkably well.

The first weekend in August, at Cork's fabulous Macau Casino, was where the winning thread was picked up again, in an Omaha/Hold'em round of each competition. I jumped straight on a plane to Edinburgh for Scotland's biggest festival of the year, the Scottish Open. Ally Myles, the former Dundee Casino manager, was now at the helm and he made me as welcome as ever, as did the natives. There was nothing other than hearty congratulations when I landed their most valuable competition, the £500 entry Hold'em tournament. As we sat down at the final table at two p.m., I told the players the game must end by six as I had a flight home to catch. The deciding hand was dealt at 5.57! By 6.25 I was going through airport security with twelve bags full of £50 notes in my pocket, hoping not to be pulled in and grilled by suspicious authorities. We were back on track.

Before my next appointment 'on the road' I had a big surprise. A letter arrived from the bank. It was addressed to Mags, but I opened it by accident. It stated something along the lines of 'As requested, repayments for your €10,000 loan, which you took out with us on June 20th 2004, will now be removed from your bank on the 2nd of each month.' I was not too happy about this. I thought we had no secrets, and if she needed money for anything, all she needed to do was ask. (If she got me on the back of a tournament win she had a chance!) I felt stupid when questioning her and saying, 'Whatever you need, just ask me. It will never be a problem.' As I prodded and probed to find out what the loan was for, Mags was forced to confess: 'It was for you. You needed it for the World Poker Championship.'

Oh my God. What a woman. Talk about faith and understanding. I wonder how many women would borrow in excess of £6,000 for their partner to play cards with.

That gave me a lot to think about when setting off for the next port of call, a pro/celeb tournament filmed in Brighton for television. I travelled over with Nick Leeson, the man famous for breaking Barings Bank. We'd met during the Irish Greyhound Derby a few years earlier and remained friends ever since. You could say we had a few things in common, particularly our vulnerable gambling mentality.

Nick, who also now lives in Ireland, was in a bit of a quandary. His wife Leona was expecting their first child and the doctors were going to induce her the following day. But as he had made a commitment to the organizers he had to be in Brighton. It was safe to say I was a little more determined than he was. That determination may have carried me to the final table, but I was disappointed with my fifth-place finish, even if it did mean another €10K plus.

On my way to the final table I crossed swords with several 'celebs' and I have to say I was horrified by the lack of basic ability, card sense, so-called educated people possess. For example, Channel 4 racing pundit John McCririck, who lists journalism and a Harrow education on his curriculum vitae, played with the skill of a dyslexic poodle. For someone who appears on television quoting prices, probability and percentages, his lack of understanding was incredible. I've also played alongside Sir Clive Sinclair. For a fella who is considered by many to be a genius, I have to question how on earth he has not devised a better strategy for playing tournament poker.

What was also noticeable about this event was the number of snooker players trying their hand at poker. I've played with pretty much every one of the world's top twenty cue-men, and all are of the same opinion . . . 'The money has totally gone in the game [snooker],' one said. 'Flying off to the likes of Northern Ireland and Malta for tournaments is great but you need to make the final to show anything like a worthwhile profit.' Whereas a pro snooker player used to be made for life following a few years at the top, now only the world championship can begin to offer a respectable payday. I think they all like the challenge poker offers and see similarities between the two games.

Television, colour television, made snooker. Pretty much unheard of in 1980, by the middle of that decade snooker was receiving near wallpaper coverage on the BBC and the players were superstars. I doubt very much a poker player will be awarded the BBC's Sports Personality of the Year award, even if a right-royal gymkhana queen and snooker players have. But I do know this: if poker ever makes its way on to the Beeb, in any way, shape or form, we can expect an explosion in popularity and general acceptance from a wary general public.

If I'm sounding a little corporate here, it's because my role as a sponsored player was changing. Tony Ure, my Messiah, had left Ladbrokes and the new management were encouraging me to take a more hands-on role. Ure had moved on to pastures new, and through his day-to-day dealings with the online poker community he suggested that the now-defunct Prima sponsor a group of London poker players. It was terribly nice of him and they received a million-pound freeroll to play any and every major tournament around the world, all expenses paid. Sadly, only one ever thanked him.

As for myself, my monthly retainer with my sponsors was not going very far at all. Tournament entry fees were in the process of going stratospheric. I was, however, still fully aware that in representing what was now Europe's biggest online card room, I had a high profile and I was in receipt of a lot more in sponsorship than 99.9 per cent of the poker-playing community.

The hands-on role led me to the BBC for an appearance on their *Breakfast Time* programme, talking about the threat online gaming poses in terms of potential addiction. It also took me on to the Ladbrokes Poker Cruise, where poker players could do what they like doing most, playing poker, while partners and wives could enjoy all the trappings of a Mediterranean cruise. Back on a roll at the time, I treated my mum and dad to the poker/holiday package. It was nice to have them on board, and they met Mags for the first time.

I finished tenth in the main event of that poker cruise, agonizingly close to the $250,000 first prize. Another disappointment was the semifinals of the Poker Million. I got my chips in first in a confrontation that would have got me to the final table as chip leader and in prime spot to land the $300,000 prize. However, none of my fourteen 'outs' against Dave Ulliott arrived. Only when friend and commentator Jesse May pointed out to me afterwards that 'the pot was worth at least $100,000' did it all sink in.

Nevertheless, poker was still evolving, as I thought it would. Prize-money was growing into incredible sums, and although I was just missing out on the big paydays, thankfully I did, as planned, have my own little slice of the action.

As a reward for leading the European rankings at the start of the year I'd received an invitation to play in the Professional Poker Tour (PPT), a free-to-enter series of events in America worth $500,000 apiece. The first of them was in Foxwoods Casino in Connecticut, the world's biggest casino, featuring three hotels, twenty-five restaurants, seven thousand slot machines and hundreds of gaming tables. This was my chance to make a name for myself on the world stage. Lederer and all those insulated Americans would no longer question my T-shirt if I could stamp some authority on this select field consisting only of major winners.

There was, and is, another way to make your mark, by playing every World Series and World Poker Tour event, but with them costing $10,000 apiece, the likes of me simply cannot continually come up with that kind of entry fee. Poker, just like horseracing and dog racing, has so much to do with money. I'm not pointing any fingers here, but we all know there are certain multi-millionaire former businessmen on poker's world stage who have the ability to spend $750,000 a year in tournament entries and play every major, including a $25,000 sit-down tournament in Las Vegas's Bellagio and a $50,000 buy-in at the Rio. Yes, they win something in their turn, but it's not reflective of their skill, only of their ability to pay their way into so many high-profile tournaments. The next thing you know they have written a poker strategy book telling people their secrets! Few truly know the value of money and I doubt any has had to sit on a street corner begging for it. Anyone can play poker, and on any given day pretty much anyone can win, but I believe only a select few are qualified or entitled to write about the winning formula. Therefore *Life's a Gamble* was never going to be a strategy book.

Before my trip back to America and the PPT I took in the final festival of the year in Dundee, knowing that I'd have to miss the Amsterdam Masterclassics by going to the States but remaining determined to fulfil my start-of-the-year plan of winning at least five European ranking tournaments.

On 5 November, despite those outrageous hedonistic ways being behind me, I woke up feeling so ill it was incredible. I got an emergency appointment with a local doctor who sent me home with enough drugs to make even Pete Doherty high, ordering bed rest and no flying for at least seventy-two hours. Bollix. I hadn't come all this way not to play, and I had to go back to Dublin the following morning as on 7 November I was flying to New York for my US appointment. I landed the Omaha competition that night, although I don't quite know how as my temperature was running into treble digits. I can honestly say I have never felt so ill. Still, the all-important fifth ranking tournament was in the bag.

On to America it was, then, where success in the inaugural PPT would mean a slice of a $500,000 pie. Moreover, it would announce an arrival on the world stage akin to a steamroller trespassing on a snail farm.

Now trust me, this place, Foxwoods, appears out of nowhere like a fairytale castle in the woods, and the size of it is something from a storybook too. It's simply huge. And what a dream the card room is, with a hundred tables packed to the capacity of a rush-hour London tube train. After wading through the hordes of players so engrossed in their games that they would have failed to notice Britney Spears walking past naked, I found the registration desk and declared, 'I'd like to register for tomorrow's tournament, please.'

While shuffling forms and looking in every direction apart from at me, the woman at the desk dismissively replied, 'I'm sorry, sir, that's for the top pros only. You can't play in that.'

'But I have an invitation,' I said sarcastically. 'Look, there's my name on the list. I'm important.'

Suddenly the tone changed as she decided it was time to be nice. 'I'm sorry, I thought you were . . . you're Scottish, right?'

'I'm whatever you want me to be. Now, can I register for the tournament, please?'

With the formalities complete, and having been told to have a nice day, I was set for the challenge ahead.

Next morning, once the speeches and photo-calls were done, it was time to rumble, and on this occasion my rumbling had to be done with the likes of Amarillo Slim Preston, recently crowned world champion Greg Raymer, and a host of other so-called poker stars. The first result was when our table, and this Scotsman, was instructed to play on the big stage – the TV table. The second came when the $5 million man, Raymer, was eliminated by yours truly. It was a simple ploy called betting straight into a Queen-high flop when holding pocket Queens. It can, and did, entice an all-in re-raise.

A TV executive suddenly appeared from nowhere and asked what part of New Zealand I was from (the information was needed for their onscreen graphics). I explained that I was actually British. Word of the local hero's demise at the hands of a Canadian (from British Columbia) spread like wildfire.

Shortly afterwards Men the Master met and was dispatched by Roy the Boy, which prompted Slim to perk up with a question: 'I'd guess you're Irish, young man?'

'Very nearly,' I replied. 'I'm English but I live in Ireland.'

He nodded knowingly before telling the player to his left that he was familiar with the European playing style as he had played in South Africa himself.

However, Slim didn't realize that Ace-King was this South African's moving hand and he too left the building when his Ace-Queen came up short.

Now I was getting somewhere as the host of names watching from the sidelines – five in total – failed to do anything other than make me a clear chip leader. Who is this foreigner at the head of affairs? It should be one of our homeboy superstars. That was the vibe about the place – and did I love it!

Conversely, did I not love my two black Queens running into an Ace-King-9 (all hearts) flop. Similarly, my Ace-Jack liked the look of a board showing Ace-2-Jack-6-10, but so did, understandably, an opponent holding Queen-King. I even limped in on the small blind with Ace-9, flopped the top two pairs yet was beaten by my only opponent on the big blind, who made a flush.

Suddenly – and, it felt, quite tamely – I was sat nursing just an average stack, ruing my luck and desperately trying to suppress a bout of tilt normally reserved for an overturned pinball machine.

Thereafter I made a move on Eric Seidel, whom I'd noted watching carefully when I previously displayed and mucked my pocket Queens as if they were disease-ridden. A full seven minutes later he reluctantly called my all-in holding Ace-King on a King-high flop. The length of his decision-making process vindicated my belief that I had earned enough respect to warrant a big lay down in a confrontation, although, regrettably, top-pair and top-kicker was simply too much of a roll-over for him.

Ending my day, I had to sign off my scorecard – as is the way on the PGA – which granted me the opportunity to enjoy one more chuckle: I was told to have a safe trip back to Australia by another staff member.

Disappointing it was indeed, but this non-American would not be forgotten in a hurry and my flight for the next PPT tournament in Los Angeles was booked immediately.

Another poker year had come to a close – well, almost. Just days before Christmas I played in a huge online tournament and finished second. My prize was $50,000, more than I'd ever won in a land-based tournament, and cause for some considerable celebration. On the back of it I booked a fly-drive holiday to Florida. These January holidays had served me well, and 2005, I felt, was going to be my best ever year.

20

Road Gambler

Nearly ten years had passed since my last visit to Florida, long before my turmoil years, my time on the streets and my discovery of poker. Mags and I travelled around a fair bit. Although the Everglades and Miami Beach were on the agenda, it was a trip to Calder racecourse and Derby Lane greyhounds that excited me most.

Derby Lane, in Clearwater, St Petersburg, was an absolute revelation. Since the last time I was there, poker had arrived. It was everywhere in the grandstands, probably a hundred tables; it was as if no one knew there was dog racing going on around them. It turned out the dog track was one of the few places where poker could be legally played in the state. It was, after all, licensed to take bets. Truth be known, if it were not for the poker tables generating profits, the place would probably close down. But dog racing has to continue; otherwise there is no licence to stage gambling.

With my enthusiasm for poker and my misgivings about an at least small number of American greyhound breeders and owners, I had mixed feelings. But, just like my first trip to the Jackpot, my head went straight into gear thinking of the bigger picture and the dozens and dozens of grandstands at dog and horse tracks in England and Ireland which lay dormant for the vast majority of the time. Shortly after this visit a dear old friend of mine, a former owner with the Walthamstow trainer I worked for some sixteen years earlier, Mick Davis, opened up Harlow dog track to poker and soon spread his empire to another five stadiums.

Here in Florida, at the dogs, a blast from the past walked straight past me: Sky Lucas. I'd felt very bitter towards him, taking all those dogs away from me, denying me the chance to get on in life as a greyhound trainer. But when I saw him and he immediately made me welcome, I forgot all those hostilities. Life's too short, and anyway, getting out of dog training was the best thing I ever did. He played his part in that. We stayed with him for a few days and visited his house – his second house, as he was based in New York. What a place! A mansion, backing on to a waterway, worth about $2 million. I wanted this life, not just the house and the money, but the family as well.

Returning home freshened up, I went to both Brighton and Luton, as I'd done in 2004, but this time there were no stunning finishes, no wins, no trophies. In fact it was not until March that I landed my first tournament, in Dublin during the Irish Open.

As always, I loved seeing the world – a never-ending perk of the job – and pro player Tony G, whom I'd met way back at the 2002 World Heads-Up, issued me an invitation to attend his tournament in Vilnius, Lithuania, in April. Tony, a far nicer fella than his on-camera persona would have you believe, also paid for my tournament entries while the casino provided me with free accommodation. Mags, now my travelling companion when at all possible, came with me, and together we explored this magical place. Trakai Island, for example, is a taste of something you can no longer find in most parts of the western world, featuring a stunning castle in a setting that is not overrun by tourists, or spoiled by demands for an entry fee with stipulations about not taking pictures.

Anyway, the story of how I won the Tony G Invitational is the stuff of legends in local parts these days.

Now, let's be clear, I like to drink when I'm playing poker. I firmly believe that alcohol, in the right proportions, has a positive effect. Firstly, time flies by and therefore a lot of the boredom the game can produce, in long tournaments, is removed. Next, just like listening to music, your perception can be enhanced. I'm serious. I've often sat in a chair having drunk copious amounts of alcohol listening to anything from Skid Row to the Shadows, and in that state where everything seems to happen in slow motion I've been able to deduce exactly when someone is strong, weak or bluffing, and in certain situations pretty much what the two cards in their hand are.

The kind people of the Grand Casino World, most notably the card room manager Evelina Vilimaite, happily plied me with White Russians from the outset. By the time I'd reached the final table I knew I'd probably had my quota, but I was on fire, eliminating people left, right and centre while also making some very big, all-important passes. One by one they fell, and I was doing most of the felling, but once down to three players

I knew the concoctions they were bringing me were no ordinary measures. Ultimately I ended up heads-up but I was in such a comatose state that I could barely see the cards in the centre of the table.

A flop hit the table, and by the best of my reckoning – you know, with just one eye open and my head spinning – a Jack or King would give me a pair, a Queen would give me a straight, and a club a flush. I blurted out 'all-in' and my Latvian opponent, clearly unimpressed and convinced he had it won, announced loudly and so seriously in a Soviet tone, 'I call!'

I was unable to focus. I knew the turn and river card had landed but I was unable to deduce what they meant to me. My opponent immediately stood bolt upright from his chair and shoved his hand towards me. I was guessing he had called with the best and won, so I shook his hand and started to congratulate him.

'No, you win!' he announced.

Oh, good-o, excellent.

I went to stand up to thank the dealer and the management, who were now circling the table, but oh dear, that was the last I can remember as I fell straight back on my chair and then backwards on to the floor. The casino security were good enough to stretcher me out and take me back to our hotel while Mags sorted out the prize-money and left behind the tips.

Because of days like this, the early part of the year passed quickly. I had the scene pretty much down pat by now. I knew where the venues were, where to stay, where to eat and who to see if I wanted something. I didn't, however, have so many players figured out. I mean, they were coming out of the wood-work. In the early days there were about fifty characters you would see regularly at a number of tournaments 'on the circuit'; this was the year when I noticed that every table seemed to have fresh faces and young Scandinavians in abundance.

Amusingly, I do recall meeting the first of this insurmount-able wave of new poker players, back in 2002 at a tournament in Paris. There I was, standing in the registration queue – which is quite futile in France as every Frenchman and his dog will always be served before a visitor regardless of their posi-tion in the said queue – perplexed as much as the young lad stood alongside me, who was not pushing, shoving, shouting, screaming or puffing on an overpowering cigar-cum-cigarette. Therefore, he clearly wasn't a local. Possibly his spiky hair, retro yellow-coloured T-shirt, orange shoes and torn Armani jeans also gave it away, but it mattered little as I needed some-one who understood English to talk to before blowing a fuse and reciting all the French swearwords my private education had taught me.

A nice kid he was too, from the Swedish city which I later discovered had an average age of nineteen, the student capital Linkoping. He explained how he was very excited as this was to be the biggest tournament he had played following his online qualification. Online qualification for a casino tourna-ment? What a novel idea, I thought. Sadly, he added that this was the only tournament he was playing during the festival, but he was in Paris for the entire week. Naturally I understood: as he was at college even the €100 freeze-out would tax his student loan. He was probably here for peanuts, so the slightly richer €200 and €500 events were absolute no-no's.

But I liked the lad, he seemed unpretentious, and there were times in my deep, dark gambling history when a near stranger had lent me a tenner to chase myself out of a hole. A few beers later, and after some romancing about the good deeds people had done for me, I purchased an entry ticket for both the €100 and €200 tournaments for the unassuming youngster. You only live once; one good turn deserves another. He was probably as hungry as hell and he could give me a share if he got a payday out of them. That was my way of looking at this rare and generous deed.

Feeling quite proud of myself, I hunted the lad down to present him with the equivalent of a Willy Wonka golden ticket to any sick poker player – free tournament entries. Following some considerable hunting I eventually found 'Scandie boy' in the *salon privé*. Never good at taking a hint, it wasn't until after I had made my unprecedented gesture of generosity that I realized the red chips on the table he was playing were valued at €5,000 apiece, not €5. Indeed, the baby-faced Swedish assassin was sat in the thick of a monstrous cash game with €55,000-plus stacked before him and was wiping out all-comers at any discipline of poker they cared to throw at him.

Well, I'm sure you will agree it was a nice thought all the same.

I digress. My annual assault on the World Heads-Up Championship, a tournament I'm still determined to win, came to nothing. Similarly, the Poker Million was a damp squib. It must have been a particularly bad performance from me as I have no recollection of it!

There was also the second leg of the Professional Poker Tour in Los Angeles. I flew over with Padraig Parkinson. It's a long flight, especially with someone like him sat next to you: he can talk for Ireland and his sense of humour can leave you with a dreadful stitch.

I had no great run there. I did, however, get a moment under the cameras by knocking out home boy and hyped superstar Phil Ivey. As these things go, despite cameras swarming all around our table, his demise never made the final cut in the show – it ended up on the cutting-room floor. I tell you, visitors are not welcome.

The highlight of that trip for me was a visit to Santa Anita racecourse, a fantastic setting for horseracing and the backdrop for the Sea Biscuit movie.

Despite firing a few blanks I still had confidence in myself and I decided to do the long haul in Vegas, the entire seven weeks of the World Series during June and July. I'd once again built up a large enough bankroll but was not enjoying a free ticket into every major competition on the planet like some sponsored players now were. In fact, my retainer was now dwarfed by the size of tournament entry fees. But I thought this was good. If I've learned one thing in life, it's that you appreciate things far more if you have to go out and earn them. It was going to be my money on the line and my losses should things not work out.

Considering the length of my stay, a budget hotel was very much the order of the day for this trip. I stayed at the Gold Coast, just next door to the World Series' new home, the Rio, offering rooms for a quarter of the price of that hotel and casino. OK, the rooms weren't akin to those found at the Ritz, but I was there to work, to play poker – lots of it – and, hopefully, turn my $50,000 roll into $250,000.

I ploughed straight into the action with a second in an event at the Palms Casino and another second in an event in the Bellagio. Combined, they netted me $35,000. I was right on track. A win and two more cashes followed the following week – another $25,000. It was like shelling peas. The trouble was, these lumpy sums were being taken to the Rio where I was unable to overcome field sizes in their thousands in World Series tournaments.

Next, the biggest headache of them all, I became bored, I lost my form and then I lost confidence. Nearly two months in Vegas is a long time. I became like a zombie. Every day was the same: wake up, go to the Rio, play in a WSOP tournament, which started at noon, play for hours on end, and after getting eliminated grab something from a burger bar and hotfoot it over to the Palms or Bellagio casinos for their nightly com-petitions, which started at eight p.m. and could last until three a.m. It was great fun for the first few weeks, but when you don't know if it's day or night outside your windowless casino environment, and when you don't know what day of the week it is, it's time to come home.

During this seemingly never-ending cycle I did play a fair amount of poker alongside actor James Woods, whose enthusiasm remained undiminished. What a terribly nice guy, full of encouragement and support when we spoke about the prospect of this autobiography.

That's the glory of poker. It's a level playing field and you often have no idea of your opponent's background. Dustmen do face off against lawyers, actors against roofers. I also played with actor Lou Diamond Phillips around this time, and my only observation of him, unknowing of his status, was, what a strange-looking beggar!

Zombiefied, I also suffered a very forgettable night playing in a Palms nightly tournament. It began when I asked the waitress if she served 'Vanilla Diet Coke'. It had just come out in England and I loved the stuff. 'Sure,' she replied, returning with a lovely glassful shortly afterwards. Having just eaten a Chinese I soon fancied another and another. In fact, by the time I'd reached the final table I guessed my drinks had been spiked because I was rockin' and a-rollin'.

'What is actually in that?' I enquired.

'Why, it's vanilla vodka and Diet Coke, just what you've been asking for.'

Oh my, I'd been drinking them by the bucketload. But why change a good thing? I mean, I was sitting in front of a mountain of chips and playing like a brain surgeon, just like in Lithuania months earlier. A few hours later I won the tournament in a state where I could barely see straight.

Twenty thousand dollars in cash, but there was a problem: I had to get back to my hotel and I could scarcely walk, certainly not past magnetic roulette wheels and blackjack tables. Just how the management let me play in such a condition I'll never know. Ironic, considering my picture was on file in the city, and given that when I won a few hundred dollars in a sane and sober state of mind on my last visit I was ejected. When you are this drunk, when you've lost all sense of reality at a roulette wheel, when chips are tiddly-winks and notes toilet paper, you have no chance of winning, and casinos know that. Why else do you think the drinks are free in these places? I woke next morning without a dollar bill to tip a taxi driver.

All in all, after a month I was happy to pack my bags and come home, but what was the point? I had to be in Vegas to entertain all the online players from Ladbrokes and I had to play in the main event, so I was forced to stay out there.

Drinking and ten-pin bowling overtook poker as the number one pastime, and every night I went to a different restaurant, most of the time with my friends John Gale, who had won over a million dollars during the past year when landing a World Poker Tour event and coming second in a World Series tournament, and Andy Black, who was unknown outside Dublin.

Anyway, on a drunken night in the Rio Hotel Andy and I swapped 3 per cent in each other for the main event. Actually, I had the vaguest of recollections of it, but thankfully Mags, who had come to visit me and was also expecting/fearing another Lithuanian incident, kept a note of it.

The history books will show Andy finished fifth in that monumental final, taking away $1.7 million. They will not tell you what a brilliant call he made at the final table, how he totally outplayed Phil Ivey when they were down to the final two tables, or what he did with a lot of his winnings. Don't worry, it's not bad: it went to charity. After seven weeks in the desert, the $51,000 he won for me meant I left with almost exactly what I arrived with.

I'd been a big fan of Andy Black since watching him in a 1998 documentary about the World Series of Poker, which like that 1999 documentary on Noel Furlong I must have watched a few dozen times at the height of my enthusiasm for the game back in the early days. In it Black made a statement that really caught my attention and which rang so true to me. 'Why do I do this when it makes me so unhappy?' he said. 'I mean, I don't even like money that much!' He went on to talk about his insecurities, his concerns about what people thought of him. I connected with these thoughts because defeat weighed heavily with me.

When I started playing in Dublin, Andy was on the missing list, having decided poker was not for him and the Buddhist way of life was. We became friends and I enjoyed writing a story about him for *Card Player* magazine. His story was interesting but, more importantly, he was clearly an awesome player. People said I was crazy posing a question to this long-forgotten player within my piece about what he would do if he made the final table of the World Series. My choice of subject matter was now vindicated. Not only did he land that mammoth payday, he went on to prove himself over and over again, most notably in Australia in the Aussie Millions and in Monte Carlo at the final table of the European Poker Tour Grand Final.

On returning from Vegas, as I knew the ropes in modern-day poker circles, we agreed I'd act as his manager with an aim of maximizing the spin-offs from his success in the World Series. I immediately sold his press conference for a serious five-figure sum, labelling him the most successful Irish sportsman ever. OK, there have been bigger achievers, but no one had landed anything like his $1.7 million prize.

However, our commercial relationship was short-lived. He turned his nose up at a €350,000-a-year offer of sponsorship, citing his belief that it was not moral to promote a gambling company which could lead to hardships and crises within families. With that kind of conviction Andy should not be playing poker at all, I thought. I clearly could not work with him.

Listen, fair play to him for standing by his guns and not compromising himself on this, but when he arrived at the televised British Poker Open where I was commentating a few weeks later wearing an internet website's T-shirt and saying to me 'I'm sponsored: so-and-so gave half the entry fee for simply wearing a T-shirt', I felt like banging my head, and his, into the wall.

What with this and Vegas I was worn down, tired. I'd done too much poker in a short space of time and I was starting to resent missing out on the riches poker was generating. I'd been there at the start of this revolution, I'd told everyone to get involved, but I'd sold myself short and had also failed to do something really smart, like start my own online poker site at the outset. TV commentary work was coming in, and I had columns in two poker magazines, and the *Irish Sun*, the *Daily Record* and the *Sportsman* newspapers, so my profile was high, but I started to realize what a never-ending merry-go-round the poker scene was. I wanted some normality. Living out of a suitcase in hotel rooms was a lot of fun but I was taking a hundred flights a year and spending over five months away from home. Normality and a family was what I'd craved deep down for years. Now pretty much everything was in place for it.

Money, financial security, was the only missing link. Every penny I had in the world was always within easy reach. It was my float, my reserve for the battles (card games) I played. A new and improved deal with my sponsors alleviated a lot of pressure. I had protested I was their front man, that in order to get results I needed to compete, and that to compete I needed to play in the biggest games.

Six grand was the entry fee into the William Hill Grand Prix in November 2005, a televised event featuring a top-class line-up of European pros. Playing too many of these with no results and I could go broke in no time. No results in these with sponsorship and I'd be sponsorless in no time.

The Grand Prix was filmed in the same studios as *Late Night Poker* had been six years earlier. That series looked dark and sexy on-screen, so you'll probably find it hard to believe that the studios are actually slap-bang in the middle of an industrial estate in Cardiff. My opponents included Peter Costa, a former *Late Night Poker* winner himself, and Willie Tann, enjoying the mantle of reigning European Player of the Year. But no one, I mean no one, fazes me at the poker table. Why handicap yourself by giving someone respect?

I landed my heat despite once again drinking way too much, and being very emotional about the sudden death of Dublin regular Pat Crowe. Pat was one of the first people I'd played with in the Jackpot and his sudden passing, as a middle-aged man, shook me severely.

That took me on to the final where I met old friends like Pascal Perrault and Liam Flood, plus Ram Vaswani, generally considered to be the best player in Europe. There was also American Phil Laak, a genuinely nice fella who made a name for himself by rolling around the floor like an infant for the cameras in a World Poker Tour final. This was the biggest final table I'd sat around and, before the cameras, it was a lot of air-time for my sponsors. I was now playing for the whole deal: the trophy, the prestige, the recognition and the money, with an eye to the future.

I can recall it being deadly quiet, so quiet you could have

heard a feather take its final fall to the studio floor. It seemed that lights glared from every direction. The silence was interrupted only by the occasional gentle shuffling of footsteps coming from the cameramen, who were clearly under instructions to tread as softly as possible. Those camera operators are always dressed in black, I suspect because if they are accidentally caught in shot you would struggle to see them on your television screen. They also wear headsets, through which they receive instructions about what to film and how to create shots that suit the moment and excite the armchair audience. I could sense the camera lens zooming in every time a big hand was played.

With just three of us remaining at this hallowed final table, which was critically billed as the finest selection of European poker players ever assembled, I was not playing for a factory worker's wage, we were fighting over the destiny of £300,000. That could do for me what the CD did for vinyl records back in the early 1990s.

Looking down at two very moderate cards, I stopped to consider . . . it's now all about what I can lose, not about what I can win. Surgically precise decisions are needed. I simply shouldn't wobble despite shooting at thousands, because I've experienced losing my last £60 in the world at a time when the rent was due, there was no petrol in the car, and only a jar of Marmite in the cupboard. That's pressure. It's also a perverse kind of buzz. I've won a million dollars playing poker and inflicted pain and misery on all around me gambling mindlessly on everything else for fifteen years. It's a deadly addictive drug.

Those thoughts helped compose me. I was in a position to

make amends, and those two cards curled up under my thumbs were pass material simply because the time was not right to get creative. Some players might have made a move with my hand, but players possessing the balls of a stallion also have the brains of a donkey. Unsurprisingly, no donkeys remained at this table.

A state of supreme calm allied to intense concentration was what was required. As a result I was no longer aware of the hordes of supporters outside in the green room watching everything on a television screen. Likewise the viewing audience, which would ultimately run into a fair few million, didn't get any consideration.

The next hand was dealt, and obviously I was praying for a monster: pocket Aces, Kings or Queens. Each is a 220/1 shot, and in addition to wishing for one of these long shots to appear I needed the all-important announcement from an opponent. I wanted to hear the word 'raise'.

My hand was, once again, not playable, but my opposition went to war – great news for me. Phil Laak, who was given the moniker 'The Unabomber' because of the hood he wears when playing, which makes him look like the photo-fit of the elusive 1980s US parcel bomber, had got all his chips in a pot clutching the worst of it. Looking cool and composed, Ram Vaswani, his opponent and the third person at the table, was in a strong position with five cards of fate, the full flop, still to land. Should his hand, a huge mathematical favourite, prevail, we would find ourselves in a head-to-head battle; if it failed, Laak would be back in the argument and three of us would fight on.

Laak found the miracle card he needed to stay in the

argument. If he hadn't I would have been guaranteed an extra £30,000 in prize-money. However, I was unruffled, only disappointed not to be a step closer to the £150,000 first prize. Ram glanced at me with an almost apologetic look as Laak scooped up the pile of chips before him. We both knew the impact this clash could have. Not only did we now have a genuine adversary, the winds of confidence were also doubtless billowing the American's sails.

Just one more hand past, Laak was still stacking his chips. Hyperactive, more enthusiastic than a cheerleader, and with only a brief look at his freshly printed tickets (cards), he announced, 'I am all-in.'

This didn't make sense to me. It was strangely uncharacteristic. If he had a genuinely big hand he would not move 'all-in'. This is a play usually made by a player who does not want to be called rather than one who does. I picked up on this immediately.

Slowly I squeezed apart my own two hole cards. I saw a 7, and gradually another 7 appeared. The whole world suddenly stopped. My gut instinct, the most important of them all, told me I had the best hand by far.

This was no £5 game at a friend's house on a Saturday night, however. Don't get me wrong, I wasn't playing with one eye on the money, I was playing with a hunger to succeed. Not making a mistake here on my quest for glory was my only concern.

I looked to my left, I looked to Ram. I could tell by his demeanour he did not have a hand to contest this huge bet, but I also sensed an expectancy about him, doubtless like the sentiment I had the hand before when he lucked out. So the action was on me, and I made the decision to call. The 'all-in' move had been made in such a way that I believed Laak was holding an Ace with a side-card, a kicker, which was very small, crucially smaller than a 7.

I took my time in announcing 'call', however, for this was a special moment and I wanted to enjoy it. I could feel my heart pumping quicker and quicker. I was excited in an inexplicable way, possibly like being on an F1 starting grid as the lights go out. I wanted this high to last as long as possible.

Eventually I muttered the decisive word and immediately enjoyed immense pleasure and satisfaction from the evidence laid out before me. Laak disbelievingly displayed his cards, a King-3. No matter what happened next I knew I had made the correct decision (it means so much as a professional). I was a 70 per cent favourite to prevail.

The heartbeat slowed but now I enjoyed a new sensation. I don't know what the medical term is, but I also float in it when watching two horses running neck-and-neck to the line when one will win me a fortune and the other will lead to my ruin. The tournament director, an oh-so-serious Austrian held up only by the starch in his shirt, announced what we all knew: 'Roy leads with a pair of 7s. Phil is going to need some help as he has King-3. Let's see the flop.'

Devastation followed as the first card I saw in this flop was a picture card, and the picture card was a King. I stood, bowed, nodded, shook my opponents' hands, wished them both well and made my way into the darkness, to the back of the studio, to the stage door and, like the infamous children's television character Mr Benn, back to the realms of reality.

But reality is a place where people do work for a living, and winning a tax-free £65,000 is not deemed a bad day at the office, even if it felt like one. Gone were the days of me wanting to lash such money out of the window. I'd got up early that morning and walked the Cardiff streets, seeing postmen and scaffolders starting work at unearthly hours to earn an honest living. Sixty-five grand, tax-free. I could be back on the streets, I could be in a factory, or delivering a hundred packages on a council estate.

Mags had come over to watch me play despite being on the back end of a thirteen-hour night shift, and it was that evening we decided to come off birth control and make plans for a baby. The time was right. A wedge was going into the bank and it could be put aside for baby's future, for his or her needs. I was as happy and content as I'd ever been. My demons had, one by one, been met head on and now only the future mattered.

There was no January holiday for me in 2006, or the usual trips to Brighton and Luton. Instead it was poker cruise time once again, our second, though this time the entire ship was full of poker players, and for me that meant a lot of niceties, a lot of hand-shaking and a lot of headaches. Once again I treated my parents to the trip, which this time left from Miami and cruised the Caribbean. On it, Mags worked flat out running the cash room operation.

These cruises are designed to be a lot of fun, and for most they are. For me they are not. They are work. I needed a holiday to get over it, and that meant making one of the trips I had always wanted to make, to St Moritz in Switzerland to see horseracing on a frozen lake and to do the world-famous Cresta Run. My other 'must visits' included visiting the pub in

Malta where Oliver Reed drank his last drink, going horse-racing in Sha Tin and Happy Valley in Hong Kong, and seeing Monte Carlo.

St Moritz is a stunning millionaires' playground. The train ride from Zurich up the Alps is incredible. It's a glass-top train which allows you to soak in the tremendous views. Horse-racing on a frozen lake may sound akin to gypsies racing ponies on a beach, but this is serious business with all the pomp, ceremony and extravagance you would expect to find at Royal Ascot. It was everything I hoped it would be and more. Tackling the Cresta Run was the stuff of dreams, too; success-fully getting to the bottom of it, exhilarating.

But at night, when we looked out of our hotel's window to see snow gently and silently falling on the picturesque town, I paused to ponder the fact that I still had plenty to prove in the poker world. There was a new wave of poker players on the scene, and in this modern era you were not a poker player until you had landed a substantial six-figure sum.

It was a ball set in motion by television producer John Duthie, who had won the first Poker Million and had sub-sequently introduced a much-needed European Poker Tour to replace the rag-tag unofficial tour which led players any and everywhere for wide-ranging field sizes and prize-money levels. Now European tournaments were for big bucks, and all were televised. It led to a revolution. Hundreds of players, like 'Scandie boy' in Paris in 2002, were qualifying for major tournaments online and almost every player was seen donning a T-shirt with an online poker room's logo. I had to prove myself all over again, but at least I was now getting some appropriate sponsorship to give me a leg up.

Deauville in Normandy, France, was my first port of call in 2006 – another beautiful place to which poker has taken me. John Gale drove me, Willie Tann and Stewart Nash down in his car via the Channel tunnel. My thirty-seventh-place finish does not sound too good, but it wasn't too bad from a field of 434 runners and it earned me a €4,800 return. I had, of course, been close enough to the half-million first prize and the six-figure payouts other final-table finishers received.

My choice of travelling companions – the average age in the car, taking me out of the equation, was upper fifties – was reflective of my new-found maturity. That's not to say it was not fun. Stu, John and I took it in turns to pose questions to Willie, a legendary gambler but not the luckiest, about how much he had lost in a single visit to a craps table, and cumulatively down the years. The poor bloke knew he had lost enough to buy five square acres of prime London real estate, but he could not help himself. 'Awe rucking well,' Willie, born in Singapore, would start his reply to every question, unaware we were having some harmless banter at his expense.

As I was still trying to execute two plans, start a family and win a monster tournament, Mags came with me to the next port of call, Paris in February, where a final-table appearance in the feature Paris Open of Poker gave me another 'close but no cigar' experience. I felt so close to a major win I could almost feel myself lofting the trophy. It was going to happen, and in my current frame of mind it was going to happen soon. I was about to get a whole lot more determined too.

On the evening we returned from Paris, Mags wandered off to the bathroom to take a pregnancy test. I had no idea what she was doing; I thought she was putting the kettle on. She returned to me in the front room and said, 'I've just taken a test but I've not yet looked at the result.' Together, sheepishly and oh so tentatively, we moved back into the bathroom to turn the small plastic pregnancy tester upright and look at the result. Simultaneously our hearts leapt as we looked at the blue line residing in the 'pregnant' area of the testing stick's window. Nothing would ever be the same again. Responsibility beckoned. I could not wait.

The news gave me a fresh enthusiasm – more so than just the desire to win, or the will to hush detractors, pay bills and live well. I wanted for our new arrival what everyone wants for their own: everything possible. My son, or daughter – I cared not one iota which, as long as our impending arrival was healthy – was going to have everything I didn't have. Some things I did have but didn't want or need were already ruled off the agenda – a single-sex school, for example.

The next chance of a life-changer came in April at the Irish Open, and once again I made an impact, finishing even closer to the money but not among it. The wheels fell off for me in thirteenth spot when my pair of 10s were futile against pocket Jacks. Had I got an amazing 'miracle 10', who knows where I would have ended up. As it was I cleared €10,000, but in inflation-rife modern-day poker that only pays for a few more tournament entries.

The very next day I banked €11,000 in another competition, and ten days later, still in Dublin, I won my €22,500 ticket into the next Poker Million. It was all coming together nicely. I could still sense that bit of luck at the right time was going to materialize and I'd be able to step off the roller-coaster ride at the top with enough money set aside to secure the future for everyone near and dear.

The World Series of Poker beckoned once again. In such fine form, maybe this was the time I'd crack that six-figure payday. By way of preparation, and conscious that our time as a couple, as opposed to as a family, was drawing to a close, Mags and I booked another short holiday, to Malta this time, to fulfil one more ambition. With Mags suffering from morning sickness and generally feeling unwell, after my mandatory drinking session in 'Ollie's Pub' and in an effort to stay out of the near constant rain, I took to playing online poker like never before. The result, from a $500 standing start, was over $50,000 in profits.

21

Biggest Pot

How could I miss in Vegas? What could stop me? Answer: a massive knock to my confidence and security. Ladbrokes called me to report that a perennial thorn in my side from north London had been on the telephone claiming he 'had enough dirt on me to go to the newspapers, who would run a front-page story and blacken the company name'. He was claiming I'd been gambling on the live televised Poker Million while commentating on it. I had! But for his own reasons, known only to him – although I wondered if he'd lost some money to me somewhere along the line – he was screaming foul play. I never really made the connection, but according to the accuser he was prepared to 'go to the *Racing Post*, who will run a story about insider trading and the ramifications of Brindley being sponsored by a bookmaker and betting on an event with the benefit of a televisual time delay. It will be on the front page for a week.'

Firstly, I doubted very much this was the *Racing Post*'s style. Secondly, there was no time delay, not even a few hundredths of a second. Thirdly, when he was asked what he wanted them to do about the situation, he said, 'I want him firing!' And he didn't stop there. He went on to make the same threats to Sky Sports, and once again they laughed at them. But I've got to say, for me, with my insecure nature, this was like being slated on a chat forum all over again. One voice does not make up a consensus, however. I had to consider that, and also to recall that saying 'it is better to be envied than pitied'. What was I really concerned about? Ladbrokes had stuck with me through lean patches, such as 2003, and the *Racing Post* were also proven loyal friends.

It's fair to say, though, that Sky Sports had had a few complaints about me down the years, but only on the back of some quips on the mic. Now and then I just hear or think of something that's catchy and find myself blurting it out in the middle of a game. Lead commentator and dear friend Jesse May once asked me if a guy could pass his hand. I countered with another question: 'Can a Hindu contract mad cow's disease?' Another time he asked what the chance was of a guy winning a hand. Considering all his outs had been passed, I replied, 'He's got a better chance of finding a foreskin in a synagogue.' Even Jordan got a mention – the old chestnut of summarizing a player's luck by announcing, 'If Jordan were to have triplets, with this guy's luck he'd be the third one, the one in the middle, the one left sucking his thumb.' To cows, foreskins and triplets everywhere, once again my sincere apologies for any offence my comments caused . . .

This knock to the confidence was compounded when another poker player made some false allegations. This time it was someone who had appointed himself the alias 'Action

Jack'. Within the pages of Des Wilson's book *Swimming with the Devilfish*, published in June 2006, this character described how he easily won a valuable heads-up game against me simply by playing like a robot. Nothing could be further from the truth. He didn't even play the game in question!

You see, there was a challenge to play me heads-up online each week. If I lost, my opponent would get $1,000; if I won, that sum and another $1,000 would roll forward to the following week. I'd gone nine weeks unbeaten so the prize was $10,000. In order to get the shot at playing me for this sum you had to play and win as many online tournaments as possible during the course of the prior week. Some poor souls logged in and played from the moment they got in from work until the early hours of the morning, and the whole weekend through. It gave them a chance at a lot of money (and also a divorce). Once the prize got high, this fella, who must have turned into some kind of insomniac as he was playing up to twenty-two hours a day, was hoovering up all the tournaments in the wee hours, the ones with smaller field sizes.

On the day in question we were both in Barcelona playing in a festival. I'd bombed out early, but he was going great guns. I reminded him about our eight p.m. online tournament, our $10,000 challenge, and asked if he wanted it suspended as he was clearly unable to make the appointment. He declined, and said it was 'all taken care of'. Returning to the casino later that night, I found him still sat in the thick of the tournament. He had in fact not played the game online, he had got someone to do it for him, and now he wanted to take the glory for the win in this book.

Call me a funny bugger, but this kind of stuff really vexes me. I don't know why I turned a blind eye to this sort of thing in the first place, but as we say in poker, 'seeing it through with a second bluff . . .' Well, that was too much for me to handle.

Around this time another swipe, a third, actually restored some of my faith in human nature. Mags and I bumped into an old friend, a marketing manager at a well-known bookmaking organization, at a darts tournament one evening where we had gone just for the craic. He was a little sheepish around me and seemed constantly to ask how I was and how things were. Pretty much couldn't be better, I confirmed. But later in the evening, with the confidence induced by more than a few beers, and while our partners had gone off to the toilet, he turned to me and said, 'I know, Roy.'

'You know what?' I replied.

'Listen, don't think I'm stepping out of line here, but I've been told about your problems.'

'Um, what problems are you talking about, mate?'

My friend totally avoided the question, I think out of fear of embarrassing me.

'Look, you've been very good to us down the years and I'd like to help,' he continued. 'I can't give you any money of my own as I don't have it, but send in an invoice to the company for a few grand and I'll sign it off for you, to help get you back on your feet.'

It was blatantly obvious he had heard I was skint, but from whom and how I didn't know.

'But, mate, things are going good. Who's told you I'm in bother?'

'Look, it's OK,' he said, 'just send in that invoice and use the money to pay off some of the people you owe. You can't hide away from them for ever.'

'What are you on about?' I protested.

'I've been given the rundown on the people you owe and how you have moved to Ireland because of your debts back in England. You've been here a few years now, so let's get it all cleared if we can.'

This type of genuine concern and a lovely offer was friendship at its best. The trouble was, it was a load of rubbish.

I got to the bottom of this story eventually. The rumours had been spread by a journalist. I never challenged the guy on it. I've never had a conversation with the perpetrator in my life, and all I've ever done in retaliation is this: I park up my Porsche and Ferrari alongside his four-door saloon at Shelbourne Park Stadium's car park.

At the time, though, these three individual glitches certainly did not make me feel more popular than Jesus. It was just my sensitive nature. But I was about to get a reminder that America wasn't my biggest fan either.

On my third quest for World Series glory I was turned away by American immigration officials. Numerous things went against me. I'd paid for my flight ticket in cash; I had ten grand in cash in my pocket. The year before I'd had a share of Andy Black's $1.7 million and the taxation forms to prove it – that surely meant I was a professional going to the States to ply my trade? Then there was the criminal record I had managed to chalk up smashing doors and vans years earlier. All in all, it was enough for them to put the 'full' sign up and refuse me entry.

The refusal hit me like a ton of bricks. I re-routed to Gran Canaria for a minuscule €300 entry tournament and tried to come to terms with missing the once-a-year feast which is the

World Series. But there was a bitter taste in my mouth, and my disappointment and concerns about never being allowed to enter the country again gave me sleepless nights. Guess what? My form took a massive dip too. Barred from the Victoria in London and now barred from the USA, I was running out of places to go.

The arrival of our baby was drawing closer but I still didn't have that big nest egg I was yearning for. In fact, between that US entry refusal and the late autumn I slaughtered fortunes playing badly and hoping somehow the tide would turn. There wasn't much money left come October. I had everything in life I had ever wanted, but I did not have the thing I needed: money. Time was running out, and I was broke. I'd even used up the Grand Prix winnings, at the wrong time.

Dublin's European Poker Tour leg in late October was another 'oh-so-close' scenario. This time I finished seventeenth, collecting €11,000; the winner made off with €550,000. If only my 10s had held up against Queen-King. At least my winnings gave me what I needed to get to Amsterdam for their Masterclassics festival, the next on the calendar and the last I'd be playing before the baby arrived.

I pulled no punches when answering questions about my need for a result during that festival and my desperation to achieve one with my heavily pregnant, ever-loyal partner at home as concerned about the future as I was. I shouldn't say it, but a win was inevitable. It was all related to my mindset, one of hunger and determination. The victory came in the €300 entry Omaha competition. So needy was I that when just two of us remained we cut a deal whereby I would finish an official second and take home €68,000. In the old days I'd've played the game to a conclusion, either going home a winner with €100,000 or taking second for €50,000.

The money did the job. I put it far out of reach where I couldn't get my hands on it. Two weeks later baby Sebastian arrived, fit, healthy and everything we had ever wanted. It was the most relaxed Christmas I can ever recall, content with our new baby, and with a nest egg stashed so far away that even Houdini couldn't have got it out.

OK, I wanted something else: more money, enough for Sebastian's future to be guaranteed. I know this is a never-ending quest for most parents, who are trapped in a cycle of working forty-eight weeks a year to provide, and pay off a mortgage which will allow them to own their own house just before they retire. But in the world of poker, at any given weekend you can make arrangements for the rest of your life, and I was now in what most would deem an outrageous hurry to do so.

Knocking and knocking ever closer, the life-changer nearly came, once more, in an EPT in January 2007. This time Copenhagen was the venue, but, despite holding more chips than a lot of people took to the final table when fifty people remained (450,000), twenty-ninth was the best I could muster.

In February there was a return trip to Paris to try to go a few places better in the Paris Open of Poker than the year before. Once again I made the final table, and once again, just like in Amsterdam, I made a deal that saw me finish second with a lumpy €48,000. I like playing in Paris as the games are soft. These are the games you want, against poor opponents. I get the impression there are a lot of people there who are wealthy and don't care about winning or losing so much as taking part and getting pleasure from the experience. They are a bit like broken slot machines: they pay you off every time.

The result meant I had now set aside € 100,000 during the past three months. Fatherhood was clearly the tonic I'd needed.

In March we travelled to Goa, India. My performance was OK – I finished twenty-second in a sizeable field – but rarely have my emotions run so high. The taxi ride from Goa Airport to our luxury resort, which resided behind sixteen feet of barbed-wire security fencing guarded by a private army, was one of the most disturbing experiences of my life. There was poverty, extreme poverty: people living under trees, huddled together, with nothing more than discarded plastic sacking to stave off the flies; children sifting through rubbish, searching for something to eat. It was heartbreaking stuff. Resisting the temptation to take the first flight home, I'd vowed to share any win I had with the incredibly friendly local community – which made the defeat all the more difficult to deal with.

Poland's EPT followed, where I blew a big stack of chips. But something was brewing, distracting me that day. It was a real chance of finally getting that life-changing result, and it wasn't poker-related.

Quietly, behind the scenes, I'd continued to gamble. Doubtless it was where some of my money had leaked away during the latter half of 2006, but it was only small amounts and done in such a way that I could neither notice or feel the desire to chase my losses. I was safer that way.

Basically, whenever I completed an online poker session I invariably cashed some money out. That involved converting my poker chips back from dollars into euros, as I live in

Ireland, or sterling, where one of my credit cards resides. It was never a round figure: $3,000 would convert into £1,579.76, say, and I'd use the odd £79.76 to place long-range ante-post bets. It was similar to what I did in 1992 when placing a host of doubles on Royal Gate in Cheltenham's Champion Hurdle and The Fellow in the Gold Cup.

This time round my selections were wide, varied and related in dozens of doubles, trebles and accumulators. I'd started the ball rolling with Kauto Star in the King George at Kempton on Boxing Day at odds of 11/4. The defeated New England Patriots cost me dear, but I did also have some bets running on Superbowl winners the Indianapolis Colts. So I'd collected some good money; yet fortunes were running on Inglis Drever in the Ladbrokes Hurdle at the Cheltenham Festival.

I was forced to listen to the race by webcast radio in my Warsaw hotel room. At no time did the commentator suggest the horse could win – indeed he was out the back and had made a mistake – but the great thoroughbred ultimately thundered up the hill to net me my biggest ever win, approaching £80,000. Victory for Kauto Star in the Gold Cup just two days later, a race I watched in a packed betting shop close to Dublin's airport among a host of €5 and €10 punters, gave me another £46,000. Furthermore, I now stood to win another lump should Manchester United win the Premiership, as they did. It was mad stuff, looking through the bets I'd placed and marking 'winner' next to every one of my outrageous long-range predictions.

I'd also placed a one-off €2,000 bet on Grand National winner Silver Birch at odds of 40/1. I'd spent thirty years trying to find the winner of the race, having last done so in 1977, backing Red Rum with my pocket money to do the unthinkable and win the race for the third time. Would you believe, I can name you every winning horse and rider of that great race during that period, and most of the placed horses to boot?

Anyway, by the time this betting spree had ended, victory for Finsceal Beo in the 1,000 Guineas on 6 May would land me another £100,000; and should Reading finish in the top six of the Premiership, I could sit back with combined winnings of over a million euros. As it was, Reading, though they still had chances on the final day of the season, stumbled at the final flight and missed out by three points. However, Finsceal Beo put up a stunning performance to win the 1,000 Guineas, which I watched in a commentary box during filming of the European Ladies Championship on the banks of the Thames. Such was the enormity of the final leg of all these bets, the producers held up proceedings midway through filming to allow Mags and me to watch the race.

After a lifetime of gambling, four years after hanging up the 'No More Bets' sign, I'd won a life-changing £300,000 for stakes that equated to peanuts.

I've heard it said that gambling really is like marriage – you know, 'for richer, for poorer'. The only difference is, gambling never ends in an amicable divorce. But I'm much happier divorced, and I got a great settlement. After more than two decades, I finally got all my money back. For a gambler, that's the stuff of dreams: chasing your losses, chasing your losses, chasing your losses and finally getting the lot back.

Was it worth it? Here, as in love and life, my head and heart tend to disagree. When I think back to how I used to live, how I deprived myself of a normal life, how I was a degenerate inflicting suffering on family members, I have to say no. But the thrill of watching that filly thunder up Newmarket's straight mile, with every galloping hoof in unison with my beating heart, cannot be explained or surpassed. Spending a week collecting and cashing five- and six-figure cheques is an unparalleled experience, and I simply cannot envisage myself spending those years, or the ones that followed, collecting a wage packet and paying off a mortgage.

Not attaining that life-changing result from poker, especially considering my string of near misses, was irksome. Unquestionably poker has given me the best years of my life. As it happens, it also gave me the ability to place bets on my unlikely string of winning selections.

Then again, just eight days after the 1,000 Guineas I took my seat for a certain televised Betfair Poker Masters of Europe and landed the coveted title along with a cheque for $120,000. It remains the biggest win of my poker-playing career.

22

Living is Easy When Life is a Game

Not a bad spot to conclude my tale, huh? But not only is life a gamble, it's a journey, one that goes on until you are placed in that wooden box.

In the summer of 2007 I sat down with a ghost writer to tell this story. But I didn't want to compromise the truth. This is not a glorious story of a man born with a silver spoon who developed the Midas touch, and it could not be written as such. Therefore our time together ultimately proved futile.

This book, like the story, is mine. I've written it word for word, about the things in life of which I am proud, remorseful, regretful and guilt-ridden. That's not an easy task, and a year on from what were due to be the closing pars and a glorious concluding high point there have been yet more twists and turns in the bumpy road of life.

Gambling, it gets you. You know, I always laugh when I see one of those leaflets on a betting shop counter or casino cash desk asking you to look at yourself, to look for the tell-tale signs of being an addicted gambler. I tick all the boxes, apart from the one that asks 'Have you ever stolen to fund your gambling?' I have begged and borrowed to place a bet, but I've never stolen. In the deluded state gambling got me into I always believed I would win and would therefore be able to repay what I had borrowed. For certain, if I'd stolen and flogged a car to place a bet, there would have been no taking it back after backing a winner.

No, leaving bills unpaid, myself without a tin of beans in the cupboard, stranded miles away from home with no petrol in the car, and humiliated by asking anyone and everyone to lend me money – all this is as bad as it has ever been.

A bookmaking associate, a guy I respect, Gary Wiltshire, who could have declared himself bankrupt following Frankie Dettori's seventh and final winner, Fujiyama Quest, laying a 12/1 shot at 9/4 on a memorable Ascot day, once said to me, 'There is nothing worse than a person who has never had money that comes into money and now does not know how to flaunt it enough.' His words stuck with me, but regardless, with my big haul I still bought myself the Ferrari sports car I had always wanted. You can often find it in the car park of a nightclub, pub or casino, but not pretentiously parked outside the main entrance. It could easily be in need of a wash, and it might have a baby seat in the back of it. That's me.

The car was the first of many mistakes I made with my money. I mean, buying the bus was reasonably cheap in comparison to any new vehicle, but after just eleven miles on the road I blew the engine sky high, leaving €30,000 worth of damage in a thousand oil-sodden pieces on the A55. That seemed to set a precedent.

Coinciding with this expensive Sunday outing, news reached

me that an online poker site in which I had bought a share-holding had gone to the wall. I was way too late buying myself a piece of the action, by about five years – from the point when I preached to anyone who would listen that poker was the future; and when the US President unexpectedly signed an act (the Safe Port Act) which basically declared that online poker was funding terrorism and barred it, I lost the majority of my Paris and Amsterdam tournament winnings in this primarily American-dependent venture. Unsurprisingly, I nearly threw a party on learning shortly afterwards that US Congressman Jim Leach had been ousted from his Iowa office when losing out in the mid-term elections. Leach was responsible for the anti-gaming legislation that was tagged on to that anti-terrorism/Safe Port Act signed by the President.

It took a while, but I finally figured out the grounds for his ferocious objections to online poker. I'll wager that he watched the James Bond offering *Casino Royale*. Just consider . . . The storyline features a rogue called Le Chiffre who is an inter-national money launderer for the terrorists of the world. Bond defeats Le Chiffre in a high-stakes poker game, a game which if lost would result in twice as much terrorist money in circulation. Surely way too many similarities to be pure co-incidence, and irrefutable proof that television and cinema, allied to a fertile imagination, are in some cases very danger-ous things.

Anyway, I've gambled and lost all of my life and I wasn't about to jump off a cliff in despair. That will never happen. I'm a gambler, it's in my blood, so I had no option other than to invest the rest of my six-figure nest egg where some kind of risk was involved.

I'd wanted to be a stock market trader since my schooldays, so if I had to save money, it was the only way to go. Of course, there have been two dramatic crashes and a steady decline in the London stock market since my big wins. I think we all know that much-flaunted warning 'the value of shares can go up as well as down', but there are extremes, and I managed to identify them. I've watched fortunes disappear from my family's reserve. Most days I dreaded turning on the computer and looking at the stock market's website to find that another £2,000 or £3,000 had disappeared overnight. The net result has been a 95 per cent drop in the value of my stock. Amongst my investments two companies have gone bust; there is barely anything left. I already knew I had the ability to lose a fortune on sporting events, but gambling with it and losing it in a way that is deemed by so many to be legitimate and respectable is kind of immoral.

There is no point in dwelling on it. You know, at the end of the day most gamblers are prepared to risk what they cannot afford in the pursuit of something they cannot have. I have all I need. Possibly not all that I want, but it's enough for me nowadays.

I appreciate everything in life, including money. By that I mean you will never see me pay for a business-class seat to Las Vegas at a cost of £4,000. Having lived on the streets, fed myself on pennies and seen poverty in India, I find such needless extravagance immoral. I'm happier donating such sums to greyhound home-finding schemes domestically, and organizations that are trying to clean up dog racing stateside.

As it happens, the US authorities granted me a visa to return to the States in 2007, and though the championship Hold'em tournament was a damp squib once more, I did place thirteenth in the $10,000 entry Omaha World Championship. Here my Ace-Ace-Queen-Queen double-suited ran into Queen-Queen-Jack-10 with every chip in the pot before the flop. I liked it that way, being an 82 per cent (2/9) favourite in a pot which would have taken me into the final table in a supreme position. The 10-10-2 flop doubtless cost me a minimum of $300,000.

The Victoria Casino was another to reopen its doors to me, although I finished unplaced in their EPT. While clocking up a few final-table finishes, there have been very few hard-luck stories just recently.

At Christmas I played Nomination with my parents – the game I mastered as a child. Alarmingly, I did not have a clue what was going on. The fundamentals of the game went over my head. After four hands I simply had no idea of what was the master trump, or the number of any suit that had been past.

There was no World Series of Poker for me in 2008 – the second time in three years that I missed the big one. This time round it was happy circumstances that kept me away: our daughter Elise Norah, named after my grandmother, made a premature appearance. I love family life and cannot wait to do the things with my children that I feel I missed out on myself. Silly things and simple things, like going fishing, or going to football matches.

Talking of families, during the penning of this book a strange thing happened: for the first time ever, my father told me he was proud of me. I was thirty-eight at the time. Furthermore, he said, 'We should go for a drink together.' Neither had been stated or even suggested before. Hopefully, Sebastian and Elise will not have to wait so long for me to lavish such praise on them. Amusingly, during this intimate conversation, I asked my father what was the most memorable day out we had when I was a child. His reply, somewhat predictably, was, 'The day we took you to Salisbury races in a pushchair and Mill Reef won his maiden on his debut.' It's a shame I cannot recall it, I suppose.

Sadly, my Uncle Roy, my mum's brother, passed away recently. He came to visit us in Ireland as this project got underway; it was the first time I'd seen him in ten years. Diabetes had eroded his bones and joints to the extent that he needed a motorized chair. His eyesight had become poor too, but he was jovial, one of the nicest men I ever knew. We talked about whale watching in the Norwegian fjords during that visit, and he was unaware that I was planning to treat him to such an excursion. Stupidly I held back until I'd had a big win. He died suddenly in early 2008. Life's too short to plan ahead. Life's for living – and there's the proof.

Walthamstow, greyhound racing's beautiful showpiece stadium, built in 1933, has closed its doors. It's being made into a housing estate. Many more tracks will follow on the back of this closure. I have mixed feelings about it. I've visited ninety-nine dog tracks in my life, and now if I drove past a new one I'm not sure I'd feel the urge to stop in and reach the magic ton. Yet I still think the greyhound is the most beautiful, graceful creature, possessing a fantastic nature, born to run, and loves doing so. I try to stick with the memories of my kennels and the dogs that lived in them with the knowledge that the vast majority of trainers in England are as caring as I was.

To the future, where I now know people's opinions of me will change. For better or worse? That's for you to decide. I'm working on my obvious insecurities, which may verge on paranoia, I don't know. I blame so much of it on being an only child (Sebastian was always going to have a sibling). Recently I met some of the serial posters on the poker forums. Once you meet these people you don't care about them any more. I actually started to pity them.

These days I'm not back gambling like I once was. I suppose I should be, inspired by my wins and tempted by the ease of those big payouts, chasing the losses inflicted by the stock market. If the right circumstances occur I'll not be averse to placing a monster bet, mind.

Everyone knows the term 'dead cert', and the vast majority will tell you there is no such thing, but if they only knew how and where the phrase came about . . .

The story goes that a bunch of fishermen used to stand on a jetty with a bucketful of crabs which had numbers painted on their shells. Each day after unloading their catch they would come together and place wagers on which crab would be last to make it off the jetty and back into the sea when the bucket was overturned. Sick gambling, huh? Not if you knew one of the crabs was dead and would sit there motionless while other people's money scampered away.

These kind of opportunities do come your way, but sadly there is a thin line between a genuine opportunity and criminal activity.

Truth be known, there has never been a better time to be a gambler. Percentages and margins are lower than ever and the internet has made placing bets far easier. It's also no longer all about finding a winner: betting exchanges allow you to seek losers, while spread betting companies give you ample arbitrage opportunities. There are more professional gamblers now than there have ever been, and each has the one quality in gambling I don't have: discipline. Similarly, they don't get the all-addictive buzz I do from placing bets. It's all a business to them. On the plus side, none of them can play poker!

These days I make a steady income grinding out cash games on the internet or in Dublin's numerous card clubs. There's PR work, tutorials, commentary and corporate presentations, too, as well as an interest in a card room and possibly a Gordon Ramsay-style television series with a poker not food spin in the mix. Combined, it gives me a good living, and I owe it all to poker.

I'll not be moving from Ireland any time soon. One of my greatest honours was being asked to captain the Wicklow team for the Irish Poker Cup, a team event featuring ten players from all thirty-two counties in Ireland at the Citywest Hotel in Dublin. Something to be proud of, that, captaining an Irish county when you are the only Englishman in a room filled with 320 Irish poker players.

After the finest imaginable pep-talk from an outstanding team captain (me), and with a stunning strategy – a cunning plan to pool together both team prizes and individual prizes and even a last longer bet between themselves – my Wicklow squad were tuned in like the Ferrari team at a home Grand Prix with Ross Brawn on the pit wall and Michael Schumacher at the wheel. Much of the strategy was very simple: hang in, hang in and hang in. So you can imagine my embarrassment when the Wicklow team finished stone last, in thirty-second place, our most successful player, the one who lasted longest, being the player who did not actually turn up to play and simply had his chips removed from his stack when it was his turn to post a blind! We all laugh about it. That's the kind of place it is.

You know, it really makes me smile when I turn back the years, cherish the laughter and remember the tears. But it's to the future, the forthcoming chapters, where my focus lies. Mags has stuck with me through thick and thin, including the difficult autopsy these pages represent. We will share this future, a better life, and she will also appreciate just how much I love her.

Right now I struggle to leave home. I miss the children so much. But when I do eventually go back out on that road I'll land that life-changing tournament win. I did say somewhere that on any given day anyone can win, didn't I? And hopefully this time I shall invest the money wisely.

Now, that investment won't be a pension scheme. I mean, some folk put every spare penny into a pension fund without considering they are only 8/13 to reach pensionable age and long odds-against to enjoy ten years of retirement thereafter. They are the same sort of folk who would be outraged at the idea of losing any sum of money in the pursuit of pleasure. I fancy I'm likely to be safe and secure for the rest of my days, long before those who have taken the short price on receiving some part of their pension scheme. In fact, I'd bet on it. After all, life's a gamble, not a destination . . .

Index